dharma punx

dharma punx

A
MEMOIR

noah levine

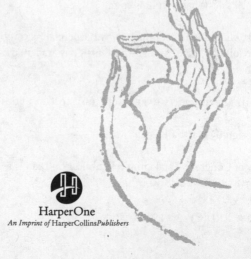

HarperOne
An Imprint of HarperCollins Publishers

HarperOne

HarperCollins books may be purchased for educational, business, or sales promotional use. For information, please e-mail the Special Markets Department at SPsales@harpercollins.com.

HarperCollins Web site: http://www.harpercollins.com
HarperCollins®, 📖 ®, and HarperOne™ are trademarks of HarperCollins Publishers.

FIRST HARPERCOLLINS PAPERBACK EDITION PUBLISHED IN 2004

Text design by Martha Blegen

Library of Congress Cataloging-in-Publication Data is available upon request.
ISBN: 978–0–06–000895–6

17 18 RRD(C) 30 29 28

For Toby Munyon,
Theresa Ferraro, my parents,
and all spiritual revolutionaries—
past, present, and future

Contents

Preface

Dharma Punx is my story and it's a story about my generation: the punks, the kids all around the world who searched for meaning and liberation in the age of Reagan, Thatcher, and the Cold War's constant threat of total nuclear annihilation.

I sought a different path than that of my parents. I totally rejected meditation and all the spiritual shit they built their lives on. Looking at the once idealistic hippie generation who had long since cut their hair, left the commune, and bought into the system, we saw that peace and love had failed to make any real changes in the world. In response, we felt despair and hopelessness, out of which came the punk rock movement. Seeking to rebel against our parents' pacifism and society's fascist system of oppression and capitalist-driven propaganda, we responded in our own way, different from those before us, creating a new revolution for a new generation. Painfully aware of the corruption in the government and inconsistencies in the power dynamics in our homes, we rebelled against our families and society in one loud and fast roar of teen angst. Unwilling to accept the dictates of the system, we did whatever we could to rebel. We wanted freedom and were willing to fight for it.

The situation was compounded by the personal despair that I and so many of my generation were facing: broken homes, addicted parents, useless school teachers, and a total lack of elders to look up to. Most of our parents were too busy to pay attention to us as they tried to survive the aftermath of the sixties or succeed in the race for riches in the seventies and eighties.

In my case, my mother was battling with addiction and two broken marriages, doing her best to raise four children. My father was so dedicated to spiritual practice and service that at times it kept him from being as available to me as I probably needed.

So I and countless others hit the streets, fueled by the music of revolution, anger, angst, fear, despair, hatred, and a total dissatisfaction with the status quo. We dyed our hair or shaved our heads, we donned a new uniform to set us apart from the mindless masses of adults and brain-dead herds of kids who were going along with the lies, buying into the great American fallacy, playing sports, going to school, and listening to the awful popular music of the eighties that carried no meaningful messages and was just another symptom of the disease of apathy and materialism that plagues our society.

Drugs and booze seemed to be the only effective escape from the feelings of hopelessness and despair. Many of us went directly to narcotics as teenagers. Eating acid like it was candy and chasing speed with cheap vodka, smoking truckloads of weed, consuming gallons of cheap beer, all in a vain attempt to get numb and stay numb. We embraced a nihilistic outlook on life. Set apart from mainstream society, we were a constant target of violence and ridicule. Fighting to survive, fighting for our views and right to be different, we often found ourselves involved in some battle or another; if it wasn't with the cops, it was with the jocks or hicks or each other.

Our lives of violence and drugs led to many early deaths: overdoses, murders, car accidents, and countless suicides. Death and grief has been a central part of the lives of all the kids who were associated with the early punk rock scene. Following the examples set by Sid Vicious and Darby Crash, our goal was to live fast, do lots of drugs, and fuck the system by dying young. Half of the kids from the crew of punks I hung out with in the eighties are dead.

This book is about those of us who didn't die young and are still around, those of us who don't go around talking about punk as "just a phase" we went through as kids. *Dharma Punx* is about those of us who, motivated by the same dissatisfaction with life that brought us to the punk rock scene, now have turned toward spiritual practice as a nonviolent form of the revolution. It is a true story about finding in meditation and service the freedom I was seeking as a young idealistic punk rocker. Having clearly seen the uselessness of drugs and violence, I and others have found positive ways to channel our rebellion against the lies of society. Still fueled by anger at injustice and suffering, we now use that energy to awaken to our own natural wisdom and compassion instead of for self-destruction.

This is a story about those of us who have taken ourselves and our struggles off of the streets. We now fight the inner battle against delusions and ignorance, yet we continue to express ourselves outwardly in our own unique punk rock ways. Having put down the booze and drugs, having let go of the violence and hatred, having lost too many friends to prison and death, we have found the highest spiritual truth, the Dharma. The spiritual path that was described by the Buddha as being "against the stream," against man's selfish desires and ignorance. This fits in perfectly with the punk rock ethic. We've turned the outer rebellion into an inner revolution.

Spiritual truth comes in many different forms and through many different spiritual traditions. While I find myself primarily engaged in Buddhist practice, some of the other Dharma Punx have dedicated themselves to the Sufi path of Islamic mysticism, to a personal relationship with Christ, or to the Hindu path of devotion and service. I use the term "Dharma" to mean the Truth with a capital T, and, as my father often reminds me, "That which is true is found in all spiritual and religious traditions." No one has the corner on the Truth.

This book will take you on an intense journey from the streets to Juvenile Hall and from Juvenile Hall to the meditation hall. It follows the life of a confused kid and his search for clarity. It is the story of not just one life but of the lives of several people who have come together to form our crew, the Dharma Punx. A group of men and women who are deeply committed to spiritual practice and engaged service in the world. These are the new faces of the punk rock scene, a group of committed Dharma practitioners who you can still find down at the local club singing along to their favorite bands and doing the occasional stage dive.

This is not a fictional tale of romantic suffering or a Hollywood love story. It's about real people, real loss, and genuine spiritual growth. This is a story of transformation, that of a part of a generation often touted as X, who now find meaning and purpose in spiritual practice and service. It is a full circle, from being institutionalized to teaching meditation in institutions, from robbing and stealing to giving and forgiving.

It's a story about finding freedom and then spending the rest of our lives giving it away.

Acknowledgments

Though a few names and the sequence of some events have been changed (to protect the guilty), this is a true story, the story of my life insofar as my imperfect memory and self-centered perception has allowed.

First and foremost I give thanks to my parents, Patricia Washko, for giving birth to me and caring for me when I could not care for myself, I love you Mom, and to my father, Stephen Levine, and other mother, Ondrea Levine, who gave me the greatest gift possible—life, love, and the Dharma, you saved my life.

Much love to my siblings, Tara Levine, Luke Valentine, Rebecca Silberman, and Aaron Silberman.

Great thanks to my friends who have supported me through the years: Toby Munyon, Vinny Ferraro, Micah Anderson, Joe Clements, Scott Sylvia, Jimmy Clarke, Mike Haber, Noelle Watkins, Russ Rankin, Jennifer Clark, Lars Fredericksen, Drew Phillips, Baron Dupont, Jason Freeland, Jason Oliver, Jason Murphy, Margie Way, Ian Clark, Mike Murnane, Gary Kosmala, Anna Sophie Lowenburg, Dave Davis, Michele Fischer, Lolly Holloway, Giovanna Windrose, Keri Richard, Brant Dobson, Darden Thompson, David Carberry, Eric Rodriquez, Vanessa Giano, Rebecca Tupper, Diana Winston, Mark Coleman, Kevin Griffin, Lisa McCool, Loch McHale, Mathew Gould, Monique Duncan, Claudine Gossett, Bubbles, Stinky, Shooter, Mark, Darren, Dave, Chris, Claudia, Gary, Adrienne, Steve, Don, Stuart, and all of my other homies I forgot to mention.

Much love to my agent, Loretta Barrett, and my editor, Liz Perle, with out you guys this book would have really sucked.

A raised fist to all of the punk rock and hardcore bands who have inspired and motivated me over the years. Since there are way too many to name them all, I will name only the important ones: The Ramones, The Clash, The Sex Pistols, Minor Threat, Black Flag, Bad Brains, Bl'ast, GBH, Agnostic Front, Judge, Shelter, 108, and a big fucking middle finger to my friends in Good Riddance and Rancid.

A deep bow of reverence to all of my teachers who have shown me the path of liberation: Jack Kornfield, Mary Orr, Ajahn Amaro, Howard Cohn, Eugene Cash, Bo Lozoff, Steven Goodman, His Holiness the Dalai Lama, Ram Dass, Thich Nhat Hanh, Suzuki Roshi, Ramana Maharshi, Hazrat Inayat Khan, Maharaji, Robert Thurman, Mark Epstein, Joseph Goldstein, Sharon Salzberg, Stephen and Ondrea Levine, and all of the teachers and practitioners on the path, all the way back to Siddhartha Gotama, the Buddha.

1

Suicide Solution

Waking up in a padded cell, my head bruised and bloody, I scream with rage at an unknown assailant. My wrists are raw and tender from the previous evening's suicide attempt. The padded walls and cushioned floor are trapping me in here with my worst enemy, myself. Death seems to be the only solution; kill the one who has created so much suffering for so long. Destroy the body that has done nothing but crave more of the substances that make me lie, steal, and fight every moment of my existence. There is no shelter, no refuge, no hope for redemption. The only thing I have to look forward to is more of the same and it's just getting worse and worse. I have no strength to continue this battle and no will to live. I must annihilate this evil mind and worthless body to ever find peace.

The years of violence and street life have finally caught up with me. There is nowhere to hide from the life of addiction and crime that I have created. I have failed at being human. I have even failed at taking my own life. Thrown in a cage to protect the world from my evil actions, the walls are padded with a hard rubber to prevent me from punishing myself. The dim fluorescent lighting gives me no clue as to whether it is day or night. I am lost in the Bardo, between worlds, unable to die yet no longer alive.

This is it, the bottom, the final depths of a teenage junkie. I have lost all touch with reality, with love, even with the hatred that once fueled my punk rock rebellion. I have nothing left to live for. I once had the fury of the anti-authority, anti-establishment, anti-everything ethic—punks versus the world—running through my veins. But all that was pushed out by the dope, crack, and cheap booze that have consumed me, which have become my only friend and my traitorous enemy. I traded in my mohawk, Doc Martens, and leather jacket for a fucking crack pipe. I traded in my belief in anarchy and the revolution for a ride on the Night Train express, head rush after head rush, nod after nod, heading nowhere, doing nothing and being no one. Pain and the fleeting rushes or comforting numbness that breaks up the monotony of the suffering is all I know.

I lie here tortured by the memories of a life only half lived yet almost over. Seventeen years old and dying. Institutionalized, locked in a rubber room crying and screaming. Deluded by the haze of forced withdrawal, poison oozing out of each cell in my being. In and out of consciousness, the walls are breathing through my broken spirit. I'm too tired to breathe, too broken to continue, too weak to fight.

Curling up into the fetal position, holding on to what's left of the once innocent child who took birth all those years ago, now as before, ready to do it all over again. Just let me die.

Sleep is as close to death as I can come, but the drug dreams are worse than the cell. The toxic horrors torment my slumber, no rest for the wicked, no escape from the hungry ghost and demonic guardians of the underworld that fill my dreams.

Rousted by Tim, the guard I know all too well, I'm told that my father is on the phone. He looks at me with suspicion and concern, says I can take the call but he will have to go with me.

My father listens to my rants and cries for help for a while and then speaks of his own youth of crime and time in prison. He speaks of his own search for meaning and offers me some simple meditation instructions, saying that it is the only thing that has ever worked for him. I listen as well as I can and thank him for not giving up on me.

Tim says I can move into a normal cell if I want to. Big fucking deal, one cage to the next. In my cell I think about what my father said about meditation. How is that hippy shit going to help me now? Suicide still seems like the only solution. I need to shut up my head; I can't deal with the torture any longer.

With no means of destruction I lie on the hard plastic bed and stare at the graffiti-covered walls. With nothing else to do and nowhere else to turn, I try to pay attention to my breath.

A week or so later some young guys come into the Hall, offering a meeting about how to stop taking drugs and drinking. I used to smoke crack with one of them so I go check it out, knowing that I have to stop, wanting to stop, but not knowing how to stop. One of them tells my life story, a hopeless junkie who used to be a punk, now he's clean and sober and says that he just wanted to die, until he found out that it was actually his addiction that was trying to kill him, and that now his life was pretty good. He doesn't want to die anymore, now he really wants to live and he is trying to use his life to help us live too. They gave me some kind of sober bible, I told them I was not interested in any religious shit but took the book anyway.

In my cell that night I read their stupid book and try to do my dad's dumb breathing meditations. I might as well be dead if I have to do all this fucking bullshit in order to become human again. But I am locked up and there is nothing else to do, so what the fuck, might as well check this shit out. Nothing I have been doing has worked, and there is nowhere else to turn, so I guess this is my best bet. The meditations do seem to help a little, at least a few seconds here and there; when I am able to focus on my breath I feel better and forget that I'm locked up. The book is confusing and talks a lot about all that God shit but I like the stories at the end. People talking about drinking and taking drugs the way that I do, out of control. There is one part that I like where it talks about getting to the point of "pitiful and incomprehensible demoralization." I don't know what that means but it sounds like the way I feel every time I use drugs, drink, steal, or fight.

2

kids of the Black Hole

Sitting on the front steps, I could hear the cries of my new little brother and sister and the sound of my mom and new stepdad arguing as usual. They met at a meditation retreat about a year earlier. He moved in with us and nothing had been the same ever since.

Making sure that no one else was around, I crawled underneath the porch and went to the place where I had hidden the steak knife I stole from the kitchen. Sunlight came through the spaces between the redwood boards, illuminating the earth in horizontal lines and giving off enough light to see clearly. I made my way to my secret hiding place, my heart was beating quickly, and I was filled with fear of being discovered.

I had hidden the knife at the foot of the stairs where only I could get to it. I had buried it in the loose dirt down there a few days earlier. For a moment I couldn't find it and was afraid that someone had discovered it, maybe my big sister, Tara. As I frantically dug around, I finally found it. The heavy metal handle felt cool and somehow comforting to my touch. I cleaned the dirt off, wiping the blade carefully on my "Hang-Ten" shorts. For a few moments I just sat there looking at my knife. It was one of my favorites; Mom had four of them. I think they used to belong to Grandma. The blades were shiny and very sharp. We only got to use them when we were having meat, usually liver and onions or something gross like that. The handles were made of metal but fashioned to look like a sort of stone or maybe wood. I had always liked those knives a lot, which was why I had chosen to bring one down to my hideout.

The blade caught the rays of the sun and threw a reflection across the ground in front of me. I played with the light in this way, amazed at how I could shine light into the darkness with my knife. Then, as I heard some more screams coming from the house, my mom yelling at her new husband and the twins crying, I remembered why I had stolen it in the first place. I turned the blade toward my stomach, gripping the handle with both hands and sat there shaking, filled with a deep sense of desperation. With trembling hands, I contemplated plunging it into my stomach, thinking that I would just instantly die like they do on the cartoons and in the movies. But I stopped. Somehow just having the knife was enough, just knowing that I had the option, that I could always get out of this life if I needed to. Even at five years old I had the sense that if I were to die it would not be the end but just a new beginning, just a transition into the next level of existence or life.

Maybe this feeling came from all the people I had seen who were dying when I would go with my father to see the patients he was counseling and teaching about meditation. Sometimes when we entered the home of one of his patients, I would know, I could smell death coming. Hopefully in my next lifetime my parents wouldn't get divorced when I was two and I wouldn't have a mean stepdad and a little brother and sister who got all of the attention. Maybe it would be easier if I just plunged this knife into my heart and started over.

Just then, I heard a loud crash in the house and the sound of something breaking. My stepfather was throwing things again. I heard my name being screamed. "Where is Noah? God damn it! Noah?" he yelled. I heard Tara saying that she saw me go out the back door. I quickly hid my knife back under the first step and crawled out from under the porch. I brushed myself off and kicked some of the dirt off of my slip-on Vans. I hesitated at the front door before opening it, afraid that I was in trouble or that I was going to get yelled at too. When I heard my name called again I opened the front door and saw my mom in the kitchen cooking dinner, a cigarette in one hand, a glass of wine in the other.

All I said was, "What?"

"Where were you?" my stepfather yelled.

I replied that I was just outside fooling around.

My mom asked me to take the compost out. "Why can't Tara do it?" I asked. My stepfather started yelling at me. "Just do what your mother says, God damn it!"

Mom yelled back at him not to scream at me like that.

That's when he started throwing things. It was the baby's shoes, one at me and one at Mom. I just picked up the old coffee can full of compost and slammed the door behind me. On the way up the driveway I began to cry and I decided that next time I was really going to use my knife, that would show them. They would miss me when I was gone forever. Then maybe they would understand how I felt. Through tears and confusion I began to think that maybe I should just kill my stepdad instead. I could sneak into his room while he was sleeping and use my knife on him. If I could just get rid of him, then Mom and me could be happy again.

I never killed my stepdad and I clearly never killed myself. But I did continue to hide under the stairs and think about it, playing with my knife and hiding from my life.

The year was 1976. I was only five years old and I already wanted to die. I knew nothing about the punk rock movement that was happening in New York and London but a few years later it would become the exact outlet that I needed to vent all of the discontent I felt. I didn't know about all of the drugs that would soon become my main way of coping with the difficulties of growing up and that would eventually almost kill me. And I certainly had no idea at all that I would ever become involved in meditation and spiritual practices. My parents were into that shit and look at where it had gotten them.

But all of this was to come, and for the meantime I decided to smoke Mom's cigarettes and start fires in the field behind our house. That was also the year I began stealing, at home, at school, and I even used to break into the neighbors' house when they were away and eat their cookies, lemon meringue pies, and listen to their autimatic piano.

About a year or so later my dad, who I then only saw on weekends and for the occasional longer visit, finally met Ondrea, who became his life's partner and new wife. It was decided that I would go to live with them in New Mexico for a while. I moved to Santa Fe with my dad and met my new big brother, James, and left my security knife under the stairs at Mom's house, hoping that I wouldn't need it anymore.

I had always wanted a big brother, but James wasn't very interested in hanging out with me. The only time he seemed to pay attention to me at all was when I bugged him enough for him to push me around or abuse me in some way. At first I really hated Ondrea. She wasn't mean like my stepdad had been, but I knew it was her fault that we had to move to that shitty house in the middle of nowhere, so far away from all my friends and the redwood trees and Santa Cruz beaches of my childhood. She tried really hard to be a friend to me but it took a while for me to let her in. I was so jealous, feeling that my dad loved her more than he loved me.

That was the year I started smoking pot, committed my first bicycle theft, and had my first fistfight with someone who wasn't related to me. In the school play of *Peter Pan* I was cast as Captain Hook. I was well on my way to a life of crime and piracy.

For the next few years I was shipped back and forth between California with Mom (who divorced the evil stepfather shortly after I left) and New Mexico or Colorado with Dad and Ondrea. Along the way I would learn new ways to get high that included drinking, huffing, smoking, snorting, and ingesting.

Which brings us to where our story really begins, in 1980, when I finally found punk rock and met my best friend for life, Toby.

As my mom's yellow and white VW bus pulled into the parking lot at the Capitola-Soquel Little League field we were still arguing about whether or not I could bring my skateboard to Little League practice. Mom was convinced that I wouldn't need it at the first day of practice but I was sure as hell not going without it so we were locked in a battle of the wills. Finally, out of frustration, she gave in and I jumped out of the bus in my new checkered Vans, OP shorts, and a T-shirt from a local surf shop, with my Duane Peters skateboard under one arm and a backpack with my uniform and cleats in the other. I knew before I even got to the field that I was more interested in skating than baseball but for some reason I had agreed to join the team. I think it was because I was ten and an older kid who lived down the hill from us played baseball and I thought he was cool so I thought I better play too so I could be like him.

But I knew from the minute I got there, just looking at all the other kids who were already in their uniforms with their short haircuts and brand-new shoes, that I had made a big mistake. I had a bowl cut like all the surfers and skaters did in the late seventies. I didn't want to play with these kids. I wanted to go skateboard in the parking lot.

A few minutes later another kid showed up and not only did he have a bowl cut and OP shorts, he also was carrying his skateboard, one of the new Rob Roscop decks that was the best skateboard around. He had ridden it to practice from his house up the street. His name was Toby. He came right over to where I was standing apart from the crowd and said, "Hey, dude, what's up?"

"Nothing, just hanging out, nice skate, can I try it sometime?" I replied.

He said, "Sure, maybe after practice we can shoot the hill."

I knew right then he was going to be my new best friend.

After the first week of practice he invited me to come over to his house to spend the night on the weekend. Our parents agreed and on that first visit to Toby's it turned out that we had a lot more in common than we thought. Not only did we both skate, we also both liked to get high. I can't remember who mentioned it first but before long we were smoking a roach that he had stolen from his aunt. I had been getting high off and on for a couple years already and so had he.

After that we were together all the time—well, as much as possible since we went to different elementary schools. We hung out almost every weekend. After practice we would skateboard, go to the beach, run around in the mountains up at my house or down by the creek at his. But most of all we tried to get high as much as possible. It's kind of tough when you're ten years old to score drugs so we resorted to stealing what we could from our relatives and got into stuff like sniffing paint and engine cleaner, smoking cloves, and chewing tobacco. Anything that would make us dizzy would do.

At some point that year my big sister showed me that our mom had a couple of grocery bags full of some kind of pot that was called "mushrooms." My sister said you didn't smoke them you ate them and they made you see cool stuff. She wanted me to steal some for her so that if we got caught I would be to blame. So I did and I kept a few for Toby and me to try the next weekend. It was perfect because we were planning to go see a surf movie with Toby's cousin, Jason, that weekend.

Toby's cousin was a few years older than we were. I guess my sister knew him from school or something. Jason was the first punk rocker I ever met: he had a bleached white flattop spiked straight up and wore big pointy-toed shoes called creepers. But he was also a really good surfer and skater. On the way to the movie Jason played a tape of a band called the Sex Pistols for us. I couldn't believe it; it was like hearing the voice of God. The high energy and fast style of music just made me want to break something, which was how I felt most of the time anyway. I knew from that moment on that I wanted to be a punk rocker too.

At the surf movie we ate the mushrooms, one each. They were the most awful, wretched, disgusting things that I had ever tasted. I almost barfed all over the place. We got Cokes to wash them down. When the movie started we smoked some pot and waited for the mushrooms to work their magic. That's what my sister had called them, magic mushrooms. But all I felt was sick to my stomach and a little stoned from the pot. I couldn't stop thinking about that music, I kept remembering one line, "There's no future, there's no future for me," and I repeated it over and over in my head. I don't know exactly when the magic hit me but all of the sudden I looked up at the screen and rather than seeing the surfers and waves that I expected, I was shocked to see only a whirling mass of color and trail-like designs that seemed to be melting off the screen and overflowing the Civic Auditorium like an old horror movie I had once seen called *The Blob*. It was both awesome and overwhelming. I felt so fully alive and at the same time completely removed from my experience. It was like I had become the movie, the colors, and the movement.

Toby and I began eating mushrooms almost every weekend for a couple months. Jason made me a couple of punk rock tapes that I listened to all the time. My big sister and I fought almost daily but I hung around as much as possible to meet her friends and find out about punk and ska bands. My mom discovered that several ounces of her mushrooms were missing; my sister immediately blamed me, and I took the fall. Things at school were bad and getting worse. Sitting in Mr. Hershey's office—he was the principal of my elementary school—I knew I was in big trouble. All year I had been getting sent to the office for being disruptive in class but this time I had been caught destroying the prized artwork of the school's most loved little finger-painters. My friend Keith and I, when made to wash all the paintbrushes as a punishment after art class, had sprayed paint on all of the other kids' art that was being displayed on the wall in the auditorium. Mr. Hershey was in a rage; this time I had gone too far. I was an enemy of art, a ten-year-old anarchist. After a long lecture, trying to convince me of the errors of my actions, staring at me with a look of contempt, expecting an apology and plea for forgiveness, he was met with nothing more than my tight-lipped smirk and blank stare.

I was expelled from the fifth grade, no longer welcome to attend Mountain School. My mom was at her wit's end. Not knowing what else to do, my parents decided that I would go back to live with my father and Ondrea.

We were at the beach in Capitola when I told Toby that I was getting sent back to my dad's after the summer. "Wow, that sucks," he said. "Let's make this the best summer ever." I had to choke back my tears and act cool, but I had never had such a good friend before and I was really going to miss him.

I lived with my dad for two years, spending most of the summer in Santa Cruz with my mom. In New Mexico drugs were easy to come by but punk rock was hard to find. I had to special-order tapes from the local record store. At school I was the only kid with dyed hair and combat boots. I really hated living there and begged my parents to let me move back to California.

While I was visiting Santa Cruz the next summer Toby and I had our first acid trip. An older kid named Chris who we used to smoke pot with sold it to us. It was hard to believe that those little square pieces of paper with the pictures of Mickey Mouse on them could have such an intense effect. They looked more like stamps or candy than drugs. We ran through the alleys of Capitola laughing our heads off at nothing. Hiding from the imagined Nazis who were chasing us. Diving into the sand on the beach as though escaping into a secured bunker. On the beach we were safe and took some time to relax before returning to the village to continue evading the troops.

3

It's in My Blood

With each slow stroke of the razor over my head, the cool breeze that was coming through the open window brought chills to my spine. Black Flag was playing on the stereo in Toby's room and it was hard for me to sit still while he shaved my head. We were going to a punk show so I wanted to have a fresh shave. I usually just used the buzzers but today we were going for the full bic bald. After he finished shaving my head he turned to me and said, "Now you really look like a dick with ears."

After I washed off my head it was Toby's turn. He had a flattop and wanted to bleach it out, so we mixed up some peroxide and bleach and

I began slopping it on his head. After about ten minutes he started to complain that his scalp was on fire and I noticed that his forehead was getting red. We washed off the bleach. His hair wasn't white yet but his scalp and neck were starting to blister so we just left it that orange-rust color of a botched bleach job. He actually liked it that color, he said it was "fuckin' punk." I started calling him carrot head, chicken little, q-tip, and rusty ass bitch. He offered me such innovative slurs as baldy locks, ko-jack, and bald baby butt head. It was great to be back with my best friend. We picked up right where we had left off.

We had been hanging out almost every day since I got back from New Mexico. It took a while but I had finally convinced my parents to let me move back to California, where I belonged. My mom had sold her house in the mountains and moved into the surf ghetto on the east side of Santa Cruz called Pleasure Point. Which was very cool for me. We lived half a block from the beach and there were a lot more kids around skating and surfing all the time.

Toby and I had both been listening to punk rock for a couple years by then but neither of us had ever been to a punk concert. Through listening to the music I knew that the punks understood how I felt and I had committed myself to live fast and die young in true Sid Vicious style. I was trained by the skate and surf punks I knew to hate all the peace punk protesting saps. To me punk rock was summed up in two words: Fuck Authority.

After we finished playing punk rock beauty parlor it was time to get ready for the show. We needed to make some shirts and get some drugs. I cut the sleeves off a U.S. Postal Service shirt I had stolen from the Goodwill and put a Bl'ast sticker over the postal patch on the front and on the back I took a big black marker and made Black Flag bars and wrote "Skate and Destroy." I was very happy with my creation. I had seen some older kids at Derby Skate Park with similar stuff on their shirts. Toby made a big Dead Kennedys symbol on his flannel and put on a Minor Threat T-shirt he had borrowed from his cousin.

We took the bus downtown and scored some acid from some hippies at the park. It was getting late so we both just put the acid in our mouths and walked over to the Pacific Garden Mall to check out the scene. We saw an older punk named Chris putting his mohawk up with hair spray in a doorway of a closed shop. He said, "You little fuckers going to the show?" I looked up to him but was also scared of him so I didn't say anything. He had bought me beer a couple times and that was cool but he was also always hanging out with the young girls and one time he told me to get lost when I tried to tag along with him to a party. Toby said, "Yeah, we're going to the show, are you?" He was bending over and spraying his hair so I don't think he heard us or even really cared so we kept walking. There weren't very many punks on the street so we just walked over to Club Culture. On the way through the bus station the security guard seemed like he was checking us out. I could feel the little piece of blotter paper from the acid still dissolving under my tongue, the familiar chills and chemical taste in my mouth. I wondered for a minute if the guard knew we were tripping.

As the acid began to take effect I could feel my skin tingling and I was unable to stop touching my freshly shaven head. As I stood in line in front of Club Culture waiting to see the first live punk show of my life, my stomach churned somewhere between butterflies and nausea.

Toby was talking to some girls behind us but I was way too high to attempt to speak, especially to these cute punk rockers. I recognized one of them from school, we went to the same junior high and I think we were even in the same grade, but I hadn't ever talked to her. She wore a blue sweater with some pins on her chest and tight black jeans that were pegged at the bottom, stopping about two inches above her yellow and pink argyle socks and white Frankenstein creepers. I knew her name was Carrie but for some reason we never hung out together at school. I had been in New Mexico the year before and when I returned to Santa Cruz most of my friends went to a different junior high. At school I just got high every day and stayed by myself or I'd hang out with the skaters.

As the line finally began to move Toby said something about getting some beers with the girls after the show. That sounded great to me but at that moment I didn't care about anything, my head felt really strange, the bald skin was so smooth under my fingers. As we passed the big window in front of the club I caught a reflection of myself and was completely surprised at the huge smile on my face. So surprised in fact that when I saw my face and the shit-eating grin I was wearing I tried to stop smiling. I wanted to look tough, not goofy. But it was no use, every time I attempted to stop smiling it just made me chuckle. I kept trying to give my best tough-guy look, squinting my eyes and glaring at my reflection but each time that just made me laugh more. Pretty soon Toby was cracking up too and then the girls behind us started laughing and pretty soon just about everyone in line was hysterical. That is, everyone except some stern looking skinheads who seemed to be scowling at us. They must have been thinking, "Those stupid little skate punks, they are probably on acid or something," and if so they were right. The laughter continued for a couple minutes and I wasn't sure if everyone was laughing with me or at me, but it didn't really matter.

As we made our way to the front we were greeted by two girls and a large black man who seemed to be counting people as they entered. One of the girls asked me for the four dollars for admission and the other one wanted to stamp my hand. This whole transaction was almost more than I could handle. I had stopped laughing but couldn't stop smiling. Inside the club there were people everywhere, street punks with bright-colored mohawks spiked straight up, girls with hair of every color dressed in plaid skirts or pegged pants, leather jackets or sweaters. There were some skinheads in tight pants, wearing clean and pressed button up shirts and shinny boots and a lot of skaters and surf punks with bowl cuts and curls wearing shorts and sweatshirts looking like they were ready to go skate or hit the beach. There was the odd heavy metal kid with long hair, a concert T-shirt, jeans, and a flannel. Even with my shaved head, we still belonged to the crew of skate punks, not the skinheads. I was most impressed by the guys who had spiked their long hair so it stood straight up in all directions so it looked like they had stuck their finger in a light socket.

I was no longer the weirdest one in the room. I was finally somewhere that I could just be myself and not worry about getting beat up by jocks or hicks. At school I was a constant target of ridicule, but here I was just another young kid hanging out. I felt accepted and I fit in. Even though we were the youngest ones at the show it didn't seem to matter.

As the first band started playing the energy that filled the room was intense; bodies began flying in every direction. Eventually the chaos became a circular pit of flying arms and thrashing bodies. Toby's cousin, Jason, came over to where we were standing. He stared at us for a minute, looking evil with his wicked smile. "Are you guys on drugs?" he asked. We both started laughing and at the same time said, "No," but continued to laugh. He grabbed us by the neck and threw us into the middle of the slam pit. I got smacked with a fist in the back of my head but the pain was invigorating, my whole body filled with a soothing rage, a comforting release of aggression. I started running as fast as I could in a large circle, slamming into people on each side of the crowded dance floor. Every time I fell down I was immediately picked up.

There was one guy who I especially noticed, maybe because he was one of the only black punks there. He had a dredlock mohawk and kept jumping so high that he landed on top of the crowd up front where the band was playing. I was so impressed by his utter defiance of gravity that I began trying some similar pitting styles. I ran as fast as I could, grabbing on to people's shoulders and launching myself over their heads, landing either on the crowd or on the floor.

All the older punks seemed to be looking out for us. Every time one of us fell down in the pit we were always picked up right away. There were some girls in the pit too and some of them were really strong and fierce. One girl with thick black eyeliner and a shaved head kept trying to go backward against the flow of the circle pit, pushing everyone out of her way, parting the massive flow of the circular sea of thrashing bodies.

In between songs we would try to catch our breath and smoke cigarettes at the same time. This was the most fun I'd had in my life. I loved it, the energy, the anger, and the freedom to be ourselves.

Between bands I realized how high I was. The graffiti-spattered walls were breathing and although the pit had stopped I saw what appeared to be a giant whirlpool of colors and smoke in the center of the room. With my back against the wall I just sat and stared at the scene before me. Punks, skaters, skinheads, new wave girls, and the random metalhead all mixing together. Toby and Jason were sitting next to me talking about something or other and every once in a while they would look at me and laugh. I probably still had that shit-eating grin on my face, happy as could be, peaking on acid.

The next group that played was the local band, Bl'ast, whose name I had on my shirt. Jason had made me a tape with them on it. They were great, one of the hardest bands I had ever heard. I listened to that tape almost every day; it had Bl'ast on one side and Black Flag on the other. I couldn't believe I was about to see them play. When they had all their equipment set up a huge crowd began to gather in front of the stage to witness these local legends perform the hardcore surf punk that was making them well known from coast to coast. The singer was a big bald guy who was wearing only a pair of black board shorts, no shirt and no shoes. He had a tattoo on his shoulder and one on his back. As the bass line began he just started rocking back and forth, shaking his head from side to side with a demonic smile on his face. He was staring into the crowd but seeing right through us. As the most powerful sound I had ever heard exploded from the guitar, he jumped up high over the stage and landed on a drumbeat with a growl that sent the room into total chaos. The room became mayhem, with bodies flying in every direction, eventually becoming a circular mass of forward momentum that occasionally spat someone out to one side or up and over the crowd to land on the stage, where they'd quickly dive back in. The pit was a pulsing vortex that sucked the rage out of all of us.

Running wildly about, I was overcome with the need to get my head above the pit. I began throwing myself over Jason's shoulders again and again. Gasping for a breath of air. Eventually I jumped on the back of a big suicidal skate punk and he carried me around in the pit swinging my arms above the crowd and singing along to all the songs I knew. I felt more alive than ever before. The pit was a realm of release. I was feeling almost no pain and was barely even aware of the abuse being piled on my body. I caught an elbow in the eye and went down, only to be scooped up quickly by an older mohawk punk. Bl'ast kept pounding out the most powerful music I had ever heard. I could feel it running through my veins, the hardcore punk rock movement had been permanently injected into me, it was in my blood.

I knew from that night on that this was where I belonged. I had found my place in this fucked-up world.

On the way out of the club Ritchie, the big black guy who ran the place, grabbed my arm and said, "Hey, kid, how would you and your friends like to get into all the shows for free?"

"Sure, what do we have to do?" I replied.

"Simple. Just come here every Thursday afternoon and I will give you a pile of fliers for the upcoming shows and you guys go around town and put them up. For that I will let you and a couple friends into any shows you want," he answered.

"Great, I'll see you on Thursday at around three-thirty," I said.

I couldn't believe it. My first show and I already had a job. Toby said, "Wow, you fucking work here now." He told Jason outside, "Noah just got a job putting up fliers. We get into all the shows for free now." Jason just smiled, knowing that meant he would get in free too. We looked for the girls from the line to see if we could try to get some beer and hang out with them but they were nowhere to be found. It was late and the buses had already stopped running. The girls probably had left earlier to catch a bus home. We were stranded downtown, without our skates, so we decided to walk home on the railroad tracks. At least that way we wouldn't get busted by the cops for being out so late. All we had to do was make it from downtown over to the boardwalk and then we could just follow the tracks all the way back to my mom's house on Pleasure Point. Getting to the boardwalk was the tricky part. We decided to stay on the levee most of the way even though the cops patrolled up there a lot. At least that way we could probably see them before they saw us and we could hide or run if we had to. The levee was right behind the club so we walked around back where the bands were packing up their stuff and a bunch of older people were hanging out drinking. Toby knew a couple of them;

they were friends of his cousin's. One of them gave us a couple of beers for the walk home.

Up on the levee there were several small groups of punks drinking and smoking, hanging out, talking about the show and stuff. I thought I saw the girls we were supposed to meet with some older guys but I didn't say anything to Toby because I just wanted to keep walking. We saw a couple having sex under the bridge at Laurel Street. There were moans and heavy breathing. I felt both embarrassed and excited but we just kept walking, wishing we were the ones ending such a great night like that rather than having to make the long walk back to the east side.

When we finally got to my house it was almost 3:00 A.M. My mom and her boyfriend were asleep. Very quietly we got some food from the kitchen and made our way into my room. We ate some cereal and bread and then tried to go to sleep. Neither of us could fall off though so we decided to talk for a little while. Toby said, "Can you hear that?" I said, "What?" He said, "Can you hear that?" I said, "Hear what?" He said, "Your brain cells popping." I just sat there for a minute contemplating what it would sound like to hear your brain cells pop and then all of the sudden I heard it. I could hear these tiny pops that sounded something like Rice Crispies just after you pour the milk on them. I said, "Shit." I said, "I think I do hear it."

"Are we gonna be like brain-dead or something if they all pop?" Toby asked.

"No, I heard we only use like a tenth of our brain anyway, so hopefully it's just the other part that we have destroyed," I joked, but it sounded good enough to me. I swore I really could hear my brain cells popping. It was so strange to just lie there listening to the destruction of my mind.

It was all worth it, the pain, the hangover, and all the dead brain cells. I had found my place in this fucked-up world.

4

Fuck Authority

At school the next week all I could think about was going down to the club on Thursday and picking up the fliers. I couldn't wait to go out and skateboard around town putting up fliers on all the telephone poles. I was incredibly excited about my new job. But on Wednesday at school I got busted with some pot. I had gotten super stoned before school and was just sitting there in my homeroom. The school security guard came into my class and took me to the office, where he and the vice principal made me empty my pockets onto his desk.

They found three dollars' cash, a pack of breath mints, some rolling papers, and a film container that was full of the weed I had stolen

from my mom's boyfriend. I found out later that the pot was so fragrant that the teacher could smell it in my pocket, so she had asked
them to search me. I was so stoned and so used to the smell of those
sticky green skunk buds that I was oblivious to the pungent herbal
aroma that was apparently wafting from my pockets. It didn't help
that I had been busted at school three times already that year for pot.
Twice I had actually been caught in the act of getting high with some
other kids in the alley across the street from school. One of those
times my friend Corey happened to have two ounces of cocaine in his
backpack that he had stolen from his dad, which we were going to try
to trade for pot after school. I hadn't seen Corey since, but his sister
told me they sent him away to a reform school or something.

Not only did I get suspended from school but they also called the
cops and had me arrested for possession of a controlled substance.
My mom had to leave work early and come pick me up from the police department. She was fucking furious. When she asked me where
I had gotten the weed and I told her I had stolen it from her boyfriend, she shut up. She didn't want him to find out I was ripping him
off and also felt guilty that I had gotten it from my own house.

On Thursday when it was time for me to go down to Club Culture
and start my new job as flier boy, I was grounded and on strict orders
not to leave the house. My mom didn't usually get home from work
until around five-thirty though so I figured I would sneak out and get
down there at about three o'clock. That way I would have a couple
hours to put up fliers. The problem was that my sister, Tara, was
going to be home so I would have to beg her not to turn me in. She
got home early and I promised I would get her some weed if she
would not tell Mom that I had left and cover for me in case she called
or something. She hesitatingly agreed after torturing me for a while,
and I was off. When I got down to the club Ritchie wasn't even there
but a woman named Andrea was in the office and she was expecting
me. She gave me two stacks of fliers for upcoming shows. One was
for an English band called the Sub-Humans that I had never heard of
and the other was for JFA and Aggression, a couple of punk bands

that I had heard over at Jason's house. Bl'ast and a band called The Faction were opening up for the second show.

Armed with a stapler I had stolen from school, I skateboarded all the way home, plastering posters on every telephone pole. The next day on my way downtown I realized that I had put posters up on only one side of the street. That weekend I recruited Toby and our other friend, Joe, to help me go out fliering. Joe was from the Point too, he lived just a couple blocks away, but we went to different junior highs so I didn't know him that well. We had told him about the show and he wanted to come so he was helping with the fliers so I would get him in. We skated from the east side all the way to Derby Skate Park, over on the west side. At Derby we got some older guys to get us some beers and then we just skated the rest of the day, totally forgetting about our fliers. I felt a little guilty for flaking out on my fliering job but I had my priorities and they were drinking and skateboarding.

At home the trouble about the pot was soon forgotten and at school the following week my friends were glad to see me. I was having a great time even with all the trouble. I had completely lost interest in school, family, and following anyone's rules. All that mattered to me was drugs, skateboarding, and sex.

I was having sex once in a while with a girl from school named Halley. We would go to her place after school and get high and then we would start making out, sometimes it ended up in sex or blowjob, sometimes it ended up with me jumping out the window when her mom or dad came home. That lasted for only a couple months until she started going out with one of my friends instead.

My mom started talking to me about possibly going back to New Mexico to live with my father and Ondrea for a while. She was planning to sell her house and go off traveling around the world for a year or so with her boyfriend. At first I said, "No way," but after thinking about it for a while I began to feel that it might be a good idea. I really hated my mom's boyfriend and I was getting in so much trouble in Santa Cruz. Plus I was missing my dad and Ondrea. Over the years we had become better friends and they gave me a lot of freedom. After some intense arguing we agreed that I would go back there for ninth grade and see how it went. I was pissed at my mom. It felt like she was just shipping me off again so she could go party with her boyfriend. My biggest complaint though was that I would miss all the great punk shows. I had finally found somewhere that I fit in and they were ruining it all.

The next week Toby and I brought some other skaters from the Point with us to the show: Joe, who had helped with the fliers, and Rick, another kid from the neighborhood who went to school with Joe and Toby. We all took the bus downtown but this time we brought our skates with us for after the show. Joe and Toby waited at the Metro while I took Rick with me up to the top of the mall to try and get some acid.

At the little park at the top of the Pacific Garden Mall there were about a dozen hippies hanging out. As we approached, several of them asked us what we were looking for. "We need some doses," I said. A crazy looking hippy with wild eyes and a dirty face brought us into the corner of the park behind a big redwood tree, where he pulled out a whole sheet of orange sunshine LSD. He told us that he had eaten half a sheet himself last week and that he was just beginning to come down. We bought four hits, for four bucks each. After he gave us our hits he chewed up the rest of the sheet. I couldn't understand how anyone could eat so much acid without dying.

We went around the corner to try and get some weed. Rick bought a dime bag from some Rasta, and we sat on the stairs by the clock tower putting the acid and weed into a cigarette pack. All of the sudden a cop walked up and said, "Hey, boys, what are you guys doing down here?" "Um, we're just waiting for some friends," I replied. Rick started shaking he was so scared. The cop asked us how old we were and then he confiscated the cigarette package. He found the weed but rather than busting us he just poured the buds onto the sidewalk and ground them into dust with his big pig boots. I gave him a fake name and said I didn't have any ID because I knew if he found out that I was already on probation he would arrest us for sure. He let

us go and warned us not to come around there anymore. I was so relieved that he didn't arrest us I didn't even care that we had just lost
thirty bucks in drugs. That's a lot of money too, but at least we weren't
going to Juvenile Hall.

After he destroyed our weed he threw the cigarette package into a
nearby trash can. He hadn't discovered the acid that was tucked into
the cellophane wrapper and I wanted to retrieve it. But he waited for
us to leave so we went around the block and came back and grabbed
the cigarette package out of the trash. The cop was gone but my heart
was racing so fast I started sweating. It was worth the risk of going
back to Juvie though. It was worth all of it to get high, to eat some acid
and see a punk show.

Toby and Joe were bummed that we hadn't got any pot and we only
had eight dollars left between us, so we shoulder-tapped a twelve-pack
of cheap beer and bought some more cigarettes. We sat under the
bridge where we had seen a couple having sex the week before. We
had three beers each and got pretty buzzed. When we were in line at
the club we all took the hit of acid. It was Joe's and Rick's first acid
trip and first punk show.

At the door the girl said I was allowed only two guests not three. I
told her we didn't have any money left and she let us all in with only a
slight bit of annoyance. We stashed our skates in the office where I
had picked up the fliers. Joe and Rick were obviously nervous and so
was I but when the music started and they had their first taste of the
pit, soon they too found a home.

The first band that played was called The Faction. The guitar player
was a pro skater named Steve Caballero. We had all heard or heard of
this band, and of course we all knew of Cab, he was a legend on a
skateboard. I was a little surprised that the turnout for this show was a
lot smaller than last time. The Faction was great but there was no pit
and we weren't about to be the ones to start it.

When Bl ast came on it seemed like people came out of the walls,
all of the sudden the room was filled with punks, skaters, skins, and a
few metalheads. I was feeling comfortably numb with my three beers
and one tab of LSD. Clifford, the singer for Bl'ast, came out again in

nothing but shorts and this time started the set by screaming out over the crowd, "Start the machine." Even before the band could begin its musical assault people began jumping up and down and the pit had already started churning. It was as if just the mere presence of these local legends was enough to incite a riot.

The four of us stayed in the pit for the whole set. Rick got smashed in the nose and was bleeding a little bit but didn't seem to care. He had a look that said, "You can't hurt me." I saw some guys going around the side of the stage and making the running, jumping stage-dive into the crowd or sometimes directly into the pit. I decided to follow along and made my own vain attempt at a dive that came off more like I stumbled across the stage and then crawled out onto the heads of the people up front. Joe was right behind me and he had a better grip on the situation. He got a running start, planted one foot on the speaker, and launched himself several feet in the air flying out above the crowd and tumbling down upon some kids who were skanking arm and arm through the pit. He got up proud and accomplished, looking over at us to make sure we had witnessed his flight.

Toby spent most of the night making out in the corner with some new wave girl who looked like Cyndi Lauper. Joe and I kept throwing stuff at them. We were just jealous that we weren't getting any.

Club Culture was not only a punk club, it also had hip-hop shows and break dancing contests. One Thursday when I was picking up the fliers I found a tape on the floor that said NYC on it. I thought that maybe it was some New York punk bands so I put it in my pocket. After a long afternoon of fliering with Joe I got home and put the tape in my little sister's pink Barbie boom box. I didn't have my own room, I shared it with my little brother and sister, who stayed with their dad most of the time but I still lived in a room full of bunk beds and Barbies. Most of the time I felt like a visitor in my own house. Expecting some loud and fast New York hardcore I was shocked by the beats and rhymes that came out of the Barbie box. My first reaction was one of disappointment but I let the tape continue to play. I had heard some of this stuff at school when the kids would break dance at lunch. But I was a punk so I never really listened to it. I just made fun of them and sometimes some friends and I would go out into the breaking circle and try to start a slam pit.

But that tape was actually really good, I liked it a lot. It had a message of disapproval of society's racist politics that seemed closely related to the punk rock I was listening to. The tape consisted of Curtis Blow, Shante, the Real Roxanne, and Whodini, as well as some other stuff. After that Toby and I both secretly got into hip-hop. We were punkers by style and conviction but you might also find us getting high and listening to the Sugar Hill Gang or Run DMC.

There was a major division between hip-hop and punk rock in the scene but I didn't care about that. I knew that I liked rap so I listened to it, even if I didn't admit it publicly. There was a Mexican kid named Ernesto at school who was one of the better break dancers. One night downtown I saw him and some of his friends out doing graffiti behind Club Culture. He let me use some of his paint and I wrote "eastside punks" on the wall with a little skull next to it. He did a head with a hat turned sideways that said "breakers" on it. The two pieces side by side looked cool and we were both proud of our creations. After that Ernesto and I became friends. We would get high together once in a while before school, but if he was with his crew or I was with mine we barely acknowledged each other.

At school the trouble continued. I was arrested five times that year for pot and once for assault (a fight). I barely graduated from junior high. I had almost failed every class owing to lack of participation but when it came time for graduation they decided to let me walk with my eighth grade class anyway. I think they just wanted to get rid of me. I was sick of being told what to do. I knew that school was all bullshit. Nothing that they taught us was useful in the real world. I learned more about what was really happening in the world from reading the lyrics of punk bands than I ever had in school. I planned some big anti-school, anti-authority protest for the graduation ceremony but when it came time I just kept my head down and walked across the stage like everyone else.

That summer I saw lots of bands and I took lots of drugs. But it was all planned: I was going back to New Mexico for ninth grade. My folks had me all set up with some little hippy school that was at some guy's house. Club Culture looked like it was getting shut down anyway because of too much violence and underage drinking. I guess the punks and breakers had started clashing around the venue too. There had been several small riots and a lot of arrests. The cops were ready to shut down the only "all ages" club in town. Everyone was pissed off but most of us were too drunk or too young to do anything about it. There were many city hall meetings and I kept meaning to go to one but never seemed to make it.

The night before I was to leave for New Mexico, Social Unrest was playing at the club. I had put up the fliers for the show and I was on the guest list but my mom wouldn't let me go because we had to leave early for the airport. We had a big fight and I was trying to leave the house in spite of her when her boyfriend came after me with a broomstick threatening to beat me if I were to leave. He was a fucking psycho, a no-good drunk. I spent my last night in Santa Cruz in my room, filled with rage, listening to my new Crucifix record over and over. My mom tried to talk to me but I wouldn't even acknowledge her. She didn't understand me, no one did. The only thing I had was my music.

That fight actually made it easier for me to move. Something to be pissed off about and someone to hate. I always hated my mom's boyfriends, partially because that's what teenage boys do and partially because she always seemed to pick real assholes.

Just after I got shipped off to New Mexico, Club Culture shut its doors forever, closing a chapter of the early eighties Santa Cruz punk scene. I had seen dozens of shows and had been ordained into a lifestyle that would influence me for the rest of my life.

5

teenage Wasteland

taos is a small town in northern New Mexico populated by Indians, Mexicans, and hippies. The only thing to do there that is halfway fun is skiing in the winter. The rest of the time there is absolutely nothing going on. I couldn't even skateboard because there were no sidewalks, just a bunch of dirt roads and a highway that runs through the center of town. My home life was a lot better though. I got along well with my parents and only fought with my brother and sister half of the time. There was a lot of love in the house but I was too stoned most of the time to notice.

There was only one other punk in Taos, his name was Francis. He was a tall, thin kid with a pierced nose and a shaved head. I was growing a mohawk at that point and we quickly became close friends. Being white in New Mexico can be difficult when you have a ten-inch mohawk and wear a studded leather jacket all summer, but in the ninety-degree heat it's even worse. We got chased by low riders and threatened by the local Chicano gangs regularly. It helped a little that we had both gone to elementary school there so we knew most of the tough guys our age but the older vatos really thought we were freaks. The only thing that saved us was that we were stoners too and the cholos loved to get high.

The party scene in Taos was mostly hippy kids and ski bums. We did all we could not to fit in but we always showed up to every party and caused as much trouble as possible. It got to the point where they wouldn't even let us into some parties anymore. There was nothing else to do, so we smoked pot every day, drank a lot, and listened to our records.

As often as possible on the weekends I would hitch-hike the three-hour trip to Albuquerque to see punk shows and hang out with my friend Steve. Francis had introduced me to Steve, who was a few years older than we were and lived in a house near the university called the Nursery with a bunch of other punks and skins. There was a pretty good punk scene in Albuquerque. At least I got to see bands like 7 Seconds, the Descendents, Life Time, Rigor Mortis, Millions of Dead Cops, and Corrosion of Conformity, to name a few, when they were on tour. I started to sell acid and weed sometimes, so I would hitch-hike down from Taos, stop in Santa Fe to sell some doses, hitch to Albuquerque to hang out for the weekend, and hitch back to Taos. I enjoyed being out on the road alone going back and forth. I got lots of strange rides and often people would get me high on the drive. A few times some crazy Mexicans would pick me up and scare the shit out of me like they were going to kill me or something but I would always just fall back on the universal peace offering, a joint. Getting high with angry locals saved my life more than once.

Francis got sent off to boarding school, so I befriended some local stoners and began eating acid every weekend over at one of the guys' places. He had his own little studio behind his mom's house that we called "the shack." That was cool for a while until I stole all his pot plants and had to try and avoid him, which isn't easy in such a small town.

School didn't go so well. I was much more interested in getting high than studying. The school was set up in a house just outside of town. There were only about a dozen kids in the high school. I had an extremely adversarial relationship with the teachers. I was stoned every single day. Since I was determined to create chaos, eventually they suggested that I do home school and just come in once a week to turn in my assignments. That way they wouldn't have to deal with my overpowering teen angst. There was a good English teacher there named Natalie Goldberg (who went on to become a famous writer) but I didn't like her very much. To me she was just another hippy trying to be part of the system of oppression and prejudice that is called high school. I ended up stealing a couple of the homework answer books and just wrote in all the answers to my homework. I passed all my classes but learned nothing.

Over the years Ondrea and I had become much closer. She was able to show me the love and acceptance that I needed. I really loved her and my dad but instead of showing it I stole from them all the time. I got along okay with James but was constantly ripping him off also. I just felt that everyone owed me something. I couldn't stop myself from stealing, trying to fill the void and get the negative attention I had become so accustimed to. Ondrea was really sick with cancer. They were doing a lot of healing stuff at home but at one point she had to spend some time in the hospital. I was too lost in my own problems to really understand what was going on.

The day Ondrea was coming home from the hospital I had been in town drinking. I had stolen a fifth of Bacardi from the local supermarket but I was supposed to get a ride home with them from the hospital. I'd only drunk a little out of the bottle and wanted to bring it home to get drunk with my brother so I tried to hide it under the seat of my dad's car. I guess he must have heard it clunking around or something because when we got home, after taking Ondrea inside, I tried to sneak out and retrieve it but he had already found it. He was really pissed, not only that I was stealing and drinking but how could I have been so stupid and uncaring. Ondrea was coming home from the hospital and all I cared about was booze. He made me take it back to the store and turn myself in. I had to work there for a few hours, sweeping the aisles, big deal. I was oblivious to having done anything wrong. The only problem that I could see was that I had been caught.

I really hated living in New Mexico and was burning a lot of bridges so I began plotting my return to California.

My mom had sold her house and traveled for about six months with her boyfriend. After they spent most of her money on traveling they split up and she was back in Santa Cruz, broke, working nine to five. She got back together with an old boyfriend who had just gotten out of prison and they were living together in Capitola. There wasn't really any room for me but she said I was welcome to stay in the twins' room again if I wanted to.

When I turned sixteen I told my parents (Stephen and Ondrea) I was done with school and with living under their roof. They were concerned for my well-being and tried to let me know that out in the world I would have to take responsibility for my own actions. We had a lawyer write up an emancipation document that said I was responsible for my actions as an adult. We all signed it and I was on the next plane back to California, planning to just stay with my mom for a couple of weeks until I could find a job and a place to live.

Being back in Santa Cruz was fucking great. There was no more Club Culture but the scene was strong. It was nice to be back around other punks, no longer the only freak in town. Things had changed the year I was away. Without the club there was no common gathering place and the different factions within the scene had really split. Some of the older punks had all bought vintage European motorcycles and got more into rockabilly. Toby's cousin, Jason, who had turned me on to punk was a rocker now and he was in a gang called the Vintage Rockers. The skinheads had started a crew called the Firm and the skaters and punks didn't seem to mix as much anymore. Joe, Rick, and the rest of my old east-side skate punk crew kind of shunned me for looking like a street punk with my long red mohawk, leather jacket, and combat boots.

Downtown, Toby was hanging out with a group of street punks called the Gutter Punks. They were a mix of homeless kids and working-class punks that included the Suicidals, Mohawkans, Misfit Punks, New York City hardcore kids, and even a few metalheads. That's where I ended up hanging out; I had always gravitated toward the streets. The Firm and the Gutters didn't get along very well and the Rockers didn't like either of us. I noticed that there was a lot of pro-skinhead, anti-punk graffiti around so I stole an idea I had seen in New Mexico and started doing graffiti with a stencil I made of a skull with a mohawk that read "Hair Force." I kept it a secret pretty much, only a few close friends knew about it. The last thing I needed was to have the Firm after me. They would have kicked the shit out of me.

I met up with some of the kids I had known from junior high and Club Culture, a crew of girls that called themselves the Hell Bitches. One of them, Jessica, was an old friend, and she had let me crash at her house a couple of times. Scooter, Talia, Valeika, and Robin looked familiar but I didn't really remember them. Within the bigger street punk scene I had a smaller crew, Toby, Jon, Bubbles, Mark, and Stinky. We all hung out with the Gutters and the Hell Bitches but when it came down to getting drugs or booze we were a separate entity. My crew were the guys who took care of me when I was broke and I took care of them when they were broke.

It was like old times with the crew back together. I was always ready for whatever chaos would ensue whenever we went out. I got a job at the A&W burger joint and after work I would head downtown to the bench where I knew I could find my crew hanging out, sparing for change and talking shit. Toby, Jon, and Mark seemed to be taking

turns hooking up with the Hell Bitches, whose signature was bloody
fingernail marks down the back. If someone got laid, they would
show off their scars and compare stories.

Toby had started shooting up while I was away. But by the time I
got back from New Mexico he was mostly just drinking a lot. I was a
little surprised that so many of my friends were using needles but I
didn't really care that much. I had always sworn that I would never
use needles but they could do whatever they wanted to.

About a week after I got home Toby, Jon, Mark, and I all got way
too drunk on vodka and ended up getting arrested for being drunk in
public. I was immediately back in the system, back on probation, and
court-ordered to stay away from my best friends. Of course that never
stopped us; it was just a big joke. Every time we were together, which
was almost every day unless one of us was in jail or something, we
would joke about how we were breaking the law just by hanging out.

I had started doing coke in Taos, mostly just snorting it, but I had
smoked it a couple times. In Santa Cruz crack was the easiest drug
to score so we started smoking crack rocks. It was cheap enough to
afford a couple rocks here and there. Unfortunately a couple was
never enough and I was spending all of my money all of the time
pretty quickly.

The A&W job didn't last too long and I had different jobs off and
on but never seemed to get enough money to get an apartment.
Whenever I got a paycheck I'd spend it all getting high. I was staying
at my mom's but tried to remind her as often as possible that it was
just temporary and that I was emancipated, that I was just staying
there until I could save some money.

Things got bad very quickly. I was feeling completely alienated
from the world and I was only really interested in consuming as
much booze and drugs as possible. I got really sick of fighting with
my mom and her boyfriend so I tried to hit the streets for good.

Slamming the door behind me, I left my mom's house swearing that I would never come back. Her boyfriend was such a fucking asshole. He had just gotten out of prison and he treated me like a jerk. So I ripped off his weed and anything else I could find around the house. On the #40 bus from Capitola to Santa Cruz, it was the same old shit—a bunch of kids and losers riding the shame train. At least my friends seemed to understand me.

On the streets we were a family. The punks stuck together. We drank together, fought together, and did whatever we needed to, to survive. Most of us had parents and homes that we could have gone to, but we chose to stay on the streets instead, eating out of Dumpsters and at soup kitchens, staying drunk as much as possible, and taking turns breaking into someone's parents' house to shower off once in a while.

As the bus pulled into the Metro I saw the crew sitting around at the bench, panhandling and harassing people as they passed our little section of the Pacific Garden Mall. Zae was the first to greet me. He had his hawk up—yellow, green, blue, red, and purple liberty spikes. I think he used acrylic paint and superglue. "Hey, Noah, check it out," he said and showed me his new tattoo. It was a homemade one of a syringe on his forearm pointing toward his elbow veins. I just said, "Cool, got any smokes?" He handed me a cigarette and his lighter, still admiring his own fucked-up tattoo. Everyone was about ready to get some beer and go down to Desolation.

Toby and I went in on a twelver of Schaefer for two bucks each. He asked how things went at home and I told him about the fight with my mom's boyfriend, that he had found out that a bunch of his weed was missing, but that I denied it of course. I said I was never going home, that I was going to see if I could stay at the squat for a while. I told Toby about how my mom's boyfriend tried to threaten me by telling me about what they do in prison for stealing someone's shit. "Good," I told him. "Why don't you go back to prison, you fucking bastard?" My mom had to step in to stop him from beating my ass. "So I split and here's the bag of weed I stole from him."

"Fuck them, fuck all parents!" said Toby. Some girl standing behind us echoed, "Yeah, fuck all adults!"

Sitting on the tracks, drinking cheap beer, and halfheartedly toss-
ing rocks at a nearby pile of bottles, I surveyed the scene. I felt kind of
cold yet sort of numb from the beer. I could hear Johnny and Zae arguing somewhere around the corner in the bushes. Toby passed me a
smoke and a light and I said, "Thanks, bro."

That was our home now, Desolation, where all the street punks
came to drink. It was really just a lagoon connected to a water treatment plant, but the trails and bushes made the place feel secluded
and desolate. It was right next to the train tracks and some abandoned
warehouses where some of the punks squatted. Once in a while some
skinheads showed up and there was either a fight or a friendly drinking match, depending on the mood. Sometimes a bum stumbled into
our lair and got rolled. But usually we were down there next to the lagoon just drinking and smoking, talking shit about the system and
how great it would be if there were no laws and no government. I felt
right at home there.

A girl named Mona sat down next to me and started talking about
how much warmer it was back in Arizona. She was a fourteen-year-
old runaway from Phoenix. All she was wearing were two pairs of
ripped-up fishnet stockings, a bondage skirt, and a little white sweater.
She looked like a nice little Catholic schoolgirl gone bad. She kept
complaining about how cold it was, so I offered her my leather jacket.
Because I'm a sucker and I really wanted to get together with her. It
was worth being cold for a while. When she put it on I saw that some
of the studs on the collar were loose so I flipped it up and started
bending the metal prongs back in. I'd had that jacket for two years; it
was the only possession that I really cared about, other than my boots.
I bought the jacket, used, with some money from Christmas when I
was fourteen, and I had spent countless hours painting it and putting
studs all over the collar and up the right arm. The boots I had recently
stolen from some poser from San Jose. Johnny and I had invited him
to come drink with us, and when we had gotten him good and drunk
we stole his brand-new boots and flight jacket. The boots were too
small for Johnny and a little too big for me, but I didn't care—a little
toilet paper in the toes did the trick. Fixing the studs on my collar gave

me an excuse to touch Mona's freshly shaven head. She left her bangs around the fringe; the skinhead girl cut. I thought she was looking great. I passed her my beer and opened a new one.

Toby and his girlfriend, Jamie, were arguing about something behind us and it was starting to get dark. Jamie had just moved to Santa Cruz from New York City and she was pregnant. I thought that she was old and gross and I had heard that she'd been doing tricks down in the Beach Flats for drugs. Toby really liked her though. So whatever—I didn't really care. She had some cool stories about New York. She saw the Sex Pistols in '77, so I put up with her.

In the distance I could hear the screams of the people riding the roller coaster down at the Boardwalk, and the breeze coming off the ocean carried the smell of junk food. I was really fucking cold and the beer tasted awful. I never had liked the taste of beer—I drank it every day but never liked it much.

I was wondering where I was going to take Mona that night, since neither of us had any place to stay. Maybe cancer-cut Scott would let us sleep on the foldout couch in his front yard. I'd slept there before, it was a lot better than the bushes. We were almost out of beer when Jerry came riding up on his cruiser with the basket on the front full of booze. Even though Jerry was a skinhead he only hung out with punks. He had "USA" tattooed across one eyebrow. Jerry was from Los Angeles, he said that the skins up here were all pussies, a bunch of wanna-be "Oi" boys. I was always impressed with how clean and shiny he kept his boots; mine were pretty fucked up.

I guess in some places the punks and skins were really united and the scene was one. That's not how it was in Santa Cruz. For some reason we small-town kids had something to prove. One-on-one I usually got along with skins but when they were in a group there was usually violence. The whole skinhead thing had come about even earlier than the punk movement in England; supposedly the skins were like the little brothers of the rude boys and soccer hooligans, listening to early Jamaican ska and northern soul. It was and still is for the most part a multiracial movement, which is why it's so weird that the Nazis are the only ones who get any attention and give all the skinheads a bad name. In Santa Cruz most of the skins were SHARP (skin heads against racial prejudice) and listened to more reggae than punk. But they were still wanna-be tough-guy thugs. A bunch of posers.

Jerry had just robbed the Safeway. It was easy and we all did it. You just asked if you could use the bathroom and they would let you go in the back room where everything was stored. There were cases and cases of hard liquor that didn't need to be refrigerated so you could just help yourself. Jerry handed us a bottle of Jack Daniels and Mona started complaining about how sick she got last time she drank JD and how she would never drink it again. Good, more for me. Same thing happened to me with tequila once.

I told her about how, when I was twelve, my big brother had a bottle of tequila—the kind with the worm in the bottom. He said I could drink it with him if we finished it and I ate the worm. He was a wrestler, sort of a jock in high school. He used to come home from his wrestling practice and try out his new moves and holds on me. I got my revenge by ripping him off and being an obnoxious little prick. Of course I drank the whole bottle with him and then I passed out. I woke up in my bed puking all over myself but was too drunk to do anything about it. So I just put my pillow over it and went back to sleep. I hadn't been able to drink tequila since.

The Jack felt good; it warmed me up. Jerry started telling us about the time he saw Black Flag play in L.A. at the Olympic Coliseum. I wasn't sure why he kept going on and on about Black Flag until I realized that I was wearing my Black Flag shirt. It had a picture of a kid beating a cop to death. It was my favorite shirt.

Some other kids came walking up but I didn't recognize any of them. They started talking to Zae and Steph. Toby and I considered fighting them for their boots and jackets but neither of us really cared enough to start any shit. Plus, I had a girl for the night and I was feeling pretty good.

For some reason in Santa Cruz we always had a feeling of superiority over the kids who lived over the hill, in San Jose or Campbell, we called them all "valleys" and felt that we could take their shit if they came into our town. Of course the same thing happened to us when we went to their towns or to San Francisco.

I wasn't cold anymore but now I was hungry. It was Tuesday night, which meant twenty-five-cent night down at the boardwalk: hot dogs, Cokes, and cotton candy for a quarter. Toby and Jamie were hungry too, so we all got ready to split and get some grub. When I tried to stand up I stumbled and dropped my bottle of Jack Daniels. It broke on the railroad tracks and Jerry started yelling at me for being a stupid, clumsy, good-for-nothing drunk. Toby and Jamie were laughing so hard that they almost fell down too. I started to realize how drunk I was but I didn't care. I felt invincible. If Jerry hadn't been ten years older than I was I would have kicked him in the teeth for making me look stupid in front of Mona. But she didn't seem to mind either; she had my leather on and was ready to go get some hot dogs.

We walked the tracks toward the beach. On the way, under the trestle, we saw Bubbles and Mark and told them where we were going and they decided to come with us. Now there were seven of us, all laced up in our Doc Martens, creepers, Converses, leather jackets covered in studs and painted with the names and logos of our favorite bands, hooded sweatshirts, fishnets, bondage belts, chains, and acne— a bunch of pubescent kids filled with angst and hatred. Together we were a crew. Safe in numbers—no one usually fucked with us in numbers. Alone we got jumped by the jocks, low riders, metalheads, frat boys, surfers, hicks, and even the skinheads who listened to a lot of the same music as we did. But tonight I felt good—I had my crew, I was drunk, and I had a girl on my arm. Soon I would have some dogs in my stomach and everything would be perfect.

On the way down to the beach some jocks gave us dirty looks and said something under their breath as I walked past them—I was used to it and didn't really care. Mona was on my arm and we just kept going. One of them tried to trip Mark and he turned around and smacked the guy with his skateboard. The other three jumped on him and start kicking him. Toby and I ran over and pushed them off. I got hit in the back of the head so I grabbed the skateboard off the ground and came up swinging, smashing one of the bastards in the shoulder and another one in the head. When the skateboard smacked his head he went down. A little blood spattered the sidewalk and he just lay there motionless. I could hear the girls screaming and some lady said she was going to call the police. The other meatheads started running down the street. For a minute I just stood there looking at the guy on the ground: he was about my age, maybe sixteen or seventeen, wearing acid-washed jeans and some big Nike basketball shoes. The fight was over and I sort of felt bad for hitting him with the skate, but he fucking deserved it for fucking with us just because we were different. They were kicking Mark's ass for no reason.

Toby was yelling at me to run, said the cops were coming. But it was too late—they were already there and I was too drunk to run. I dropped the skateboard and tried to start walking away, but the cops came from both directions and pulled their guns on us. "Face down on the ground, hands where I can see them," and all that shit. Mona was gone and so were Jamie and everyone else. It was just me, Toby, Mark, Bubbles, and Johnny. Some lady was saying we were the ones that started it and pointed me out as the one who hit the boy with the skateboard. He was sitting up by then, holding his head. He had a good-size cut on his head, either from the skateboard or from the sidewalk, I don't know which.

We all got handcuffed and stuffed into the back of the riot van. At the station the cops went inside and left us sitting there for a few minutes. Toby managed to get his zipper down, stood up on the bench, and pissed through the screen barrier: all over the cops' seats and on a jacket that was hanging on a hook behind the driver's seat. When the cops came around back to open the van Bubbles and Johnny were spitting at them and screaming, calling them baby rapists. Johnny was saying, "I'll fuck your dog, you baby raper." I was laughing so hard I almost pissed myself, until I caught a billy club on the shin. Then I wasn't laughing anymore, but I don't fight with cops. I had seen too many of my friends beaten to a pulp.

Inside the station they hog-tied us because Toby and Johnny wouldn't stop spitting at them. They had our hands and our feet cuffed together, so we were face down on our stomachs. Toby's pants

were down around his knees and there was blood on his shirt. I didn't
know if it was from the fight with the jocks or from the beating he received from the cops for pissing in the van.

I was the only minor. Toby and Bubbles had just turned eighteen
and Johnny was twenty. They pulled me out of the holding cell at the
boardwalk and sent me up to Juvenile Hall. Staring out the window of
the cop car as we drove through the beach flats and then downtown, I
saw the bench at the corner of Pacific and Chestnut and wondered if
any of the punks noticed me in the back of the car. If they did would
they have really cared? Leaving town we headed up Graham Hill Road
to the Juvenile Detention Center. It was an all too familiar experience,
handcuffed in the back of a cop car, again.

Outside the trees looked cold and lonely. I wished I were lost in
those woods rather than on my way back to jail. I had been in and out
of that place for years. I came up there every other week to see my probation officer. A few weeks earlier I had gotten a dirty piss test for
cocaine and my PO said I would have to do some time if it ever happened again. I had made up a stupid story about how someone had
passed me a cigarette with coke in it at a party. She was pretty cool but
I couldn't seem to stay out of trouble and her hands were tied. She
had let me off a million times but this time I knew I was going down:
assault and battery or assault with a deadly weapon—plus, if they
threw in a drunk-in-public or an intoxicated-minor charge, not to
mention it was a violation of my probation to have even been with
Toby and Johnny and I was sure they would find my bag of weed
when I got strip-searched. I'd probably have to do a few months.

In the Hall everyone knew me. Tim looked disappointed to see me
again but was very friendly. He had worked there for a long time, seen
me come and go. He was probably in his early thirties, thin, short
blond hair and wire-rim glasses. Nice guy for a cop. Well, he wasn't
really a cop, but he might as well have been, he held the keys that kept
me locked in the cell.

I was fucking starving and he got me some leftover cheese sandwiches and a carton of milk. Tim knew who my dad was and told me
he had read some of his books, so he was perplexed about why I was

so fucked up when my father was such a wonderful spiritual teacher. Another woman named Jennifer, who worked there, was also a fan of my dear old dad. I thought they might be a couple, but they would never tell me.

I didn't even know what my dad's books were about, I had never even read one—some hippie shit about being nice and passive, I figured. Meditation and all that boring crap. Not for me. Everyone knows that the hippies failed. A bunch of drugged out, dirty rich kids talking about peace and love. No fucking way. The only thing that was going to make a real change was to abolish government. Anarchy was the only solution. It was too late for peaceful protest—we had to fight the oppressors and the brain-dead followers of the dictates set up by the capitalist system. I got so mad thinking about all of this and how I was there for standing up against a bully, fighting against the oppressor, caught up in the system.

6

No Remorse

I had to do only a couple of weeks in the Hall. The kids we fought with weren't pressing charges and the regular juvenile judge was away. When you're locked up every day it's the same old shit. Up early for breakfast. Make your bed, military style. Line up by your door and wait for the man with the keys to come by and let you out, get your shoes on, then stand in front of your door until they call your name to come get in line for breakfast. Then walk single file to the dining hall, where you're fed some kind of disgusting slop or other.

After breakfast we were locked back up for a couple more hours while groups of five or six were taken down to the showers. Everyone showered every other day. Then we had school. I had dropped out two years earlier in tenth grade, but they made me attend anyway. So I worked on some GED prep books and drew a lot. At noon we had lunch. Same drill, single file, called by name out of class. More greasy mess hall chow. Seconds if you dared.

After lunch we usually got to play ball or do some sort of exercise in the guise of PE. When we were out on the baseball field I always fantasized about making a run for it. There was only one twenty-foot fence between me and freedom. Everyone got caught who tried it. You could easily get over the fence before they caught you but there would be a hundred cops waiting for you on the other side. After we played ball for a while we got locked back in our rooms for an hour or so before dinner. I usually read some horror books or looked at the *Maximum Rock n Roll* (a punk rock magazine) that I had already read a hundred times.

Dinner was at five and then we got locked in our cells again. The whole day was based on a points system. You got points for behaving the way they wanted you to. If your bed was made as they had directed and your room and toilet were clean, you got five points. If you didn't cause any disturbances during the meals then you got a certain number of points. Same with school, showers, PE. Basically every part of our day was judged and if we acted like robots, doing only as they dictated, then we got all our points. The points were used as leverage. Based on the number of points you had accumulated, or hadn't lost, during the day you were awarded a certain amount of time out of your cell in the evenings. If you had lost too many points then you stayed in your room. Perfect points stayed out until 9:00 P.M. and then there were various amounts of free time under that based on points, 7:30, 8:00, or 8:30. They often showed a movie in the evening and if you had an early down time then you had to go back to your cell in the middle of it.

Most days I got out of my room for at least an hour. Very rarely did I get to stay out till 9:00 P.M. All the structure and rules got me down, I felt so confined and scrutinized all the time. It was hard to stop myself from just snapping and trying to hurt someone, or hurting myself. The only other emotion besides depression I could feel was anger: rage at the system, society, at my fucked-up predicament. I must have been lonely, scared, even sad, but it would all just come out as anger.

There were a couple of cool guards but most of them were just pretend cops who seemed to get off on the power trip of controlling our lives. Tim was the only one in the place who seemed to genuinely care about me. But he still held the keys and still locked me in my room several times each day. I knew some other kids from the streets in there and I also got along with some of the gang kids from Watsonville, probably because I grew up with so many Chicanos in New Mexico. The kid in the cell across the hall from me went by the name Shady Boy; he was from a gang called the Nortenos. He was there the last time I got locked up too. They were just waiting to ship him off to Youth Authority. He shot three kids from the Surenos gang at a party. He told me that he was drunk and just protecting his territory. None of the kids he shot died but he would still be spending several years in prison. Shady was cool with me, always trying to tell me stories and shit through the windows.

We also had to shower together since we were on the same unit. One day in the shower he explained to us how to make a Fifi—a prisoner's pocket pussy. He explained that all you needed to do was "get a toilet paper roll, some of that plastic wrap shit, and a little Vaseline. Stuff the plastic wrap real snugly into the toilet paper role and then put in the Vaseline. And that's it, then you have a nice Fifi to get you through these long and lonely nights in the Hall." It sounded like a good idea but I decided to stick to using my hand. Shady also liked to demonstrate his ability to swing his dick around in a circle like an airplane propeller while we were showering. Sometimes I tried to ignore him but in some ways I looked up to him as an elder in the Hall, a long-timer who lived there. I knew that I was just a visitor to his world. He was going to live in places like this for the rest of his life.

My friend Billy was in the Hall too. He was a metalhead I knew from downtown. Actually he was from the mountains like most of the metalers but he hung out downtown with the Gutter punks sometimes.

Billy kind of bugged me but at least he was a familiar face. In the evenings during "free time" we talked about mutual friends and girls we knew. He kept me posted on the progress of this cool pencil drawing he was working on that he had named "Juvenile Hell." It depicted all of the guards as demons torturing us in an evil scene.

(One day after we'd both gotten out Billy ate too much acid and we found him running around downtown screaming and hiding in the bushes on the Pacific Garden Mall. He didn't even recognize me anymore. He was yelling something about the Nazis coming and dove into the bushes, and then he took off running across the street, almost getting hit by a car.

A couple days after that, while some of us were getting drunk down at Desolation, Billy came stumbling out of the bushes. His pants were stained with piss and his Metallica T-shirt was so dirty and filled with stickers and mud that I could hardly read it. His arms were covered in dried blood and scrapes from the bushes and cement. Someone asked him what the fuck happened but he just kept walking. There were paths all through Desolation but he just walked directly through the bushes and trees. Like a zombie.

I felt bad for him but just laughed it off with everyone else.

I didn't see Billy too much after that but I heard he finally got locked up in some insane asylum or something.

Years later I saw him around downtown once in a while and would say hello but that was about it. Billy ended up having a kid with Scooter, one of the Hell Bitches, but they were both totally strung out on heroin by then, pulling scams and dealing dope. Once in a while I would see them pushing the kid around in a stroller down in the beach flats copping some dope.

They found Billy's body floating in the Santa Cruz yacht harbor in 1996. All his teeth had been smashed out and his bloated body lay wedged in the rocks at the harbor's entrance. Word on the street was that he had been ripping off a lot of people and that it must have finally caught up with him.

Last I heard, Scooter has gotten clean and is working at women's rehab helping other women get off the streets.)

After a couple weeks in the Hall I went to court and was released on home supervision. That's when they let you go home but you are not supposed to leave your house unless you are at school or work or one of those fucked-up drug counseling groups. The deal was that your probation officer knew where you were supposed to be and would randomly drop in on you.

While on home supervision I broke into the neighbors' house and stole their VCR; I stuck it in a duffle bag and rode my little sister's pink ten-speed downtown to trade it for drugs. I scored two crack rocks at Louden Nelson Park and quickly returned home to smoke the rocks in my front yard. I made a pipe out of a car antenna using a Brillo pad as a screen. It was an incredible California day, sunny and hot. I was already sweating from the bike ride but when I smoked the rocks I was really pouring sweat so I pretended to pull weeds in my mom's front yard, keeping an eye on the road, waiting for my probation officer to arrive.

Each time a car pulled around the corner my heart began racing even stronger than it did when I inhaled the toxic smoke of that chemical crack that I loved so much. She did finally come by, but just for a minute. She didn't even get out of her car, she just rolled down the window and asked me how it was going, said the yard was looking good and that it was nice of me to be helping my mom out around the house. She split and I was free, at least for the rest of the day. When the crack was all gone I decided to go out and get some beer to help mellow out my jones.

I shoulder-tapped some old surfer at Quality Market in 'Tola who bought me a six-pack of Mickey's big mouth with the money I had stolen from my little brother's piggy bank. I went under the Capitola wharf and drank all six beers alone. That sent me on a run that seemed to last for several weeks.

Breaking the window at Ian's mother's house, I carefully reached my arm through the broken glass to unlock the door.

Ian was a kid I met at the continuation high school I had been court-ordered to attend. When I met him he was a really nice skater kid. Toby and I started hanging out and skating the half pipe he had in his back yard. I think it was our friend Tim, Toby, and me that gave him his first hit of crack. We were skating his ramp and smoking some rocks and he wanted to try some. After that we all got high every day for about two months.

Ian became our supplier. He had his mom's ATM card and we would take as much cash out as possible, usually about three hundred bucks a day. After a few weeks his mom realized she was a few thousand dollars short in her account and canceled the card. Then he began stealing her weed. She had a couple pounds. We would get at least an ounce a day and trade most of it for crack rocks, saving a little to smoke with the beers we drank to come down from the crack high, trying our best to soothe the intense craving for more.

Ian ended up getting arrested a couple times for possession and then sent off to a long-term rehab. Tim also sort of dropped out of our drug crew. He was still using but I think he got sick of sharing with us. So there we were, Toby and I breaking into Ian's mom's house. I guess we felt like if he could rip her off so could we. We were so strung out there was no longer any sort of bond of friendship. It was every junky for himself.

Once we were in her house we started looking for her weed but got scared she'd come home so we settled for a Rolex, a VCR, and a handful of gold rings and necklaces from her jewelry box.

Toby and I took our day's loot and quickly skated away, making a beeline for the beach flats, where we traded the VCR for half a gram of coke and two joints. Later that night we ran into a surfer kid named Jimmy who Toby knew and we went out drinking and driving around in the mountains with him. He had an old Toyota Corolla but it was in its last days. His brakes weren't working very well anymore so he had to pull the emergency break to slow down around the corners. That worked pretty well until it started raining. We started sliding out sideways, coming dangerously close to skidding over the edge of the cliff or smashing into the side of mountain. I was so drunk that I was beyond being scared, it was just fucking exciting.

We still had beer and some gold and the Rolex so we decided to head back into town and get some more drugs. Coming around a sharp, steep curve, Jimmy pulled the brake too hard and we spun out, crashing into the side of the mountain; the car completely flipped over onto the roof. Somehow the motor caught on fire and we were all trapped upside down in the burning car. Toby and Jimmy managed to crawl out the windows in the front seat but I was in the back and the windows wouldn't roll down and I couldn't get the door open. Toby was yelling at me to get out. He was fucking freaking out and running up the hill thinking that the car was going to blow up any minute. I finally started kicking the window and it broke but I decided to try and save the beer and the gold before I got out of the car.

There I was searching around for my booze and drug loot in a burning car oblivious to anything but my next fix. We just left the car there upside down on fire in the middle of the road and walked away drinking our last beers.

A few weeks later, on a visit to my folks in New Mexico, I was smoking some coke with this crazy Mexican hippie named Wild Man Mike. He told me that smoking this shit was a waste of time and that we should have really mainlined it. I had never injected drugs before but it was beginning to sound like a good idea. He told me that we could score some rigs at the pet store. "Just tell them that your dog is a diabetic," he said. I was too scared to do it but I paid him ten bucks to get me a couple of bags of needles the day before I went home.

Back in Santa Cruz some of the Gutter punks shoot dope but most of us just drank a lot. I sold most of the needles to kids on the streets but kept a few for myself and told Jamie and Toby that I wanted to try some heroin. I had smoked it a few times but I always liked crack better.

Toby and Jamie had an apartment in the Beach Flats, in a small complex of ghetto apartments that a lot of the punks and skins lived in, in those days. Theirs was a one-room flat with a hot plate for a kitchen and the bathroom was so small that you could stick your feet in the shower when you were sitting on the toilet. I decided that I wanted to put to work a couple of the rigs that I had saved.

Jamie copped some heroin from one of the many dope dealers who lined the streets in the Flats. After cooking up the heroin in an already burnt spoon and soaking up the tarlike brown substance I was the first one to get high. Jamie tied the bloodstained torn piece of cloth tightly around my bicep and probed for a vein. The sting of the needle was exhilarating. My heart was pounding with anticipation of the rush that I knew would follow. A flash of blood entered the syringe and Jamie pushed down on the plunger, forcing the full contents of the rig into my bloodstream. A warm and comforting rush of the most pleasant sensations filled me from head to toe. The anxiousness of the anticipation was replaced with the delight of being free from all worry and remorse. My mind began to swim in the mucky waters of the narcotic.

Pleasantly numbed and warmly flushed, I sank back into the tattered armchair and in the distance I watched Toby and Jamie begin the ritual of their own fixes. I watched them as though through a peephole, seeing them but being completely removed and protected within my own private room of the heroin's house of pleasure. After what seemed like hours but was more like a few minutes the full body heat rush began to fade but the mind state continued for some time. I began to feel as if my stomach was being twisted in knots and I knew I was going to be sick. Stumbling across the room to the bathroom, I fell in front of the toilet, sitting down on the edge of the shower, and a release of my twisted guts shot forth my breakfast and the three beers

I had drunk for lunch. But this was nothing like puking from being too drunk. The pleasure of throwing up was almost as great as the initial rush of injecting the dope. I was in love with the toilet, filling it up with an ambrosia. Feeding it as a bird feeds her newly hatched chicks. Staring down into the beer and Cheerios, I was as happy as I had ever been in my life.

Later that day we began mixing the heroin with coke, shooting speedballs. I knew I had found a new friend. Unlike smoking rocks, shooting dope was actually relaxing and it lasted much longer. Still loving the head rush of cocaine, I was partial to the speedballs. Over the next few weeks I injected several times with Toby and Jamie. Eventually we ran out of new needles and started sharing the ones we had left. Probably not the smartest move considering Jamie was occasionally prostituting and Toby had shared needles with several questionable characters himself. But I was beyond care or concern, living my life with the understanding that there is "NO FUTURE."

7

Live Fast Die Young

Drinking vodka and fruit punch for breakfast was always fun. Toby passed me the plastic half-gallon container and I happily turned it up-side down, drinking the last of it in a long and powerful chug. My stomach complained of hunger but hesitantly accepted the day-old mixture of cheap booze and red-colored sugar water instead of real food. Another liquid meal to pass the time and kill the pain. Toby asked me if I had any money left. He knew I didn't have shit but now that we were drunk it was more of a statement than a question. He was basically saying, "What are we going to do now?" So rather than saying, "No, I don't have any money," I said, "Fuck it, let's try and get some real drugs." I looked at my watch and it was only eleven o'clock on Friday morning. We had both gotten super drunk and passed out over at our friend Bubbles's house the night before. Sitting in the park staring at the polluted river water flowing toward the sea, Toby said, "Yeah, let's get shy." Getting shy was what Toby called it when we were doing hard drugs, coke or heroin. We were both feeling pretty invincible from the booze so we stumbled out of the bushes in San Lorenzo Park where we had been enjoying our liquid breakfast and walked over the footbridge that crossed the San Lorenzo River.

I was wearing some weird LSD shirt that some friends had stolen from some hippies' van. It had a big flying eyeball on it that I thought was pretty cool but I had written in thick black letters across the back, "Never Trust a Hippy," just so that it was clear I liked drugs, not fucking hippies. Toby had a Broken Bones T-shirt on; it was a skull wearing a helmet of spikes. Neither of us had been home in a couple of days. We were filthy and hungry but right now what was on the top of the list was getting some real drugs. I had my long board but Toby didn't have a skate with him so I was just carrying it. On the bridge we began speculating on how we were going to get money for drugs. We had both already stolen everything we could from our families and it was a little bit early to find someone looking for weed and rip them off so we both agreed that our best bet was breaking into cars in the parking lots downtown.

Maybe we would find a purse or wallet or maybe we would steal a car stereo that we could trade for drugs down at the Flats. The biggest question on my mind was, coke or heroin? I liked the body rush and warm swirling effects of dope but I missed the bell-ringing, head-about-to-explode high of a hit of coke. I guess that's why I found speedballs to be so attractive—two highs in one injection, the full bell-ringer mind explosion followed by the comforting vomit and heat flush of the cheva.

For a moment the thought entered my mind that I had a piss test the next week and that maybe it wasn't a good idea to do dope so close to it but then I realized I had already missed two appointments with my probation officer, who probably already had a warrant out for my arrest. (Not to mention that Toby and I had been court-ordered not to associate with each other.) I had gotten a dirty piss test the last two times I had gone in. That's why I stopped going. So why was I even thinking about it? I must have been drunk.

In the parking lot of Lucky's I jumped on my skateboard and tried to skate between some parked cars to see if any were unlocked but I kept running into them because I was too loaded. I hit one car hard enough to actually break the skin on my thigh when I slammed into the corner of its fender. I was screaming and my skateboard went flying out in front of a car that slammed on its brakes. Toby was laughing at me and he picked up my skate. It was almost noon and all I had in my stomach was booze and cigarettes and we were almost out of those. I felt desperate and consumed with the need for some real drugs.

Toby went into the store and stole a couple packs of smokes. He even got our brands; I smoked Camel filters and he smoked Lucky Strikes. I was happy to have smokes but instead of thanking him I said, "You should have got some food, asshole." We crossed Front Street and cut through the parking lot behind the Del Mar movie theater into the lot behind Warehouse Liquors. Toby spotted a stereo that was only half installed in a white Volkswagen Jetta. All the doors were locked so our only choice was to smash the window and make a run for it. I grabbed a big piece of broken concrete from the corner of the lot behind the theater and walked over to the car. My heart was pounding and I was feeling kind of paranoid. I kept looking around. Toby was at the corner of the parking lot keeping a lookout. Just before I was going to throw the rock through the driver-side window some old lady came walking around the corner. I dropped the rock right there next to the Jetta and walked away, straight past her. For a minute I considered trying to grab her purse and making a run for it but I remembered what happened last time I tried that (I got a felony strong-arm robbery charge and almost went to prison but the lady didn't press charges) so I just walked past her with my head down.

She got into an old Ford pickup truck and pulled out of the lot. Toby came back around the corner and said, "Are you gonna fucking do it or do I have to?" I told him to go ahead if he was in such a fucking hurry. We argued for a few minutes and then without even looking around I just stumbled up to the car, grabbed the rock, and slammed it through the window. Glass shattered everywhere and in one clumsy movement I unlocked the door, climbed in, and started yanking at the car stereo. A few of the wires broke easily but one of them didn't want to let go. I had to get out of the car and use all my strength to rip it out. Just as I got the stereo free a big man with a tight T-shirt and crew cut came around the corner and as soon as he saw me running away with a car stereo in my hand he started yelling for me to stop. He chased me across the street, with the stereo in my hands, wires trailing behind. I was so drunk that I made no attempt to hide my new possession, which I intended to trade promptly for some drugs in the Beach Flats.

I tried ditching the guy down some alleys, running between the brewery and the thrift store. I ended up behind Kinko's with Toby nowhere to be seen. The man in the tight shirt was still in close pursuit. I threw the stereo under a Dumpster and ran into the back door of a building and hid in a bathroom for a few minutes. When I finally caught my breath and no one had broken down the door yet, I figured I was safe, that they hadn't seen me go in there. Suddenly I realized that I was hiding in the bathroom of the old Club Culture, a place that just a few years earlier I had avoided like the plague. Back then we would piss outside rather than enter the putrid toilet of the scummy little club that we loved so much. Now the bathroom was cleaner and uglier than ever. It had been remodeled and painted lavender with a trim of green and yellow floral print. The colors were starting to make me sick and I thought that it might have been safe to exit. After a few more minutes of nostalgia I caught my breath and poked my head out the back door. No one was around.

First thing I did was check to see if the stereo was where I had tossed it under the Dumpster but it was gone. I looked around the corner of the building and some young guy with curly hair on a ten-speed bike saw me and started yelling, "He's over here." I took off running again, stumbling over myself in a drunken escape. The bruise on my thigh from the car in the parking lot was throbbing. Running behind the buildings that backed up to the levee, I ended up in a used-car lot and quickly crawled underneath one of the cars. I pulled out my knife and decided that if anyone tried to apprehend me I would just stab them and take off. I was trying to catch my breath when I heard Toby being questioned on the levee behind the lot. The cops had Toby and I could hear him saying, "It wasn't me, it was Noah," and he was giving them my fucking address and phone number.

I was so furious, I swore vengeance. It was all I could do to stay hidden and not come running out of the lot and tackle him right there in front of everyone. I promised myself I would give him a good beating when I caught him. In the meantime I was lying in a puddle of oil underneath a used car. I had my knife in my hand and was ready to stab anyone who tried to fuck with me. I was so drunk that I may not have even been fully underneath the car, my legs were probably sticking out. Just then I was ripped out from under the car feet first. I dropped my knife and tried hitting the guy but he was huge and just smacked me a couple of times and restrained me. It was the man with the tight shirt and crew cut who had been chasing me the whole time. He said he was an off-duty police officer. I was too drunk and too scared to continue fighting with him so I just surrendered.

There was a cop car waiting for me in the front of the lot. They took me back to the parking lot by the liquor store where I had just minutes earlier smashed the window and snatched the stereo. The curly-haired kid on the ten-speed had taken off with the stereo. He was supposed to bring it back to the crime scene but had decided to keep it for himself. I tried some drunken lies about how I was just playing hide-and-seek with some friends in the car lot and that this big asshole had assaulted me for no reason. The cop was not even listening to my pathetic attempts to absolve myself. He just called for backup to fill out the rest of the report while he took me in. I told them that my name was Noah Peterson (Peter is my middle name) and that I was eighteen years old, so that they would take me to jail instead of Juvenile Hall. All of my friends were older than me and when they got busted they were always out within a couple of days but since I was a minor I always ended up spending a couple weeks in the Hall waiting for court and probation to figure out what to do with me.

In the backseat of the cop car with handcuffs on that were way too tight I began to question my decision to get sent to jail instead of Juvie. Before they took me in the cop stopped at the bus station and picked up a drunken homeless guy who a rent-a-cop security guard had arrested for pissing in the lobby. He smelled more like he had pissed on himself than in the lobby. He was yelling at the cops and trying to kick out the window of the cop car. He was screaming some shit about having fought for this country in the war. He didn't even seem to notice me; I guess I was just another POW to him. We exchanged no words and I didn't join him in his fight against these fascist pigs who were ruining our day.

At the county jail the cops took the old homeless veteran into the receiving cell first. From where I was sitting in the back of the cop car, I could see into the holding cell through a small window. What I saw made me change my mind about wanting to go to jail instead of Juvenile Hall.

Several cops entered the room and beat the homeless veteran with a frenzied repetition of fists and batons. All I could see were angry cops punching and hitting the homeless guy whose only crime had been urinating in public. I was really scared that I was going to be next. I imagined they were thinking, "Okay, we got the bum, now let's get the punk." I had been beaten up by cops before but only when I had resisted. That day I was not resisting. I had resigned myself to my fate. I was just looking forward to getting out of those fucking handcuffs and eating some of that all too familiar institutionalized food.

When the cops had finished the poor guy off it was too still. I thought that maybe they had killed him. The city cop who had brought me in came out to get me, his face red and his forehead wet with sweat from the violence I had just witnessed. As he approached the car with anger in his eyes I began admitting to him that I had lied and that my real name was Noah Levine and that I was only seventeen and that I was on probation and that I had an ID stuffed in my sock. I begged him to take me to Juvenile Hall. I told him my probation officer's name and my mom's name and phone number and when I was done with my monologue of reasons why he should take me to Juvie there was a satisfied smirk on his face that seemed to say, "Yeah, we scared this little fucking punk." He was right. I was scared and hungry and still fucking drunk and the last thing I wanted was to get beaten by a bunch of crazy cops and then raped by some other fucking fascists in jail. No thanks; I wanted to go back to the Hall, where I knew that at least I would be fairly safe. Juvenile Hall had become all too safe and familiar to me. In the last year and a half I had been in and out consistently; not four months had gone by between my arrests. I was beginning to accept that it was just what my life was going to be like, in and out of institutions until eventually I became a permanent resident or died.

The city cop took my ID out of my sock and went back inside the jail to make some calls. After a few minutes I thought he was coming back out but it was just one of the sheriffs looking through the window to see if he recognized me. My mind was spinning with visions of the morning and all of the rage and shame I felt at what my life had come to—a blur of jail, the streets, and being strung out on crack and booze.

That's when I made the decision to follow through with the suicide pact I had made with myself at five years old: "If it ever gets bad enough, I will just kill myself." Well, it was bad enough. All I wanted was to escape from this life, from this cop car, and from the jail cells that I knew were waiting for me.

The next morning I woke up in a padded cell, my head pounding and my heart heavy with fear and regret. It took me only a few minutes to realize where I was and why I was there. I began coughing and the black chunks I spit on the faded yellow walls brought back the previous day's events. I recognized the state-issued white T-shirt and starched jeans I was wearing and began to remember what had happened.

My head exploding with pain, wrists red and raw, the wounds throbbed angrily from a half-assed suicide attempt the night before with the Juvenile Hall issue comb. I was going to be the first inmate to comb himself to death. When that failed I had started slamming my head against the concrete walls, hoping to spill my brains all over the cell in a dramatic and horrific ending to an only half lived life. My mind had been filled with fantasies of revenge and violence. I became so distraught and despondent that suicide seemed like the only solution. I was eventually restrained and thrown into the padded cell where I had just woken up.

I was overcome with the pain and sorrow that was fueling my downward spiral. I was only seventeen years old and there I was locked in a cell, "to protect you from yourself," they said but I knew it was really to protect the rest of society from me and my path of destruction.

I spent the first few hours crying and yelling at the guards. My head was red and swollen from the night before. After exhausting the tears and my voice I was left with nothing. My mind began to replay the scene from the day before and the years of drugs and violence that had brought me there.

Sitting in my cell, I thought about what had led me to this life where all I did was take drugs and steal, lie and fight, all just so that I could do it all over again and again. My whole life had become a quest to escape from reality. I had traded in my leather jacket, Doc Marten boots, and mohawk for a fucking crack pipe. I was losing touch with the only thing that I could relate to in this crazy world, the punk rock scene, whose loud, fast, aggressive music gave me the only outlet I had found for the rage that I felt at the world. My connection with other punks was gone and with it any sense of belonging. I had once had a community on the streets. Bonded in drinking together and fighting together, standing up for what we believed in, a dream of anarchy and revolution. Drowning our teenage angst with drugs, sex, and violence had, in the end, made me lose my punk rock ideals in what became nothing more than the pursuit of oblivion.

Even the homeless gutter punks with their pet rats and filthy
clothes covered in metal studs and patches, who I spent most of my
time with in those days, had started to shun me as a junkie. The skinheads had hated me the most because I would rather do drugs than
drink their disgusting ales and dark beers with them. I recalled the
time years ago when I used to drink with the skins and skate with the
east-side punks but that was all lost. Now I was eating out of soup
kitchens and Dumpster diving or sneaking into my mom's house during the day while she was at work to shower and see what I could steal
for my next fix. I was finding companionship in only the lowest of
punk junkies, prostitutes, and dope dealers.

This time in Juvenile Hall something was different. I could see
where I was and it scared me. It was more real and for the first time in
my life I knew that where I was and what I had become was my fault. I
was the only one to blame. I had always blamed everyone else: the
cops, the system, society, my teachers, my family, everyone but myself.
I was a victim of my surroundings, product of my environment. But
none of that was working anymore. I began to see that I was the problem. I was the one stealing, taking drugs, and hurting people. I was the
one who had broken the window to steal the stereo to get a fix. I was in
jail because of my own actions, not because of anyone else's. I had no
one to blame but myself. This was the consequence of my addiction to
drugs and this was what happened to drug addict thieves like me.

I had lost all hope; death was all I had to look forward to. But I
couldn't even succeed at that. "What a fucking loser, can't even kill
myself."

On the phone with my father I told him about all the regret and
fear I was experiencing. He suggested that some simple meditation
techniques might help alleviate some of the pain I was feeling. He explained to me that by "bringing the mind into the present moment,
the present experience of being, [I] may be able to find some freedom
in that moment from the regret of the past and the fear of the future."
He said that much of the pain I was experiencing had to do with replaying the events of the past and making up stories about the future.
He reminded me that in the present moment I had food to eat, a bed
to sleep in, and clothes to wear. Although I was still quite uncomfort-

able from all of the abuse I had put myself through I could see that he was probably right.

I had always had some faith amid all of the craziness that I would be okay no matter what happened. Even if I died. That was probably a message that I got very clearly as a child that had somehow stuck with me through everything.

My dad had been telling me things like this my whole life but I had never really heard him until that day. He said, "The best way to keep the mind in the present moment, in the beginning, is through awareness of breathing." He offered me the simple instruction:

Bring your awareness to the breath by focusing your attention on the sensation of breathing. Attempt to stay with the sensations of each breath through counting each inhalation and exhalation, trying to count to ten, breathing in, one, breathing out, two. Whenever the mind wanders off to the thoughts of the future or past, gently bring it back to the breath and start over at one. If you can actually stay with the breath all the way to ten, then start over again at one.

After talking for a little while about other things I thanked him for the suggestion about meditation and said I would give it a try.

Back in my cell I reflected on how he too had spent some time in prison in his early life. I was happy that he was so accepting of me, and for the first time I felt really bad for putting my family through all this shit. I decided to try out this seemingly oversimplified meditation technique, wondering what good it could possibly do for me when I was going to spend the rest of my life in prison. I probably had done too much damage to my mind to be able to get any benefits from this, I thought. After all, I had been taking drugs and drinking since I was a kid. With these same negative thoughts I sat in my brick cell with the stained yellow walls from years of kids spitting and doing graffiti on them. Right there on that hard concrete bed with the thin plastic mattress I closed my eyes to attempt to "count my breath."

This turned out to be the beginning of a meditation practice that would be one of the main focuses of my life.

One night a few days later I was sitting in the recreation room waiting for the evening movie to start and a group of young guys came into the Hall to host a twelve-step recovery meeting, as they always did, and as I always did, I ignored them. But this time I actually knew one of the guys from the streets, this dude named Joe who was the brother of my friend Hank. Joe, Hank, and I had all gotten high together a couple of times so I knew that he was at least sort of cool. Hank had told me later that Joe had gotten "sober."

Only a few months before that Hank had been sent to prison for murder. He had beaten a man to death and chopped up his body and left it in the bathtub of his house. They arrested him when he went back to the house to steal the dead man's stuff and sell it for drugs. One day when I was down at the crack park Hank had told me that he knew about this place where we could steal some electronics or something but I didn't go with him for whatever reason. Probably because I was afraid of him. He had ripped me off a couple of times and I must have already had a pocket full of rocks or I probably would have gone. I'm not even certain if it was the same place but it seemed like it was just before he got busted. I didn't even realize how close I might have been to being involved in that whole thing.

Hank had gotten life in prison, Joe had gotten sober. Now he was right there in Juvenile Hall talking about twelve-step recovery and how good it was to be straight. For some reason all of the sudden I didn't feel too cool or too tough, so I went to the meeting to check it out. Joe and two other guys, Drew and Baron, told us all about the way they used to do drugs and booze all the time and how they were sober now and how much better their lives had become.

Drew told his story of how he was a mohawk street punk dealing drugs and committing crimes, in and out of institutions, and how he finally lost touch with the punk scene in a never-ending quest for drugs and total oblivion. He talked a little bit about how he was staying away from drugs one day at a time, and how important it was for him to be surrounded by other sober people. I sat dead still, shocked, feeling naked. He was telling my life's story. I began to admit to myself that I might also possibly be in need of some recovery and that there was possibly some hope for me.

I had actually been to a few meetings in the past but had never thought that any of it applied to me. I was just going because the courts or my probation officer had sent me. At the time all I had seen were a bunch of adults and adults were the enemy. But I could really relate to these guys. When I went back to my cell I was armed with some books about recovery to read that they had given me, as well as the meditation instructions from my dad. I let them know that I wasn't interested in any of that God shit but that I would check out the books.

Although that one meeting had given me some hope, I was still quite angry. I was not at all interested in anything that was "spiritual" or in any way related to peaceful hippy types or Bible thumpers. After all I was a punk and the punks knew that all of that shit was for weak-minded followers. I just needed to stop doing drugs, that was my problem. If I could just stop doing drugs then everything would be all right. If I could get a job and a place to live on my own and stay away from all the trouble, then I would be happy.

In my cell that night I fantasized about what life would be like if I didn't spend all my time getting high. I thought about all the shows I could go to and how I wanted to get my leather back and get some new boots. Sometimes all I could think about was how I was probably going to get sent to Youth Authority and what kind of hell that would be. When I got really frustrated with all the shit going on in my head I would try to do the meditation that my father had taught me and it did seem to help a little. At least if I was counting my breath, I wasn't thinking about prison or killing myself.

The day my court date came I was terrified. My mom and my little brother and sister brought me some pizza. I was too scared to really enjoy it, which was shocking to them considering that I had put on over ten pounds in the short weeks that I had been there. I had become so skinny from the last month's diet of drugs and very little healthy food. I was convinced that I would have to do some time and the only thing that helped was trying to pay attention to my breath coming and going.

By some miracle the regular judge was not there that week and the one who was sitting in for him decided that he just wanted to keep me off the streets until I turned eighteen. He sentenced me to a group home for boys. He didn't hesitate in letting me know that he would be glad to send me to prison if he ever saw me as an adult. I was so relieved I instantly forgot about breathing and began fantasizing about the future. I couldn't fucking believe it, a group home, no big deal, better than Youth Authority, and I was going to be eighteen in like eight months or something.

They could have sent me away for seven years just for the auto burglary charge, and with the two other felony charges and all the other misdemeanors and violations of my probation on my record, I was shocked that I was basically being set free. I knew kids who were in group homes; they still went to school and had jobs and everything.

My mom wasn't as pleased as I was because the judge was basically saying, "You can't control your kid so we are taking him away from you and placing him under state supervision." But she was also relieved that I wasn't being sent to prison. At least if I was in a group home we could still see each other sometimes. Eventually I would even be able to come home for weekends and holidays.

I had to spend a few more weeks in the Hall while they tried to find a placement for me. My probation officer was hoping to find something local so that I could be closer to my family. While locked up I continued to attend the meetings with Drew and Baron. Joe never came back in with them. I guess he had just come that one time as a guest or something. I committed to them and to myself to stay sober. At night I read some of the books and once in a while I tried to meditate but after court, when I knew I wasn't going to prison, I didn't need it as much. Instead I spent most of my time planning about how everything was going to be different this time. I would stay away from the drugs, get a good job, maybe buy a motorcycle or old car, hopefully find a girlfriend. Life was finally going to be good.

8

Nailed to the X

From Juvenile Hall I was shipped off to a group home. The man from the boys' home who came to pick me up was named Jim. He looked like an old surfer/stoner with unkempt curly hair, wearing a wrinkled button up shirt, jeans, and flip-flops. He was giving me this whole talk about the rules of the place and how this was my last chance. "If you fuck up, that's it, no second chances," he said, then he offered me a cigarette.

I was so happy to have a smoke that I forgot to be pissed at him for taking me to some place where my freedom was being taken away for the next several months. I was relieved to be enjoying a smoke in his little Toyota Corolla and not shackled by the hands and feet on an armored bus headed to prison. A part of me knew that this was going to be a good thing. If I wanted to stay off the drugs it was going to take something like this to help me stay away from the old crew. One thing I did hear at those meetings in Juvie was that it was important to have sober friends. The only people in the world I knew who were sober were those guys I had met in the Hall.

In the group home I shared a room with some African American crackheads from East Palo Alto. We had a lot in common except they were into hip-hop and I was into punk rock. I actually really liked hip-hop a lot but was still a little afraid to admit it. The scene in the group home wasn't too bad. I got along pretty well with the kids I roomed with; even though we were all teenage crackheads, we had our differences. I was still a white punk rocker from hippy parents and they were black ghetto kids from the inner city.

The people who ran the house were these hillbilly types. They seemed to have good intentions and did the best they could with a house full of juvenile delinquents. We were allowed to smoke cigarettes but no more than one pack a day. I was sent to a continuation high school in Watsonville, where I continued studying for the GED. I had missed way too much high school to even attempt to graduate, so I was just waiting until I turned eighteen to take the GED test. School wasn't too bad, mostly gangbangers and group-home kids. Nobody messed with me and I pretty much kept to myself. Eventually I was allowed to get a job and work part-time, which allowed me to save money for when I was released. I got a job at a pizza place that I had worked at for a short time before I got locked up. I told the owner all about my troubles and the group home and that I was staying sober now and he was cool enough to give me a job.

After I was in the group home for a couple months they gave me a home pass to go see my mom for a week or so. I immediately looked up Toby. I thought he would understand my decision to be sober. When I found him he was living in a little room that had been constructed by putting up two walls in the corner of a living room with several other punks and these beautiful bisexual dominatrix girls. I had been sober for about four months and it had been even longer than that since I had gotten laid. I may have been even more excited about meeting his roommates than seeing my old friend. Toby gave me the news about where everyone from our crew was. This kid Brant who we knew and some other guys had all gotten sent to Youth Authority for beating and robbing someone at an ATM. Mark was doing time for possession and Bubbles had moved to Texas with his girlfriend. Most of the other punks were still around, still drinking down at Desolation.

(That wasn't the end for those guys. After doing a bunch of time locked up, Mark became a Suicidal vato loco punk. He continued living the street life and in the end they found Mark's body in the bushes on the side of Highway 9, where whoever he was with when he overdosed had left him only a few hours earlier.

Brant ended up doing six years straight. From Youth Authority he was shipped directly to the state penitentiary, where he picked up more time for doing what he had to do to survive in those hell realms. When he finally got out in 1996 he was no longer the nice skate punk kid I had once known, he was a man, an institutionalized man, hardened from having been six years down. But Brant was luckier than Billy or Mark, whom we had already buried; he got out and stayed sober.)

Toby wanted to get some beer so we got a twelve-pack and he started drinking and I was telling him all about how I was sober and all the stuff I had learned in twelve-step recovery. He was not very impressed and said that he thought it would probably be cool if I just had one or two beers to celebrate my freedom. Without even thinking about it, I decided he was right. A couple of beers couldn't hurt me. After all it was the harder drugs that were the real problem anyway. So I cracked open a nice cold can of Schaefer beer and drank the whole thing in one long slow chug.

The booze felt great in my system after having been sober for so many months. So I just opened another and drank that one down. With two beers in my belly I was feeling pretty good and it seemed like a fine idea to have another and another and another until all of the beer was gone. At that point the only logical thing to do was to get some more. Once I started drinking I just couldn't stop. It was as if I had totally lost control. There was a voice in my head repeating all the stuff I had learned but I just couldn't stop my hand from grabbing another beer. Internally there was a war going on between my head full of recovery and my body full of booze. My head lost and I surrendered to my addiction.

Later that evening when we were both good and drunk the dominatrix girls invited us into their room to play some cards with them. I was extremely fucked up and really hoping to get together with one of them. They proceeded to make out with each other and I passed out in the corner. When I came to I was in Toby's little room on the floor and the familiar smell of burning chemicals told me that Toby was smoking some crack. I looked up and saw him sucking on a glass pipe with some crazy looking hippy dude. It was all I could to just roll over and go back to sleep.

When I woke up the next day I couldn't believe what I had done. I swore to myself not to drink again. My experiment with drinking had proven what I had been hearing: "Alcoholics cannot stop drinking once they begin." That same night I was with Toby at some surf punk's house down the street and someone offered me a beer. Without even thinking about it, I took it and drank it down as fast as I could. Same thing happened that night: once I started drinking I just couldn't stop. This only had to happen a couple more times for me to start to see the pattern and to remember what my sober friends had told me: "One is too many and a thousand is never enough." It also helped me a lot when, shortly after that, Toby checked himself into a rehab, seeking his own recovery. It was the motivation that I needed to go back and start over on my sobriety.

With lights out at ten o'clock at night in the group home, I often lay awake in bed with nothing to do but think. I often felt lonely, cut off from my family and friends. Sometimes I would recall the meditation instructions and begin to pay attention to the rhythm of my breath, but more often I would just drift from fantasy to fantasy, planning all of the ways that I would be happy when I got back on the streets for good. My mind swam in visions of fast cars, loud music,

beautiful women, tattoos, motorcycles, and the freedom to do whatever I wanted, whenever I wanted to do it. In those fantasies I was always sober. Drugs and booze had gotten me in this mess in the first
place and I had barely escaped alive. From now on it was going to
have to be drug free for me.

The group home was not about any kind of rehabilitation or anything, it was just a storage facility to keep kids like me off the streets.
The last stop before the Big House. At first that was fine with me but
after my relapses into drinking I realized that I should probably get to
some recovery meetings since my way was clearly not working. This
proved to be more difficult than I thought. It was inconvenient for the
house parents to take me to meetings and I wasn't allowed to go out
alone yet. So after some finagling I finally got to some meetings. I
wasn't sure what else to do, not wanting to drink but not wanting to
do any of the things that were suggested in the meetings or literature.
They wanted me to pray and admit all kinds of shit. I wasn't about to
do any of that crap but at least maybe I could find some sober friends.

At a meeting, I reconnected with Drew and the guys I had met in
Juvenile Hall. They became my new friends and on my home passes I
would hang out with them and go to meetings rather than look up
Toby and my old crew. Somehow or other I stayed sober and out of
trouble. It was strange: by not subjecting myself to the people and
places where I used to get loaded I was able to stay clean. All of a sudden I had a few months sober and just after I turned eighteen they let
me out of the group home. I felt a little lost, not yet fully in recovery
and no longer having the structure of being institutionalized as I had
been for the last year.

My mom let me stay with her until I could find an apartment.
Since I had passed the GED just before I got out of the group home
my dad said that he would help me with rent if I wanted to take some
classes at the junior college.

A friend of mine named Gina and I got an apartment near downtown and I began taking classes at Cabrillo College in Aptos. My ex-
stepdad, whom I still couldn't stand, hooked me up with his old car, a
1967 Bonneville. I still had my job at the pizza joint and with the

money I had saved while in the group home I went out and bought
some new boots, a leather jacket, and began collecting the records and
tapes of all my favorite bands. My dreams were quickly being fulfilled.
I had the fast car, new clothes, and freedom. Now I just needed a girl
and a bike and I would be perfectly happy.

I was committed to staying sober and still going to meetings but I
started hanging out with some of the street punks again. A couple of
the Suicidals were trying to get sober so I was going to meetings and
punk shows with them, getting into fights and picking up on girls.
Not all that much had changed but now I had an apartment, a car, and
I didn't get high or drunk anymore.

I became really good friends with this older Suicidal punk named
Shooter. He was twenty-two and I was eighteen. He started coming to
meetings with me and even got off heroin completely for a while but
he never wanted to stop smoking pot, he felt like it was different, like
it wasn't part of his problem. I was just happy to have some other
punks to hang out with who weren't strung out. We spent a lot of time
driving around in my '67 that was lowered to the ground and blasting
out punk rock tunes. We still hung out downtown with the street
punks but when it was time to go drink we usually went to a meeting
or just went off and drove around or something.

Shooter had grown up in Los Angeles and had been affiliated with
the Suicidals since he was a kid. He had great stories about the punk
scene there in the early eighties. He also had seen more than his share
of violence and addiction. He had stories about everything. He was one
of those people who you could just listen to for hours but he was really
good at always including you in his stories, asking questions and then
going on with his story before you could reply. He was always saying
how much he hated the world and how adults were our enemies. He
swore that everyone over twenty-five was untrustworthy. He was sticking to our suicidal philosophy of living fast and dying young.

*(After some time I lost touch with Shooter. He started shooting dope
again and I had stopped hanging out with the street punks. A couple years
later he killed himself on his twenty-fifth birthday, sticking to his word, not
wanting to join the enemy.)*

On a visit to New Mexico to see my parents I was hanging out with the Albuquerque punks I knew from the time I spent growing up out there. My friend Steve had gotten into Straight Edge in the year or two since I had last seen him. Straight Edge was a movement within the punk and hardcore scene that was adhering to drug-free principles. No smoking, no drinking, and no casual sex. A set of moral standards that I would have previously laughed at, but after all the trouble I had been in over the last few years and with my true desire to be drug free it was the perfect philosophy for me: still punk rock, just sober. The only part that I had a problem with was the restriction on my sex life but I chose to interpret that one as I liked. Straight Edge developed out of the Washington, D.C., punk scene and it was signified by wearing black X's on the tops of your hands. By the late eighties, when I got into it, Straight Edge had become a huge movement within the greater scene of punk and hardcore.

Steve introduced me to bands like Youth of Today, Chain of Strength, Bold, Judge, Wide Awake, No for an Answer, Insted, and Uniform Choice. I was already quite familiar with Minor Threat and 7 Seconds, but when I heard all those hardcore bands screaming about a drug-free way of life I knew I had found the answer to my dilemma: "How can I be a punk but not a drunk?" It was a lot like the first time I heard punk when I was a kid. I resonated so deeply with it; again I had discovered a whole movement of youth that felt the same way I did.

Getting into Straight Edge probably saved my life. The twelve-step program was offering a spiritual solution to my alcoholism that I wasn't ready to accept. Straight Edge was just a bunch of punkers helping each other stay clean through peer support. In the Straight Edge scene there were actually two factions. One talked about unity in the punk scene and overcoming our differences through positivity, a lot of emphasis being put on brotherhood and a set of moral standards. The other was a harder and more violent sect that put more energy into judging those who drank and used. This hard-line movement got its strength through feeling superior and separate from everyone and anyone who didn't believe what it believed.

In Santa Cruz there was no Straight Edge scene at all. For a while I thought that I was the only Straight Edge punk around and felt pretty isolated until I finally met Russ. I had seen him at some meetings but we had never spoken. Then some girl at school told me that there was another kid running around with big black X's on his hands. When we finally met we became good friends, and as we started hanging out other kids who were into Straight Edge slowly started showing up. That was the beginning of what turned into the Santa Cruz Straight Edge Crew, which lives on today.

(Russ ended up staying sober and his band, Good Riddance, has become one of the most popular modern punk bands around. He spends most of his time these days touring internationally and spreading political and spiritual awareness through his lyrics.)

At a hardcore show at Gilman Street in Berkeley I was amazed to see hundreds of kids with X's on their hands. It was surreal to be surrounded by so many kids who all believed as I did in being drug free. There were kids passing out literature on vegetarianism, Hinduism, and social action. I was still just staying clean out of pure fear of what would happen if I drank, but at that show I began to open up to the possibility of actually doing something positive for the world, like becoming vegetarian or doing some sort of service for the community.

When Uniform Choice came on there must have been fifty kids on stage singing along to the anthems that we were basing our lives on. The flying fists and thrashing bodies in the pit were a perfect expression of our discontent and commitment to positive change by any means necessary. I was higher than I had ever been on drugs. The purity of my belief and the power of the adrenaline pumping through my veins transported me to another way of life.

It was just after I got back from my first Straight Edge show in 1988 that I started getting tattooed, mostly Straight Edge symbols and images. I had wanted to have tattoos since I was a kid. Most of my friends already had them. I'm not sure why I never got any while I was on the streets. A lot of the kids I was hanging out with did but for some reason I never got around to it. But I was glad I had waited, because now I really had something I believed in to mark my body with.

My first tattoo, of crossed hammers and a fist with an X on it, is on my left shoulder, signifying my commitment to Straight Edge and my belief in the working-class ethic. At that point it was my intention to enter the trades and become a carpenter, thus the hammers. I was so proud of that little tattoo, I would roll up my sleeves so I could show it off. Driving around with my arm hanging out of the window of my Bonneville, I felt so fucking tough.

It wasn't long before I got another tattoo on my other shoulder and then on my back. It hurt a lot but was worth it. I really wanted to tattoo my forearms but decided that it would be a good idea to wait until I was older for that, just in case I wanted to work somewhere that having visible tattoos would be a problem, so I decided to start getting my legs tattooed.

While I was getting tattooed in Monterey I met a guy named Scott Sylvia. He was just learning how to tattoo but he had also recently gotten sober so we had something in common. We talked only a little bit but he made a lasting impression on me. It was just cool to meet someone my own age who was also sober and into tattoos.

Not long after I got out of the group home I got in a bad car accident with some friends. I suffered some minor whiplash and back injury pain. After a few months of chiropractic adjustments I was in good health again. The insurance company offered me a few thousand dollars in an out-of-court settlement. With the money from the settlement I paid back some of the people I had ripped off, attempting to make some amends to the more immediate family and friends I had stolen from in my addiction. With the rest of the money I bought myself an old European motorcycle.

Most of the street punks had shunned me for being a sober asshole by that time. So I started hanging out with the Rockers. Toby's cousin, Jason, was one of the leaders of this gang of ex-punks and skins who had all gotten into vintage motorcycles and listened to either fifties rock 'n roll or this new form of music that was a mixture of punk and rockabilly called psychobilly and was mostly coming out of England. Some of the old punk bands like Social Distortion had also adopted a greaser style that I thought was pretty cool so I got into the whole psychobilly scene for a while. Growing my hair into a pompadour and cuffing my jeans, I liked it but was still just a punker at heart and a Straight Edge one at that. I wore a Minor Threat patch on my biker jacket and still went to a lot of hardcore and punk shows.

The Rockers would fight with the Mods, those wanna-be English kids on the scooters with the silly army jackets and the fur collars. I was always trying to start shit with them. They were just a bunch of fancy rich kids, they weren't hurting anyone, but I saw it as my duty to act out some ancient Rocker versus Mod war that no one really cared about anymore. I guess I had seen Quadraphenia one too many times.

After hanging out with those guys for a while and getting in plenty of incidents with the law for speeding and reckless driving on my motorcycle, my bike was eventually impounded and I lost my license for a few months. It's crazy that I was even hanging with those guys; half of them were racist assholes. The funny thing was that although some of them were fascists the rest were Asian and Latino and I am half Jewish so it never really made sense that I was into all that crap. I even wore a Confederate flag on my jacket for a while, trying to fit in and liking anything that was offensive to the masses and an excuse to become violent. Through all of the fighting and tough guy image I didn't have to look at myself. It was so much easier to hate everyone else. I could ignore my own pain through inflicting it upon others.

One of the leaders of the Rockers was an older guy named Mike. He was one of the old punks who had started the motorcycle club in the early eighties. He had been a punk in '77 and then got really into reggae and even went to Jamaica in '80 and saw Bob Marley. After that he was a northern soul skinhead listening to all the old Jamaican ska until he eventually got into psychobilly and started the VRCC (Vintage Rock Cycle Club) and the Rockers. I really looked up to him. He turned me on to a lot of the psychobilly records and taught me some stuff about working on my motorcycle. He drank and fought a lot and I admired that; he was my mentor in some ways. I was always trying to start fights knowing that I had this whole crew and especially Mike backing me up.

Mike was always trying to make me drink with him but I was way too committed to staying clean. It didn't bother me much that he wanted me to drink or that he called me a pussy for not drinking. I liked the attention and was willing to put up with it to be accepted by the Rockers.

In the early '90s Mike ended up moving to San Francisco. I went up to San Francisco a couple times to hang out with him but he was always so drunk that it wasn't very fun. So I stopped visiting and didn't see him again for several years.

After I lost my license I started skateboarding again. I realized that I had started to lose touch with my Straight Edge identity so I decided to start doing pro Straight Edge graffiti. Being a compulsive egomaniac, I liked seeing my tags on the walls so much I would go out painting several times a week. I started writing "Noah Core" and "Just Say Noah" as well as tags like "STR8 Edge" and "EDGE 1." Still seeking the negative attention I had been getting since I was a kid. Trying to prove my existence and place in this world by writing my name on the wall.

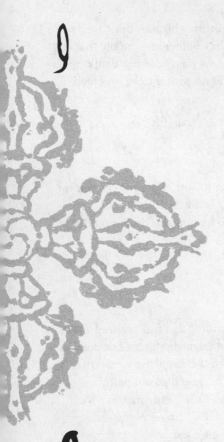

9

I Need Your Shelter

One day, out the window of my apartment, I saw a sheriff's car pull into my driveway. I quickly ducked down so he wouldn't see me. Hearing the car door close and the footsteps of the Santa Cruz County sheriff deputy coming up the stairs, I quickly hid in my closet. My heart was beating loudly in my ears and I tried to be as still as possible so he wouldn't hear me. I remembered the meditation instruction: "Watch your breath and soften your belly." I heard those instructions in my father's voice but it didn't seem to work. I was fucking terrified; I didn't want to go back to jail. I had come too far for that. But there I was, hiding from the cops in my closet, two years sober and still living a life of crime.

I could hear the sound of something being slipped under the door and his footsteps going back down the stairs. The sound of the cop car starting and driving away, down to the corner and left toward the free-way, allowed me to relax a little. But I stayed in the closet, closing my eyes, wanting to be anywhere but here. I was so sick of that shit; that feeling of fear and adrenaline was way too familiar. Sometimes it seemed like it was all I knew.

I was leaning back against my laundry basket, the smell of dirty socks filled the small space where I was hiding. The cops were gone and now I was just trying to hide from myself but couldn't seem to get away. The booze and drugs hadn't worked and now all the steal-ing, violence, and graffiti didn't seem to be working either. I had been trying my whole life to find something but I just kept fucking everything up.

I was too freaked out to move so I resigned myself to just staying put for a while, reflecting on what had brought me back to this famil-iar place of demoralization. It had been over two years since I'd had a drink or any drugs. On the outside my life looked pretty good—I owned the motorcycle I had always wanted, I had a cool job at a record store, I was going to school, and I even had a nice apartment that I shared with my big brother.

Yet there I was hiding in my closet from the cops, living in an apartment full of stuff I had bought with credit cards that I'd stolen from work. I had been working at this record store and once in a while when someone "forgot" a credit card I would pocket it. I had mostly just bought clothes and music but I had also recently pur-chased a whole home stereo system and a bunch of art.

Everywhere I went lately someone was telling me that the cops had been around asking about me and my graffiti. I guess spray-painting "NOAH CORE" probably wasn't very smart, but I loved it, seeing my name all over the city. It was such a rush to be out there in the middle of the night, skateboarding around and spray-painting the walls.

A few nights earlier at the pool hall I had asked this girl if she had ever heard of Noah Core and she started talking all this shit, said she had heard this and that, that he was so mean and blah blah blah. When I told her that I was Noah Core she was really embarrassed and tried to backtrack. I had thought it was hilarious, I was fucking famous, everyone knew me. Before I left she gave me her phone number, said that she was sorry and asked me to give her a call sometime.

But my life was a mess. I was still living like I was on the streets when I was strung out, only now I was stealing from my job and starting fights at school instead of drinking down at Desolation. All I could think about was that I was going to get sent to jail, at two years sober, for stealing and spray-painting. "Why can't I get my shit together?" I had seen some other guys get sober, and they seemed to have found a better way to live than this.

Drew and the guys who helped me get sober at Juvenile Hall were all doing pretty well. They were always talking about serenity and how happy they were now that they had done the twelve steps. I had always thought the steps were a bunch of bullshit—God and all that stupid crap. I never wanted any part of the peace-and-love fantasy. I hated hippies and all that peaceful shit. I'd rather fight and fuck any day. But I really didn't want to feel like that anymore. I didn't get sober to be hiding from the cops in my own fucking house.

I woke up to the sound of the front door slamming, and for a minute I didn't know where I was. Then I realized that I was still in my closet and I remembered the cops—maybe they had broken down the door. A chill ran down my spine and I closed my eyes, trying to shut out reality.

I heard the refrigerator door open and my brother's voice from the kitchen. "Hey, cocksucker, you home? There's a letter here from the pigs." I must have fallen asleep. I wondered what time it was. My bedroom door opened and I knew it was just my brother but I still felt really scared and embarrassed, so I didn't say anything. I could hear him walking around in my room and all of a sudden the closet door slid open.

"What the fuck are you doing in here?" he said, half laughing.

"I'm hiding from the cops, what does it look like? How did you know I was here?" I said, feeling like a chump.

"I saw your motorcycle in the garage so I knew you were home." He and I had been living together for about six months. He had been living in Colorado for a while but I had finally talked him into moving out here to beautiful California. Those days he was hanging out with all the rockabilly Nazi bikers we knew. We both had old European bikes—his was a Ducati and mine was a Triumph. My brother James looks a lot like Andrew Dice Clay so we had taken to calling him "Dice." We got along pretty well but tended to ridicule each other a lot, a leftover habit from our adolescence.

I got out of the closet and we went into the living room to check out the letter that the cops had left. It said that they were investigating me for several counts of malicious mischief, that they had witnesses and spray cans with my fingerprints on them, but that they wanted to give me a chance to rectify the damage I had done. If I agreed to do some graffiti cleanup and pay some restitution they wouldn't press charges. Blah blah blah, call me soon, Detective Lofrano, Santa Cruz County Sheriff's Department.

James was just laughing at me, saying, "Busted." I felt relieved that it didn't have anything to do with the credit card shopping sprees, but I said that we needed to get rid of everything just in case they came back. He agreed to help me and I made a few phone calls and arranged to give all the stolen stuff to a friend who happily agreed to take my brand-new stereo system and some framed art I had bought at the mall. I didn't think they could trace any of the clothes but I got rid of some of them anyway.

After we got rid of everything and I cleaned out all of the spray paint from the garage we kicked back and watched some TV for a while. I began to wonder: "Should I call the cops and turn myself in?" James said, "No fucking way. They can't prove shit unless they catch you in the act."

The phone rang and like an asshole I picked it up. It was Detective Lofrano. He was going on and on about how much evidence they had. I felt sick to my stomach and really confused. I didn't know what to do so I argued with him for a while, told him he had the wrong guy, just because my name was Noah didn't mean it was me. He asked me if I remembered Warren Berry from school and I did. He was my little brother's water polo coach then. Lofrano said that Warren was on the police force now and that he was one of their main sources of info. I recalled telling Warren about some stuff a while ago but I wasn't sure if I should believe him or not. After a long conversation I told the cop that I would think about what he had said and call him tomorrow.

Later that night I called Drew and told him what had happened and asked him for some advice. Of course he went on and on about how the steps of recovery were the only place that he had ever found any relief. Drew was supportive and understanding and he seemed to have his shit together. His story was just like mine. He was a few years older than I was and had been sober since he was twenty. I really trusted him and knew that he was one of the only people in the world who understood me.

He suggested that I get a sponsor to help me work the steps but had no advice on what to do about the cops. Great. Now what was I supposed to do? I needed some real help, not all that "just pray about it" crap.

I didn't sleep very well and was up most of the night thinking about my life. "What should I do next?" What I had been doing wasn't working very well. I thought a lot about what Drew had said to me about the steps and how his life had really changed when he surrendered to a Higher Power. Lying there on my bed, I just stared at the posters on my wall: "New York City Hard Core, The Way It Is" and "Suicidal Tendencies, Join the Army." Oh, and the little picture of Claudia Schiffer on my dresser. I started thinking that maybe I should just pack up all my shit and move to NYC, just fucking escape from all the shit. Then, for a half second, I thought about joining the army, going over to Iraq to be a medic or something, but that thought was quickly replaced by the realization that the army sucks and war is useless. "Maybe I could go down to Venice and hook up with Mike Muir and the Suicidal Tendencies crew." I didn't really care where I went, I just didn't want to feel so fucked up anymore.

I woke up to the sound of the phone ringing; I tried to ignore it but heard James in the other room. "No, he's not here," he was saying. Then through the door I heard him say, "It was your pal the detective." I got up and showered. I tried to eat some toast but still felt sick to my stomach. I picked up the phone, my hand trembling, and dialed the number on the letter from Detective Lofrano.

We talked for a while and I told him that I had decided to confess, that I just wanted to make amends, that I knew it was wrong, and that I was willing to clean it up. "I am done with graffiti," I said. "It's over and I'm sorry."

They made me come down to the station and get fingerprinted and everything. They also made me do some writing samples of my tags (Noah Core, 8edge, and Psycho).

When I got home I called up this guy named Don who I knew from the program and asked him to be my sponsor. He said sure and suggested that I begin by really admitting to myself that I was powerless, that my life was unmanageable. He wanted me to write about it and call him the next day. So I started right away, writing about how fucked up everything was and about how I always seemed to fuck everything up—very unmanageable. I wrote for hours, about how much I hated the world and how I wanted to change it. In the end all of my problems seemed to come down to being powerless.

Before I went to sleep that night I tried to meditate for a little while, concentrating on the sensations of my breath coming and going. It helped some, and I fell asleep feeling pretty good, like I was finally doing something positive with my life.

I called Don the next day and read to him what I had written. He mostly just listened and laughed a couple of times, then invited me over to talk more with him that evening. Just after I hung up Toby called and started telling me about some girl he was seeing. He asked if I wanted to come hang out with them and her friend, who was super cute. I was tempted but after I told him about everything that was going down with the cops and his only concern was that I didn't mention him I was pissed that he was so worried that I would turn him in that he didn't even ask if I was okay. We did graffiti together sometimes; his tags were "uncle-T" or "T-bone." Toby was doing a lot of drugs still but we were good friends anyway. I assured him that I hadn't said shit about him or anyone else. "I will go down alone. I don't need to take anyone else with me, not like you the time we got busted and you fucking tried to turn me in." I had never beaten him up for that but I hadn't forgotten it either.

"I'll talk to you later. Have fun with the ladies," I said, more than a little annoyed. Toby had tried to get sober when I did but he couldn't seem to stay away from the shit. It was kind of sad but I loved him anyway. We had been through so much together, I was not going to turn my back on him now.

Don was a big man, 6'1" and about 250 pounds. He wore a flattop haircut and usually sported shorts. He was big and strong but also very gentle and understanding. I had known him since I got out of the group home. I met him through Baron, one of the guys I had met while I was in Juvie. Baron and I ended up working at Round Table Pizza together while I was still in the group home, and he used to live with Don.

He had always been cool to me and he had been sober for ten years, so I figured he must have known what he was talking about. We got together and talked about everything that was happening in my life and he explained how the steps could help me if I was willing to really have an open mind about spirituality. I started going off on a rant about how religion is for weak-minded followers and how I didn't need God, what I needed was some real help. He explained to me that it was all about sanity, that my own thinking continued to get me in trouble and that by coming to believe in a Higher Power, I could be restored to sanity. He said, "It doesn't have to be God"—it could be anything that I considered to be a power greater than myself.

After talking with him for a while and contemplating the whole thing I said, "Okay, I've got it. My Higher Power is the feeling that I have always had that I will be okay, no matter what. Even when I was a kid I always knew that if things got bad enough I could just kill myself and I would be all right, so my Higher Power is that feeling of everything will be all right, even if I die." Don's expression was one of bewilderment, but he said, "Fine, if that is your Higher Power, that's fine." Really, I had no idea what a Higher Power was, but all of the sudden I was totally willing to try the steps, to be open-minded about growing spiritually. I was even willing to try Don's suggestion that I start praying. My next assignment was to pray three times a day for my Higher Power's guidance. I was supposed to turn my will over to the care of a loving, caring power greater than myself.

I felt like such a jerk. All of my life I had made fun of religious freaks and there I was, on my knees praying. It took quite a while to get used to it and I didn't tell anyone except Drew and a couple other sober friends. Prayer was like my meditation practice, something I did alone and never talked about. I was actually a little ashamed that I had become so weak that I had stooped to spiritual practice. This was not punk, and certainly didn't fit in with my anti-everything attitude.

But it really worked. The more I prayed the better I felt. For the first time in my life I was beginning to feel comfortable in my own skin. I was starting to have faith that everything was really going to be okay, that I wasn't going to have to kill myself. It was such a relief to begin to rely on this Higher Power stuff, to not have to control everything all the time.

I questioned my dad and my therapist, Forest, about the whole Higher Power thing. They both tried to give me some spiritual, Eastern philosophy about how actually it was more like there was an inner power than a higher power, they were saying that ultimately it is non-dual but I couldn't understand what they were pointing me toward. I felt so lost and beaten down at that point. All of my best ideas and attempts had just constantly brought about more trouble and pain. It didn't seem like I had much of anything good or positive in me. I needed to seek some external help. So the Higher Power praying thing worked okay for me. I was willing to accept some direction and try something new.

By the time I went to court for the graffiti bust, I was already well into trying to turn my life around. The day of my hearing the front page of the *Santa Cruz Sentinel* read: "Notorious Graffiti Vandal,

8edge, Apprehended." In court the detective and district attorney who had promised to allow me to do just restitution were now begging the judge to put me in prison. Fucking prison! I had so many counts of vandalism that they were carrying a seventeen-year maximum sentence. The DA asked for a minimum of two years in the state pen. I was really scared that I was going back to jail, but I kept praying and trying to be in the present moment and that seemed to help a little. I was really relying on whatever God's will was for me but I couldn't help but think that I was going to be leaving the court in handcuffs.

The judge ended up being very cool and let me off with $10,000 in restitution and 500 community service hours to clean up graffiti. It was a lot of money, but anything was better than prison. I felt a huge sense of relief. I didn't even care about all the money or community service hours. I knew I was on the right track, the path to redemption and forgiveness.

Outside the courthouse the news reporters attacked us, yelling questions and chasing my mother and me all the way back to her car. For weeks I got calls from angry people threatening me and saying they were going to come over and spray-paint my house. "See how you like it, you little bastard." It got so bad that we had to move—I got a studio apartment in Seacliff and James moved into a place downtown.

Prayer and meditation quickly became a more integral part of my life. They were helping me make sense of everything. I was beginning to find some sense of purpose in my life. Being an addictive type, when I find something that makes me feel good I want to do it all the time, so I did, I turned my life toward recovery and spiritual practice. I had tried everything else. Drugs hadn't worked, material accumulation hadn't worked, violence certainly hadn't worked, and the negative attention ego trip of graffiti, gangs, and lawlessness had just almost gotten me locked up again. I knew that this spiritual practice shit was the last hope for me.

10

Serve the truth, Defy the Lie

In 1991 I attended my first meditation retreat with Jack Kornfield and Mary Orr at Mount Madonna Center in Watsonville. I chose that retreat because my father had told me a lot about Jack and I had read one of his books. Jack had been a monk in Thailand for several years in his twenties but had been teaching meditation in the West since the early seventies. My father had attended courses with him in the early days and now it was my turn to dive a little deeper into this meditation stuff.

Arriving at the retreat, I was filled with both excitement and fear. I was looking forward to giving my spiritual practice a jump-start but afraid of being bored stiff. It didn't help that I was the only twenty-year-old there and certainly the only punk rocker. Looking around, I didn't see anyone even close to my age. This was my father's scene, not mine. But when the retreat started and we began the sessions of sitting and walking meditation I knew I was in the right place. With my eyes closed and my mind focused on the sensations of breathing, I began to forget about all the differences between me and everyone else. The retreat was not without its challenges and several times a day I considered leaving, making up all sorts of reasons why I shouldn't be there.

It was helpful that Jack had known me since I was a kid and when I introduced myself to him he was very kind and seemed genuinely happy that I was there. Mary was also very supportive. In the interview about my meditation practice I told her I was thinking about leaving early. She said that she understood, that it was natural to want to leave. That she too wanted to leave retreats sometimes but was always happy that she had stayed when they were over. She reminded me that there was only one day left and said that she had faith in me and that she knew I could make it. I believed her. I wasn't so sure about myself, but if she had faith in me that was enough. It turned out that Mary was from Santa Cruz and had a couple of weekly meditation groups. It was good to meet her and nice to know that there were groups I could attend.

After my talk with her I went for a walk and thought about what she had said. I sat down under a huge redwood tree and began to meditate. Her confidence in me gave me confidence in myself. As each breath came and went I let go a little bit more each time, surrendering to the present moment. My mind began to wander to the days of my childhood playing innocently among the redwoods. I was transported to a time in my youth when I had sat down alone in the woods near my house and felt peaceful. I relished the memory or fantasy or whatever it was for a while before bringing my attention back to the present time. I must have sat there for some time because when I opened my eyes it was getting dark. It was time for dinner and then the nightly Dharma talk. In the morning, after breakfast, I could pack up my stuff and get out of there, but for now I was contented to stay till the end.

That night, it was during Jack's Dharma talk about meditation and spiritual life that I got my first sense of inspired purpose. As I sat there listening I began to fantasize about becoming a meditation teacher. It was almost as if I just knew that eventually it would happen. One day I would teach. A quiet sense of direction took me to a place I had never been before.

I knew that even though the retreat had been difficult I had found a meditation practice that I deeply resonated with. The simplicity of the technique and the profundity of the results had already given me a glimpse of the freedom and happiness I had always been seeking.

After living alone for a while and slowly transitioning out of the whole tough guy/biker/hard-line/Straight Edge identity, I began really getting more involved in the program of recovery. I now focused my time and energy on meditation and service. I ended up moving in with some friends I knew from the program. I was going to lots of meetings and trying to help other alcoholics and drug addicts. I was going to junior college and trying to turn my life toward some kind of career that would be in the helping professions. I decided that working in the medical field would be a good way to give back to society. Through helping people who were sick or injured maybe I could begin to repay my debt to society for all of the damage I had caused in my insanity and addiction.

It was around that time that my friend Darren accidentally killed himself while building a house for himself and his fiancée. The skill saw had slipped off the wood he was cutting and severed the femoral artery in his thigh. He was alone and bled to death fairly quickly. Darren had been sober for a long time and I had known him from the streets from when I was still drinking. When I got sober he was one of the only friendly faces in the program. At his funeral I ran into some of the street punks I hadn't seen in years. Everyone was dealing with the grief in their own way. Toby was way high on smack. Johnny, Mark, and Stinky were all drinking beers in the parking lot. Talia and Louie looked like they were doing pretty well, dressed nicely and sitting up front with the family, but I didn't get a chance to talk to them. I was feeling pretty torn up and confused. Although we hadn't been the closest friends Darren was one of the only kids I knew from the streets who had been in my life consistently since I got clean. When he died I had to question my beliefs and practices. Why would the so-called loving Higher Power take the life of someone like him? Unable to feel my sadness, I got so angry I couldn't even stay at the funeral so I left early.

I was kind of crazy for a few days after the funeral, annoyed by all of the dramatic attitudes of the people in the meetings who hardly even knew him. I walked out of meetings as I had walked out of his funeral. It took about a week before I could feel the sadness of his loss. It was when I was alone, in my car listening to Suicidal Tendencies, his favorite band, that I began to realize how much I was going to miss him and how much it had meant to me to have him around.

As each of my friends have died so has a part of me, my past. This time too I was left here to deal with the world and all of life's difficulties. I felt totally alone and friendless, with Toby still getting high and all the others spread out across their lives.

11

My Friends Look Out for Me Like Family

few weeks later Vinny walked into Marino's BBQ and Catering in Soquel village where I was working. I recognized him but wasn't sure where from. I didn't know then that this East Coast Italian kid with the gold earrings and hip-hop attitude would become one of my closest friends. He ordered a chicken sandwich, BBQ chips, and a Sprite.

Neither of us acknowledged the other. I was just kind of checking him out, trying to remember where I had seen him. I got the feeling that he was doing the same. I later found out that he was so impressed by my haircut that he phoned home to the East Coast and used me as an example of how fucking crazy people were in Santa Cruz. I can imagine the conversation went something like this: "Yo, Johnny, you wouldn't fuckin' believe the kind of freaks they got out here. I got a sandwich today, down at the BBQ pit, from a fuckin' guy that had his whole fuckin' head shaved except for a four-inch fence of white hair sticking straight fuckin' up on the top of his head. Yo, that dude is fuckin' crazy."

A few weeks later, when we were properly introduced by our mutual friend, Boyd, we were both like, "Oh, you're the dude from the BBQ pit." Vinny, Boyd, and some other guys had started a men's support group for guys who were in recovery from addiction. It was this small, you had to be personally invited, thing. I guess they decided that I was cool enough and extended the invitation. I started going to that group with them every week and Vinny and I started hanging out.

Vinny grew up back east. Both of his parents were pretty hardcore dope fiends. His father was in and out of prison while he was growing up and his mom did her best to raise three kids. Vinny started getting loaded when he was a kid and was totally strung out on crack by the time he was a teenager. His mother died when he was seventeen. For some reason he felt like it was his fault. Losing hope and having no idea how to deal with the grief of his mother dying, he hit the streets and the crack pipe with a vengeance.

After going in and out of institutions for several years he got sober when he was about twenty. Living in New Haven, Connecticut, where he had grown up, he became very involved in twelve-step recovery. But Vinny wanted out, away from the past, away from the wreckage. So he moved to California to try to get away from it all.

I hadn't had such a good friend since I met Toby. There had been other guys I hung out with, but no one as close as Vinny. It was strange because we came from really different backgrounds, but we were both recovering crackheads so that was definitely a bond. I was into punk but I liked rap; he was an old metalhead who was pretty much only into rap now. He turned me on to a lot of cool hip-hop groups and I turned him on to the best music in the world: punk rock.

We were hanging out all the time but I was vehemently working the steps at that point, trying to get spiritual and change some of my negative behaviors and attitudes. There were several times when I felt like my friendship with Vinny wasn't very supportive of the changes I wanted to make. We spent most of our time talking shit about other people and trying to pick up on girls. I was really wanting to change some of those behaviors and when I would bring it up to Vinny he would get really defensive and pissed and we would get into a fight about it. His usual response was, "Don't be such a girl." He felt like he had already done enough of the steps and recovery stuff and now he was just going to enjoy life sober and have some fun. It was challenging for me at times but our friendship was always strong enough to endure all of our differences. Perhaps our strongest connection was the laughter we shared. We laughed at ourselves and everyone else until we cried.

We got ourselves into some crazy situations and would often compete over girls and battle our wills about how to act. After we had been friends for a year or so Vinny invited me to go back to the East Coast with him to visit some friends and family. It was on that trip that I met Micah, an old friend of Vinny's who was a lot like me. He was playing in a punk rock band and had been into the hardcore scene for many years. We spoke the same language and had a lot of mutual interests. He was also in recovery and had just started getting more into Eastern philosophies, primarily Buddhism and Sufism.

Micah's parents met in the seminary. His father was in training to become a minister and his mother was an ordained nun. They fell in love and left the life of the cloth. Well, his mom did anyway; his pops became a pastor. Like the rest of us, Micah dutifully rebelled against his puritanical roots and started drinking and getting high at a young age. His parents lived near a golf course so he and some friends would often be found running around on acid or drunk driving on the golf carts. His parents, not knowing what else to do, sent him off to rehab at fourteen.

Being a searcher and recognizing that what he was looking for would never be found in drugs and booze, he allowed the twelve steps to do their thing and he was one of thousands of recovering teens in the mid-eighties. Being a punk rocker and a sober one at that, he too got into Straight Edge. By the time we met he was beginning to get more interested in the spiritual traditions of the East than the Western model that he had grown up with and that is offered in the program of recovery.

Micah and Vinny knew each other from meetings in New Haven. Vinny once told me that Micah was wearing a sundress when they met. He had lost his mind on some hippy peace punk crap, but by the time I met him he had regained some sanity and was singing for a melodic punk band that was about to get a major recording deal. The first night I met Micah his band was playing a festival in downtown New Haven, and the next night they played in New York.

On that trip we spent a bunch of time in NYC. I was really excited about being there. A lot of the bands that I grew up listening to and almost the whole Straight Edge scene that I was into was from NYC. We went to the world famous CBGB's, the club where all the early punk and hardcore bands got their start; it was all just legend to me. We hung out down in the Lower East Side and saw some shows.

One night we went out dancing and when we left the club it was 4:00 A.M. so we thought that we would just hang out in the city until morning. We ended up in Washington Square Park trying to sleep on some benches but these huge rats kept attacking us. Looking back I see that Vinny was often attacked by strange animals. It must have been some sort of strange karmic connection he had, some old shit he was working out.

Not long after that trip Vinny decided to move back to the East Coast, which, although I knew I would miss him, was somewhat of a good thing. Our friendship had continued to be challenging and I felt like he wasn't a very positive influence in my life at times and I was really trying to commit myself to the spiritual path.

Vinny and Micah lived together for a while and Vinny opened up a store called 10 Times Dope that sold all the hip-hop, graffiti, and streetwear stuff. The store was a great success and Vinny really enjoyed all the connections and prestige that went along with it. He was in NYC several nights a week hanging with world famous graffiti artists, rappers, and DJs. We kept in touch and I went out to visit several times but I was headed in a different direction.

12

No Spiritual Surrender

I started hearing about Matthew before I had ever met him. He was somewhat of a legend in the Santa Cruz twelve-step recovery scene. He had a whole flock of sponsees and they were all the ultra spiritual characters in the program. My friends Jason, Baron, and Drew were all working with and for him. What I mean is that Matthew was both their sponsor and also their boss. Matthew was a musician and had his own recording label. He had this whole setup where people would work for him going out to big events and conventions and setting up booths to sell his records.

When I first started working the twelve steps with Big Don, I was tentative. But now I felt like I was really ready to give this spiritual practice shit a try. I looked around the program in Santa Cruz to see who was really working the steps. I knew I sure as hell wasn't and I had already been sober for almost two years. So I asked Matthew if he would be willing to be my sponsor but he said no, said he was too busy. He suggested that I go and work the first nine steps with one of his sponsees, a guy named Shawn, and when I was through with them I could come to him for ten, eleven, and twelve. Matthew said he wanted to be more like a spiritual adviser to me than a sponsor and that sounded better than nothing.

I was a bit disappointed but I was very willing to take suggestions at that point so I gave Shawn a call. We arranged to meet a few days later at the Shivering Denizens group that meets on Thursdays at 6:00 P.M. in the little red church in downtown Santa Cruz. Shawn was a big man with long hair. I hated guys with long hair but I was so willing to do whatever I needed to do to get through those steps I was even willing to let go of my judgments.

I spent almost a whole year working the steps with Shawn before Matthew invited me to begin spending time with him. My relationship with Shawn became very close. I would see him every week at Shivering Denizens and we would meet and talk about the steps several times a month. All of the sudden I had an incredible willingness to take suggestions and to do all I could to change my negative behaviors. The steps were really helping. I had incredible experiences of forgiveness and letting go over and over.

Just praying regularly helped a lot but I knew I needed to start taking action to rectify all of the bad shit I had done. I had to write down all my resentments, fears, and a sexual inventory. Getting all that stuff down on paper and out of my head was both difficult and extremely freeing.

When I finished with it I read it to Shawn in a little shack behind his dilapidated Victorian house. He listened intently and once in a while asked me a question about what I had done to retaliate against some of the people I had been resentful toward. The whole time he was writing down the names of everyone I mentioned and making a list of the defects of character in me that he was hearing. You know, all the basics—fear, anger, lust, pride, self-centeredness, greed, envy, and self-esteem issues. I shared with him everything from my whole life, all of it. It was the first time in my life that I had told one person everything. I had talked about some of it with various friends and counselors over the years but never had I been completely honest with one person about all of the people who I felt had harmed me and the ways that I had tried to get revenge. He shared with me some very painful and embarrassing things from his past to try and make me feel more comfortable about the more difficult things I had to tell him.

When I finished I felt like I had just dropped a hundred-pound bag of shit that I had been carrying around my whole life without even knowing it. When I left Shawn's place that day he suggested that I take it easy, that I spend some time reflecting on what we had just done. He said I might feel a little different in the coming days and he was right, I did. I had skateboarded over to his house that afternoon and when I left the sun was just about to set so I skated down the street to a park that overlooked the boardwalk and the beach. I felt like a kid with brand new shoes on. My skateboard was so light under my feet and everything seemed to look different.

Sitting alone on a bench in the park, I watched the sun setting over the ocean and heard a group of kids playing basketball off in the distance. I just sat there thinking about my crazy life. I must have been sitting there for quite a while because by the time I left it was very dark and starting to get cold.

Over the next several weeks I prayed every day for the willingness to let go of all my defects of character and shortcomings, all those things that had come out of my inventory. The more I prayed and paid attention, the more I saw how much of my life was lived out of fear. It got to the point where I felt like every word, action, and thought I had was somehow coming from fear, greed, lust, or anger. It seemed like I was just one big walking, talking defect. But gradually as I continued to pray about it and be aware of what I was saying and doing some of the more gross shortcomings began to fade. I stopped lying and stealing. I began to be a little nicer, even to people I didn't like very much. It became less and less important to be cool and tough and more and more important to be kind and honest.

It was then time, Shawn told me, to start making amends to all the people I had harmed in my life, both while on drugs and while sober. He explained that this was a very necessary and important part of my recovery. That it was by making amends and cleaning up the wreckage of my past that I would begin to forgive myself. By forgiving others and taking responsibility for all the harm I had caused I would be able to open more deeply to the spiritual experience I had already begun to taste. I knew he was right and I wanted to continue with the steps and everything but I had done some really awful shit. How do you make amends for robbing an old lady or beating someone up or robbing someone's house? And what about all the people who had hurt me first? Shawn said that I didn't have to do them all at once and that I should just start slowly, but steadily. He explained that naturally I would be afraid to do some of them but that fear was not an acceptable excuse for inaction. He reminded me that if I held on to any of my resentments I would very likely drink again. That resentments, for alcoholics like us, were poison and eventually, if not dealt with, led back to drink and drugs, or at least a life of misery and confusion.

So I went out and began to make reparations to the people who were on the list I had from my inventory but that list wasn't enough, I had to add a lot of people—everyone I had hurt or ripped off, many of whom I didn't even know.

By now I had gotten a job working at a medical clinic as a nursing assistant. I was making pretty good money and I had also been involved in another car accident where I reinjured my back and received a few thousand dollars from the insurance company for "pain and suffering." I had some extra money, which made the financial part of the amends easier, but it was getting over my pride that was the hard part. I had already sort of apologized to my family for all the trouble I had caused but this was different. Now I was just making a sincere attempt to rectify the wrongs and heal all of the broken relationships, to mend that which I had destroyed: people's trust, faith, and love. The hard part was staying on my side of the street, taking responsibility for my actions, and not focusing on what they had or hadn't done.

But even though this was incredibly difficult, the more amends I made the more I began to forgive myself. It became easier to look people in the eye. I didn't have to continue to hide from or avoid anyone. Every opportunity I got I pulled people aside and asked for forgiveness for any way that I might have harmed them, committing to behave differently in the future. For a while it seemed like this was all I did; I couldn't walk down the street without running into someone who had made the list. I even made amends to my ex-stepfather that I had hated for so long, taking responsibility for all of the ways in which I had retaliated against him, asking him for forgiveness. I did the same with my big brother, who, although our relationship had changed a lot over the years, I still had resentment toward from our childhood. I asked for his forgiveness for all of the times I stole from him and all of the ways I had been unskillful in our relationship, completely putting aside all of the reasons why I had felt justified in my actions at the time and just taking responsibility for what I had done. After I got a good chunk of it done I met with Shawn again and he told me that I really needed to continue with it, that I could actually finish it within the next few months. He promised that one day we would be able to sit together and I would have a clean slate, free from resentments and loose ends. It sounded good but I still had a lot of names on my list and some of the scarier amends to make. Like all the people I had robbed or cheated. I was scared but the willingness and desire to be free was greater than the fear. I knocked on doors of homes that I had burglarized and offered an amends and some cash to rectify the past. I even paid back some drug dealers I had ripped off.

Once I went to make amends to this lady for whom I used to babysit, who lived down the street from my mom. I had stolen her VCR while I was strung out on crack. I knocked on her door with two hundred bucks in my pocket. I was so fucking scared she was going to call the cops or something. But when she answered the door and I told her why I was there and offered her the money and made my amends, instead of yelling at me or calling the cops she invited me in. She thanked me for coming and talking to her. She said that I could keep my money, but that I could make amends in another way. It turned out that her teenage daughter had a friend who had been staying with them recently and she really cared about this kid but he was in jail right now because like me he had stolen someone's VCR. He too was doing a lot of drugs. She said that if I would be willing to, the best amends I could make would be to help him get sober. Of course I agreed to try to help. I told her that I would talk to him if he wanted to but that it was my experience that you had to want to stop yourself, that no matter how many people had talked to me I didn't stop until I was completely beaten and finished. She seemed to understand and was satisfied with my willingness to help if he was interested.

This was one of the times that I walked away knowing that I was on the right path, really feeling like God was working in my life. It was one of those spiritual experiences that inspired me to continue, even when I was terrified.

Over a period of several months I made over a hundred direct amends and paid back thousands of dollars to all the people I had stolen from. At the same time I was doing community service and making monthly payments for restitution in the graffiti bust. My life was very full of the work of recovery and trying to deepen my spiritual practice. Some of my old habits and attitudes were still quite strong but my life was changing so drastically that many of the old ways of being just didn't fit anymore.

I began to notice that other people started treating me differently too. The whole world seemed more friendly, people rarely wanted to fight me anymore. Women seemed to be much more interested in dating me. More and more people started actually asking me for advice, calling me to help them with the steps or to just talk about stuff. That was truly incredible: people actually thought that I had something to offer that would be helpful. It was the first time in my life that I began to understand why so much emphasis is put on service work both in the twelve-step programs and in most spiritual and reli-gious traditions. Because it just feels great to be able to help someone who needs you. Through the act of helping others I temporarily got out of my own self-centered thinking. I had always felt pretty indiffer-ent about other people's problems because I had enough of my own problems. But when I did start helping people I realized how much it really helped me too.

One day when I was at a meeting with Drew the topic was gratitude and I had shared about how I was feeling grateful for the steps and prayer and meditation, how I had tried everything else and that it had been the only thing that ever worked to give me any feeling of peace at all. After the meeting this guy named Jim approached me and asked me if I would be his sponsor, if I would help him work the steps. I gave him my phone number and said he could call me and set up a time to get started. On the way home with Drew I felt kind of proud that someone actually wanted something that I had. Jim and I began meeting regularly and talking about recovery. He was really eager to do the steps and before long he too was sponsoring people. After that more guys started asking me to help them and all of the sudden I was helping other people all the time. Rather than being so self-absorbed with my own problems, I was trying to help others stay sober and deepen their spiritual understanding.

Even my old friend Joe, from back in the Club Culture days, who had been strung out on heroin for years, gave me a call. He had just gotten out of rehab and wanted some help staying sober and needed some other punks to hang out with. It was incredible to feel like I was someone people called for help when just a few years earlier I was someone people crossed the street to avoid.

I was really enjoying working in the medical field. I felt like I was actually helping people on a daily basis. After working in the medical clinic for about a year I got a job at the local hospital as a laboratory technician. I loved doing that job because I would just walk all over the hospital drawing people's blood for their lab tests. I could visit each different unit and see both the newborn babies and the dying el-derly every day.

I was then ready to meet with Matthew, the man who I had asked to help me so many months earlier. I ran into him at a meeting and told him that I was almost done with my ninth step and that I was praying every day and meditating pretty regularly. He said that he would be happy to meet with me and that Shawn had told him how well I was doing.

13

Who Killed Bambi?

Matthew sat in front of the stacks of recording equipment in his home studio with a comfort and style that felt oddly familiar and deeply inspiring. His spiritual understanding and monetary success were attractive and gave me some extra motivation to continue to seek spiritual wisdom. He told me stories of his youth in Santa Cruz, surfing and drinking, of his twenties playing music in local bars and restaurants, of fighting and being quite the ladies' man. He told me the story of how he had gotten sober and of how the steps had led him to a spiritual awakening that completely transformed his life. I was impressed and I knew I wanted what he had. I wanted the inner peace and freedom that he was talking about. I had already had a glimpse of that freedom and my life was getting pretty good but I knew I still had a lot of work to do. After talking for a while about my life and what had brought me to wanting to learn more about spiritual practice we just sat there looking out the window in silence. From his house perched on the top of the mountain overlooking Santa Cruz we had a view of the whole Monterey Bay. I had the feeling that my outlook on life was beginning to expand. I was starting to open to the true meaning of life, to have a spiritual perspective on things.

I began coming up to his house regularly. We would meditate together and discuss spiritual teachings. I was doing mindfulness meditation but also beginning to study Adviata Vedanta and to do some Hindu devotional practices. Matthew knew a lot about the Bhagavad Gita and I had a lot of questions for him about the nature of God and self. These were all questions I was also asking my parents and I was sort of checking out the answers I got from each of them. They seemed to have slightly different perspectives on things but there were no major contradictions. My father was very supportive of my newfound interest in serious spiritual practice and would suggest books that I should read and teachers I could check out.

I always had some dilemma or question that I was struggling with and Matthew's gentle acceptance and loving encouragement to deeply explore all of these questions was exactly what I needed. It was so unlike any relationship that I had ever experienced. He was much more than a sponsor or a friend; he was truly my teacher.

After I had been studying with him for several months he became very adamant about the danger of sexuality for the serious spiritual aspirant. I had heard that he had lost his sexual desire years earlier after some intense spiritual experience or something. I didn't know all the details but I heard that he had just gotten so spiritual that he could no longer connect with his wife in a sexual way. By the time I came around they were already divorced. I guess she had left him; no sex equaled no marriage. Yet there he was suggesting the same thing to me.

I began to consider what the celibate life would be like. Sex was definitely something that I was really attached to. I felt like I was just discovering my sexuality and now this guy was telling me that if I really wanted to be spiritual I should consider abandoning my sexual desire or at least my sexual practices. He suggested that in the beginning I should either stop or at least cut down on masturbation. He felt that masturbation was especially unskillful because it not only increased the sexual appetite but was also a form of mental rape. He explained that when one fantasizes about others without their consent, it is like sexually taking them against their will. I wasn't sure what to make of all that but I was really willing to do whatever was suggested if it was going to help me find more understanding and peace. It did fit in with what I was studying in the Buddhist and Hindu teachings. The Buddha was celibate and so were a lot of the Hindu gurus and yogis. So I took a thirty-day vow not to masturbate. I was still dating a lot and having sex quite often so the no jacking off thing wasn't all that difficult. After the first thirty days it seemed to be going pretty well so I decided to continue with abstaining from masturbation.

I was still being pretty promiscuous though, even as I had started to become more aware of how my actions affected others. I was also beginning to see that my spiritual practice did suffer when I was spending all of my time either chasing girls or having sex. If there was someone else in my bed I usually didn't do my morning and evening prayer and meditation. I still wasn't comfortable enough to do it in front of other people. I was still somewhat in the closet spiritually. I thought that being spiritual was uncool, that it wasn't punk to pray and meditate. Yet I was really beginning to experience a sense of peace that I had never known before. Three months after my vow of abstinence from masturbation I decided to take a vow of complete celibacy. The girl I was dating at the time was not too happy about it but I was really motivated to progress on the spiritual path. Matthew was very pleased and totally supportive of my decision to give up sex in order to go deeper into my spiritual practice.

I was continuing to study the Eastern systems of spiritual awakening and attending Buddhist meditation groups and Hindu gatherings, but Matthew was my main teacher. We would sit on the porch of his house and discuss the Bhagavad Gita or Adviata Vedanta or Buddha Dharma. He had studied much of what I was studying but his awakening did not fall under the guise of any particular paradigm or spiritual philosophy. We spoke a lot of God and ultimate reality but our relationship was a simple one and it mostly consisted of meditating together.

A couple times when we were sitting in his living room looking out over the mountains and ocean and I was inevitably asking some esoteric question about the ultimate nature of reality, instead of answering my question he would go into a sort of trance and then place his hand on my chest, right in the center over the solar plexus. What happened is hard to explain. It felt like he was infusing me with his wisdom or some kind of energy. I had read about shakti and kundalini so I guess I just figured that was what was happening. But the experience was a little like heroin: a warm rush filled my whole body and whatever question I had seemed answered not in words but experientially. I wasn't sure what to make of it. Was it magic? Was he really enlightened and this was just one of his spiritual powers? I knew that the Buddha was said to have had a lot of magical powers so it seemed like it all made sense. I didn't talk about those experiences much. They felt too sacred and I wasn't sure if anyone would believe me anyway, so I just kept them to myself.

My life had truly been transformed in those first couple of years of serious spiritual practice. Many of my negative and destructive behaviors, such as stealing, lying, and all forms of physical violence, began to fall away. The more I practiced kindness and humility, the more the world seemed to appear friendly and manageable. I was sponsoring a bunch of guys in recovery and volunteering at Hospice on my days off from work. An incredible willingness to help others was suddenly present in my life. Being celibate allowed me to spend my time doing spiritual practice rather than looking for love. It was truly incredible to me that I was able to resist temptation. At times it seemed that women would come on to me just because they knew I was celibate.

The practice of celibacy alone was opening me up to a deeper sense of the way the mind-body connection works. I saw over and over that my mind and body could be filled with desire and that no matter how intense the craving was it would always pass. I didn't have to satisfy every desire that arose in my mind. I began to understand impermanence through direct experience rather than just intellectual theory.

This was the first time in my life that I began to question my identification with punk rock. I was so deeply engrossed in the beginning stages of spiritual practice that I thought that the negative vibe of hardcore punk rock would bring me down. I had always loved punk because it was an outlet for my anger but now I had a new outlet and it seemed to be working better than punk ever had. Within the punk rock scene there were other kids getting spiritual too. There were even some hardcore bands, like Shelter and 108, that were preaching Krishna consciousness. I also started trying to get into other forms of music like jazz, soul, and reggae but although I thought some of it was cool, nothing ever moved me the way punk did. I continued to listen to punk and rap and still went to shows but as my perspective on life began to change so did my resonance with some of the negativity and violence in the hardcore scene. I even started listening to some of Matthew's music, which was way too mellow, but since I appreciated him so much I even started to like his records. Matthew knew I was into punk but we never talked about music. He was always giving me CDs of his music to listen to. It was okay if you were just hanging out or meditating but not something you wanted to blast in your car.

As I began to identify more with the Krishna Core scene, I realized that some other kids who were into it also, like my friends Joe and Russ. Even within the punk scene I had found a place where it was cool to be spiritual.

On a trip to the East Coast to see Vinny and Micah, while we were all in New York City, I visited Equal Vision records, which was the main force behind all of the spiritual punk that was coming out. The people who ran the record label were Hindu practitioners mostly following the teachings of ISKON, the International Society of Krishna Consciousness, founded by AC Bhaktivedanta Swami Prabupada. The

Krishnas had really made an impression on the hardcore punk scene. It's not surprising really: we got into punk rock because we knew that society was fucked and that the material world would never offer us happiness, so most of us just got drunk all the time in an attempt to escape. When we heard that there was actually an escape from this world that was lasting and eternal some of the kids really went for it. It was really crazy for a few years there. Every time you went to a punk rock show there would be a bunch of young devotees passing out literature and food.

Inspired by what I had been learning from Matthew, my celibacy, and the plethora of spiritual books I had been reading, I decided to go to another meditation retreat. I had been to a couple of my parents' weekend workshops about death and dying and conscious relationships. A woman who organized my parents' workshops told me about a retreat they were organizing for a Buddhist monk. She said that she thought I would really like him so I decided to go check it out.

It was there that I met a monk named Ajahn Amaro who would become my next teacher. He was an Englishman who had become a monk in Thailand about fifteen years earlier. When I met him he was living in a monastery in England after having trained in Thailand for several years. A nun by the name of Sister Sundara co-taught the retreat with him. She too was a Westerner who had renounced the world to live the life of a celibate Buddhist monastic. There was a small group of Americans who invited him to come teach retreats in California each year. The retreat was being held in a Chinese Buddhist monastery in northern California called the City of Ten Thousand Buddhas. It's located in an old state mental hospital, one of the old brick and concrete ones with the shock treatment bathtub chambers and the vibrations of years of torture and overmedication. It reminded me a lot of the movie *One Flew over the Cuckoo's Nest* and also of all the time I had spent in jail. The retreat was much more formal and austere than the first one that I had attended with Jack Kornfield. Here I had to bow all the time and chant in some weird foreign language. We didn't even get to eat dinner.

After trying to meditate all day I went back to my room, which was a little bit too much like a holding cell with its brick walls, an uncomfortable bed on the floor, and that hospital-like institutional smell that sat just under the surface of the incense. I was questioning what the fuck I was doing. Why did I think that I could do something like this? I wanted to leave but I also knew that it was important that I stay. I was learning something new and I was even willing to be uncomfortable in order to find a new way of living my life.

Ajahn Amaro deeply inspired me. I was definitely intimidated by the robes and all the ceremonial aspects of being around him but there was something else that was stronger than my fear and intimidation, there was a sense of acceptance that I felt from him that I had rarely experienced in my life. I felt like he was sincerely happy to see me and that he was completely content to be doing what he was doing.

During the retreat I got the opportunity to help offer the midday meal to him and Sister Sundara. I was nervous and felt awkward about not knowing how many times to bow and when to hand them the food. They were very kind and understanding about my ignorance of the traditions that surrounded their mealtime. They asked me a couple of questions about my life and about my parents. I couldn't believe that I was actually talking to real monks; what a totally different universe than what I was used to. Before I left the retreat I got to thank them and do the customary bowing three times. Ajahn Amaro encouraged me to keep up the practice, assuring me that it eventually would get easier. I decided I would take his word for that and made my swift departure. I felt good about what I had experienced on retreat but was definitely looking forward to getting back to three meals a day, loud music, and sleeping in.

For weeks I told all my friends about the retreat with the monks at the monastery. They thought I was crazy. "Why would anyone want to get up at four o'clock in the morning, do nothing all day, and then go to sleep hungry?" they asked. I had the same questions. While I was there, at times, it was like torture but afterward I was really fucking psyched I had done it and I immediately wanted to do it again. I had seen the possibility of living happily and contented as a full-time meditation practitioner. For the first time in my life I understood that the highest happiness comes from the simplest things.

That was when I began fantasizing about becoming a monk some-day. I had been so inspired by Ajahn Amaro that I hoped to someday follow in his footsteps, the footsteps of the Buddha.

I had grown up in some of the most beautiful and wild areas of this country, the redwood forests of northern California and the high deserts of New Mexico, but I had always preferred to spend my time in town, on the sidewalk. I was never much into camping or hiking; that shit was for tree huggers and cowboys.

When I first got sober and started in on recovery and would hear about serenity I always equated it with some place outside of myself. I had a picture in my mind of a peaceful meadow filled with wildflow-ers, butterflies, and grazing animals. I felt that peace was for hippies and that as a punk rocker it had been my duty to fight against those passive, useless people, to foster some real changes, or at least to leave a path of destruction so that someone would know I had existed. My vision in those days was to enter the serene meadow with a flame-thrower, smoking a cigarette, and burn down the whole fucking place, destroying everything and killing Bambi.

I was really afraid of what I would find in the quiet moments. I was afraid of being bored and boring. Filled with the grief and rage that had fueled years of drug abuse and violence (even in sobriety it was still there), I was still afraid of what I might find if I slowed down enough to see what was really behind my negative attitudes and actions.

Yet after having practiced meditation for a while I began to truly ex-perience moments of serenity and my fear of peace began to lessen. Once I saw that serenity had nothing to do with nature and was sim-ply another state of mind that could be experienced in any surround-ing I became more and more attracted to spending time in the mountains and on the coast. The more my mind began to quiet, the more I found myself wanting to be surrounded by natural beauty. I began taking hikes and spending afternoons on the coastline of northern California, between Santa Cruz and San Francisco, just wandering about offering prayers and practicing meditation.

Just after my retreat with Ajahn Amaro and Sister Sundara, I decided I was ready to do some solitary practice, alone in the wilderness, sitting under a tree like the Buddha had.

I packed up my car with a tent, a sleeping bag, some food, and a copy of my father's book, which was my meditation Bible at the moment, *A Gradual Awakening*. I was working full-time at the hospital and taking classes at the junior college so I had only a couple of days to camp. My friends thought I was crazy. "Why would you want to go camping alone?" I was asked. I just said I was going to do some soul-searching or something and they were like, "Whatever, dude, you're turning into a real fucking hippy." They were right, I was. But I was a lot fucking happier than they were, so fuck it.

I chose Big Basin State Park as my destination for that first solo outdoor practice period and adventure, partially because it was close to where I was living in Santa Cruz at the time and partly because it is home to some of the largest and oldest redwood trees in the world. I felt drawn to being in the presence of these ancient trees and figured it would be a safe and inviting place to come to some sort of peace with my fear of being alone in nature.

On the drive up to the mountains I stopped at a small Burmese monastery that was on the way and sat in the shrine room for a few minutes. Before departing I offered some incense to the Buddha image and asked for protection on my journey. My mind was filled with the comment a friend had made about how I was turning into a real fucking hippy. But I knew I was following a path that led to somewhere I had always wanted to be.

As I pulled into the parking lot of the campgrounds Ice Cube was busting on my stereo, "I ain't the one to get played like poo butt, see I'm from the streets so I know what's up." I turned off the car and jumped out. Before walking over to the ranger's station to reserve a campsite I took a few deep breaths of the fresh mountain air and bent my head back to see the sky through the tops of the redwood trees.

NWA was still reverberating in my mind but that was fine, I didn't feel like there was anything incompatible with my love of gangster rap and my spiritual aspirations.

The very cute girl in the ranger station was sweet and helpful. I asked if there were any campsites that were more secluded and she showed me maps of the different available sites. One was located at the very end of the campground, blocked off by a large fallen tree— she said that she had been there and that it was one of the best sites they had.

"I'll take it," I said. For a moment I was tempted to invite her to come with me but I resisted the urge, partially out of fear of rejection but mostly just because I knew I needed to be alone for a couple of days.

Driving from the ranger's station up to the area where my campsite was, I turned off the music, feeling that I had already arrived at my destination and that it was time to begin my practice and start relaxing. Pulling into my parking space, I tensed up, seeing all of the other campers and how close together everyone was packed in. I had come for solitude, not to hear the hillbillies next door getting drunk all night. With more than just a little annoyance, I packed up my gear and made the hike through the very full campsite, past the little kids with peanut butter and jelly smeared across their faces, past the guy with the three cases of beer and the portable radio, past the group of hippies with all the newest North Face camping gear—until, finally, I reached the end of the campground.

For a moment I couldn't even find my spot; every other site I had passed seemed occupied. At the end of the trail where the path began to turn back down toward the parking lot there was a huge fallen redwood on my right and beyond that a hill. After a moment I remembered the map the ranger had shown me and I realized that my site was on the other side of the great big tree. I noticed a small trail that led around the tree. I took it and as I turned the corner I saw my campsite. There was a picnic table, a fire pit, and a large smooth surface for my tent. I instantly breathed a sigh of relief. Even though there were other campers just a few yards away, at least they were out of sight. I felt like I was really alone but also found some comfort in the fact that I was not too alone.

I began setting up camp. Starting to feel pretty hungry, I pulled out some of the trail mix I'd brought and had a snack. It tasted better than I remembered and I took my time chewing it, recalling the instructions for the eating meditation that I had learned on retreat: chew slowly, taste every mouthful, don't add anything to it. Setting up the tent was the next order of business. I had borrowed the tent from a friend so it was somewhat of a puzzle as to how to put the thing together. I struggled for several minutes, attempting to set the damn thing up. I didn't have a clue about what I was doing. I gave up and searched the carrying bag for the instructions. They were clear and easy to follow; once I knew what to do the tent was set up in a matter of minutes. I faced it toward the mountain to further give myself the sense of being alone with the wilderness.

I unloaded the rest of my pack and stored my clothes neatly in the tent. I put my books on the picnic table and got my food organized for the weekend and then I began to gather some wood for the fire. Once that was done and I was all set up, I sat on the picnic table for a while, surveying the scene, taking in all the sights and sounds. The smell of someone else's campfire was in the air. I realized that this was the first time I had ever set up a tent alone. I had been camping before with friends but this was the only time I had set everything up myself. I felt a moment of pride and had the sense that my life was finally going in the right direction—hoping that all the trouble was behind me. I just wanted to spend the rest of my life trying to help others. All I wanted was to find more of the happiness and satisfaction I had been discovering through spiritual practice.

I picked up *A Gradual Awakening*. It opened at the chapter on daily meditation practice. I realized that in all the busyness of packing and preparing to come camping I had not yet done any meditation that day, not counting my mindful munching of the trail mix. I read a few pages and felt inspired to do some meditation but I also felt pretty hungry—and it was going to get dark soon. So rather than meditate I decided to get the fire going and cook some food.

It was Ramen noodle soup and some fresh vegetables for dinner. I had been attempting to go vegetarian. I was still eating fish sometimes but I had renounced all the other flesh foods. I also had some fresh sourdough bread for sandwiches the next day but thought it would go well with my vegetable noodle soup instead. The fire was blazing and I got the water boiling quickly, so I added my carrots, onions, and broccoli. The noodles and soup base went in last and about five minutes later I had a fragrant pot of campfire soup. I let it cool down and then dipped in a piece of bread to get started.

My meal tasted incredibly good. I intentionally ate very slowly, trying to taste every bite and remembering to put the spoon down between each mouthful. Sometime ago my dad had been speaking with me about mindful eating—hadn't he said that he thought it could be as powerful a practice as sitting meditation? The taste of the noodle soup under the evening sky certainly brought me into the present moment as much as paying attention to my breath ever had.

I was just about finished eating and the twilight was well set in. Something was moving nearby, rustling in the bushes on the hillside above me. I looked up and saw a deer, carefully picking its way down the slope. I became very still, sitting, watching the deer as she continued her walk down the hillside. She stopped a couple of times to nibble at some leaves or to straighten up, lifting her head to listen for the sounds of a possible predator.

My mind was strangely calm—I was amazed at the sight of the lone deer moving toward my camp. I had never been so close to a wild animal before. A couple of experiences I had as a kid flashed into consciousness: smelling the stench of deer jerky hanging to dry in the garage of our neighbor's house in Santa Fe when I was seven and, when I was eleven, being sickened by the sight of a deer killed and gutted by my friend Ricky's father in Colorado. Now, looking at that exquisite, delicate, living being that was almost at my tent, those disturbing memories evaporated.

It seemed like she was playing some sort of game, to see how close she could get without freaking out and running off. I sat as still as I possibly could, watching and waiting to see when she would realize that I was sitting there, then turn and take off, back up the hill to find the rest of her family. She continued past my tent, sniffing around while carefully avoiding the fire pit, then walked right up to the table where I was sitting. She was only a couple of feet away. She stopped and looked directly at me. For a moment I had no idea what to do; I was mesmerized by the dreamlike experience of being face-to-face with this being. Then, very slowly, I picked up a piece of bread and held it out—my palm was flat and the bread just sat there as an offering on my outstretched hand.

She tensed for a moment, but instead of making a break for it, she took a step forward and her wide eyes relaxed. She sniffed at the piece of sourdough I was offering her. She made the final step and was right before me, within arm's reach. She began to nibble on the bread in the palm of my hand. I could feel her little lips scraping my hand as she ate. I was perfectly still but my heart was racing with excitement by then. I was amazed at the unfolding of the scenario—I couldn't believe that it was happening to me, of all people.

I decided to try to take it a step further. Slowly, I reached up with my other hand and lightly touched her head and nose. She continued to eat, not seeming to mind or even really notice that I was stroking her gently between her eyes. They sparkled in the dim light and her fur felt silky. I tried to pet her ears as well but she shook her head.

She finished eating her piece of bread and, without even looking at me again, walked off, just as slowly as she had approached. I watched her until she disappeared over the crest of the hill.

For a long time I sat contemplating what had just happened, wondering what to do next. I found myself making up all kinds of elaborate fantasies: that she must have been sent by God to tell me that everything was going to be all right; that I had been forgiven for all of my early life's violence against nature.

Later that night when I was tucked snugly into my sleeping bag I reflected on the stories my father had told me of Ram and Sita when I was a child, and I remembered the tale of the evil Demon King Ravana, who had one of his sidekicks turn himself into a golden deer to lure Ram and Laxman away from Sita so that she could be kidnapped.

I recalled the childhood stories of Bambi and Thumper—how I had taken to saying I wanted to burn the fields of serenity and kill Bambi. No! I didn't want to kill Bambi anymore, I didn't want to kill anything anymore, I just wanted to live my life and let go of the past.

14

Love Sick

About a year and a half into my celibacy, and almost two years into my study with Matthew, things started to get weird. One of Matthew's senior students was a woman named Monique. She had been working with him for many years running his recording label and she also acted as a teacher for some of the other women who studied with Matthew. Out of the blue, Matthew announced that he and Monique were going to get married. This was really shocking, owing to Matthew's stance on sex and what I thought I knew of him. When I asked him about it he told me that it wasn't what it seemed and that it

was more for others than for himself. He explained that since most of
their students were parents and had families it would be better for
them if their teachers were also a family. He went into this whole
weird esoteric description about how if he were to kiss Monique it was
more like the smelling of a flower. Basically I guess he was saying that
they were beyond celibacy, that they had transcended the realm of
human desire and were meeting on another level.

Matthew and Monique had their ceremony up on the hill at his
home on a sunny day at the beginning of summer. At the wedding
Jason, Drew, Baron, and I talked about how weird it was that they
were getting married. I didn't really know Monique because I had
never worked for Matthew's record company but all of the other guys
had worked there and they were all talking about what a psychopath
she was.

After the wedding Matthew moved in with Monique in Scott's Valley and asked me if I wanted to rent his place up on the mountain and
share it with another student, named Vanessa. Vanessa and I knew
each other from meetings although not very well. I decided to move in
there because Matthew was saying he thought it would be good for
me to live with someone else from our spiritual community. At the
time I was living alone in a beautiful cottage in the mountains in
Aptos. I had the perfect setup with cheap rent and a nice place all to
myself. Matthew's place was twice as much rent but I had a new job at
the hospital and was making good money so I could afford it.

I asked Matthew if he thought I was ready to be back in intimate
relationships. He said that he was very pleased with my progress and
level of understanding of spiritual principles and that he thought that
it would be fine, if I felt moved, to enter back into relationship as long
as it was based on love and mutual commitment to spiritual practice.

When we were sitting together that evening he told me that he was
going to be in New York for a couple of months working on some new
recordings. He said that if he thought that they would listen to me he
would have asked the other students to start taking spiritual direction
from me while he was gone. But since I was the youngest one in the

scene and most of the other students were almost twice as old as I was, they probably wouldn't be able to take that. He even used as an example a physician from the hospital where I was working who was also a student of his. Matthew said, "I wish Nick could learn from your example. He suffers so much. If I thought he would listen I would have you teach him about meditation."

This was great news. I felt a real sense of pride and accomplishment. Not only had my teacher just told me that I could break my celibacy, he was also saying that he was personally proud of my progress. This was the first time he had encouraged me to begin teaching meditation.

I'm sure that a big part of my desire to be back in relationship was that if Matthew was going to be in relationship so was I. I wanted to be like him so I did what he did. I thought it was kind of weird that he got married, but I was getting pretty tired of being celibate anyway.

I met Lola at the Red Room, a small bar in downtown Santa Cruz where I used to go dancing once in a while. She was a friend of a friend's girlfriend. Actually, I had met her best friend, Kim, first and we had been flirting a little but I wasn't really interested in dating her. Lola has long red hair, a petite build, and angelic features. She was half Japanese and half English but when I first met her it was hard to tell that she was Asian at all, she just looked so delicate and exotic. She was so beautiful that she looked otherworldly. I was instantly mesmerized. It was love at first sight but I tried to ignore and discount my feelings because, after all, she drank and I figured she had no set spiritual practice or discipline. How could I even think about being in a relationship with someone who was not practicing spiritual principles?

After our first date, when I was dropping her off at her apartment, I gave her the speech that I was used to giving girls in those days. "It was great hanging out but I need to tell you that I'm not interested in more than friendship. Spiritual practice is the most important thing in my life and I am practicing celibacy." I believe I may have added that I was ready to enter back into relationship but that it would have to be with someone who was also committed to the spiritual life.

Her response totally blew my mind. She began to cry and told me all about her love for God and her inner spiritual search that had led her to a deep connection with images of angels and spiritual deities. She spoke of her practice of journaling and how she would often write of her vain search for happiness and feeling of homesickness for God.

That was all I needed to hear. I was hooked, I longed so deeply to be in relationship, and we were falling in love. Within a week I had broken my celibacy. During our first lovemaking I began to weep; the emotional connection and physical pleasure of our union was over-whelming. The bliss of sex while in love was much higher than any-thing I had ever experienced. There was some confusion and hesitance; I had conditioned myself for so long to turn away from de-sire that it had become an ingrained habitual response. But it didn't take long for me to re-embrace my lust. In no time we were making love daily.

At home I could tell that Vanessa's relationship with Monique and Matthew was very different from mine with them. She seemed to put them on a level of spiritual attainment that we could never reach, as though they were just higher beings than we were, not just further along the path. As it turned out, Monique was asking her about my lifestyle, wanting to know what I was like to live with. So Vanessa had been reporting that I was constantly reading some spiritual book or another and that I spent a lot of time on the phone or with friends. She told Monique about all the statues and pictures that I decorated the house with, mostly Hindu and Buddhist images, and that I had a tendency to listen to loud music sometimes. It wasn't anything bad. I was pretty mellow in those days.

Monique and I had planned to meet and talk about the spiritual practice. I had heard mixed things about her but really trusted Matthew. He had just married her so she couldn't be all bad.

At our meeting Monique said that she had been "instructed" to tell me that I needed to go deeper into a practice of renunciation. This was just the opposite of what Matthew had recently told me. She said that I needed to "no longer initiate physical contact with people, no hugs or embraces." She felt that I thought I had something to give in that way and that she wanted me to experience total solitude within myself. She also said that I needed to take down all of the pictures and statues in my home and not read any books or teachings from other spiritual traditions, that I could get everything I needed from her and Matthew. I was also instructed to not listen to any music but Matthew's, and to cap it all off she told me I shouldn't get any more tattoos.

This of course meant that I couldn't be with Lola. I was really blown away. My whole world turned instantly upside down; I wanted to tell her that she was fucking crazy, but I couldn't. I wanted spiritual awakening so badly that I had lost trust in myself, and my better judgment. I obeyed Monique even though I knew inside that her direction and contradiction of Matthew's previous instructions was totally wrong for me.

At home I took down all the pictures and put away all the books as I had been instructed. I called Lola and told her we were going to have to take a break from our relationship, said that we couldn't be physical for a while. She was devastated, asking, "What are you talking about? What's wrong with you?" She didn't understand what was going on and I was too confused to explain it properly. So we just got in a fight about it instead and I fell back on the "I told you from the start my spiritual practice is the most important thing in my life." And that was that, end of conversation. We had been together for only about a month at that point and she had completely quit drinking, but that night she went out and got drunk.

The next day my friend Dave called. He had just gotten out of jail and wanted some help getting sober. I took him to a meeting but couldn't give him a hug or anything. Internally I was a mess and I started to get kind of depressed. Here I was trying to help a friend who was in a really bad place and I wasn't supposed to give him a hug and tell him that I cared. I started getting angry, angry at Monique, at Matthew, and at myself for being such a sucker as to have gotten involved with them in the first place.

After a couple more days of that confused haze I called my father and talked with him at length about all of what had happened and how everything felt like it had been turned upside down. I could tell he was concerned by the tone of his voice. He suggested that I speak directly with Matthew to find out why such conflicting instructions were given and if he really agreed with Monique. If so, if these folks were really that confused, then maybe it was time for me to reconsider my relationship with them.

Matthew was coming back to California in a few days so I made an appointment to see them both. In the meantime I decided that I wasn't going to continue with the no-touching shit. Lola and I got together and I told her what had happened and that I was really sorry. We decided to try to work things out but she was really struggling with her sobriety after her relapse. I didn't know what to do. She said that she thought that she was probably an alcoholic and wanted some help. After she told me about how much she was drinking before we got together it was clear to me that she had a problem. She promised to start going to meetings and to stay sober. I was unclear about what to do about the relationship but I knew I was deeply in love with her. She was the first woman I had truly fallen in love with and although we had a lot of problems I wanted to work everything out.

When Matthew returned I went to meet with him and Monique at their home. I was sitting with him and Monique, discussing the recent events. Monique did most of the talking. Matthew seemed somehow different—not his usual easygoing self, almost withdrawn. I told them that the contradictory experiences I had been having with each of them had left me confused and that my trust in them was in question.

Monique was spouting some bullshit about how she knew that I was-n't "ready" yet and that she had set all this up just to demonstrate that fact to Matthew and to me. She said that she could already see the time (and date) in the future when I would be "ready" and that I would come back to them then. I was surprisingly calm despite feeling somewhat angry and anxious—it was strange and unsettling to be questioning everything that I had learned and experienced over the years with Matthew.

After some time Monique left the room for a while; Matthew was standing with his back half turned to me, almost as if it was impossible for us to meet face-to-face. The silence was awkward.

Eventually I asked him about what his awakening experience had been like and who his teachers had been. I already knew that he never really had a teacher, that he considered God to be the only teacher necessary for awakening, but I wanted him to say that again. I knew I was leaving him, my teacher, for good and looking directly to God for guidance from then on. I wanted to force him to acknowledge that I was following his example by leaving.

He was unable to answer my question. He froze up, and then called Monique back into the room. "Noah's got a question for you to answer. Ask her, Noah," he said.

"But I asked *you*. Why should she answer? I don't get it . . ." I replied.

"Ask her," he said again, in a flat tone.

"Okay. What was Matthew's experience of enlightenment like and who were his teachers?" I asked. The heavy blanket of tension and dis-comfort in the room muffled everything.

"Matthew is not really of this world—he is from another, sacred realm," Monique replied, in her creepy way. "He has only come here to help us. He is pure love; we should be completely devoted to him. As for myself, I am a spirit who walks between both worlds—that's why I have been trying to teach you discipline. Matthew can't do that because he is only love. It's only someone who knows both worlds who can give the kind of guidance that you need."

I just sat there for a few minutes in disbelief. I didn't know if I was enraged, confused, or just freaked out. She was basically saying that they were here to save the world like a pair of fucking new age messiahs. Inside, however, I started feeling a strange sense of relief: it was getting clearer and clearer exactly how confused they were—I almost felt compassion for the delusion they were lost in.

I was done, ready to move on, my head was spinning. My heart was heavy with the grief of deception and confusion. But I knew I had grown a lot over the years of studying with Matthew. I knew that although he and Monique had obviously lost their minds, it didn't negate the genuine experiences I'd had. I was finally able to trust myself and know that I didn't need them or anyone else in order to be on the spiritual path.

"Thank you for all of the time we spent together; you helped me a lot," I said, trying to express to Matthew my deep gratitude for the spiritual teachings that had been shared. Then I got up and said goodbye. In spite of Monique's instructions, Matthew and I attempted a friendly hug, although as we embraced each other it felt as though there was a wall between us. To myself I swore I would never return.

I moved out of Matthew's house and went and stayed with a friend who understood what I was going through. She had had a similar experience with Matthew and Monique and was really able to support me and give me the space I needed to allow everything to settle. As it turned out, since Matthew and Monique had married, several students had left.

Years later I heard that Matthew left Monique, saying that she had been manipulating him into all kinds of crazy delusions for years. Monique was completely deranged and obsessed about the whole thing. Her twelve-year-old daughter claimed that Matthew had been molesting her. It may have been true but only they really knew. There was so much paranoia and fantasy in the air, no one was really sure of the line between fact and illusion by then.

Matthew ended up going to jail for a little while, and then he moved away to begin afresh on the other side of the country.

(The saddest part of this chapter of my life was that, because she believed all the lies that Monique and Matthew had told her, my old roommate Vanessa was devastated. To her, God had just been convicted as a child molester and, even worse, when he got out of jail he left town and she was all alone.

Her body was found hanging from the fan in a hotel room.)

Lola and I broke up and got back together several times. The first time we split was shortly after everything went down with Matthew and I had left that scene and I was still in so much pain and confusion about all that had gone down. The only thing I knew was that happiness and peace was what I was looking for and spiritual practice was the only place that I had ever truly found it. I had searched for it in drugs and violence and never found it. I had gotten all the material things I ever wanted but was still feeling empty.

I had already been doing Buddhist meditation practice for several years but it was through that painful experience that I came to fully commit to Buddhist practice as my primary spiritual path. I thought about running off to join Ajahn Amaro at the monastery in England but it wasn't really feasible. So I began sitting more and more with Mary Orr, who taught a couple of meditation groups a week in Santa Cruz.

As well as looking for some comfort in the Dharma I also fell back into looking for comfort in sex. I had a whole list of women whom I had been attracted to over the years of celibacy. So I went out and got together with several of them, falling back into looking for happiness in sense pleasures rather than in spiritual experience. My meditation practice was affected by the fact that I was putting more energy into getting laid than into practicing. I had become pretty sensitive to other people's feelings in the years of abstinence so it was not without a price tag. I caused a lot of undue pain to the women I was using to try to escape from myself. I was always very honest, but I believe that if we know that our actions are going to hurt someone, it is our responsibility to protect them. On the other hand it was incredibly fun to be back in the dating scene. All the attention and sex did give me a little reprieve from the confusion about what had just happened with Matthew.

I knew I was trying to fill a spiritual void with sense pleasures but was unable to stop myself. Not only did my compulsion not work, but it created further difficulty in my relationship with Lola. After a couple of months of slutting around I realized that all I was really looking for was love and that Lola was the only woman I had ever truly cared for. She had always had a fairly unreasonable sense of jealousy about my relationships with other women. When we were together she would often question me about other women I knew, and since I had slept with several of them, when she was upset she would often bring it up. After she found out about the women I had always claimed were "just friends" she was more insecure than ever.

When we got back together we started going to meditation groups together sometimes and when my parents came to town we went to a workshop they were teaching in Oakland. Lola was tremendously sincere about her desire for awakening but still battling with her personal demons and struggling with depression. Her formal spiritual practice never really seemed to develop. I was really attached to making everything work out with her. I tried to take care of her, but with my own confusion and immature spiritual practice it wasn't possible for us to maintain an intimate relationship. I felt like she was making me her Higher Power and she felt like I was trying to play therapist. The result was that I ended up being really pissed that I wasn't getting what I wanted and I needed out of the relationship. I loved her but couldn't be her boyfriend. We split up again, with the understanding that we both just needed to work on ourselves for a while.

I had been working in the hospital for a couple of years and found that work pretty fulfilling but I wanted to do more counseling so I got a job at the county health department's AIDS program as an HIV test counselor, putting my blood-drawing skills to work but also getting trained to counsel people about the risks of HIV. It was the perfect job for me at the time. People were so freaked out about their lives and the possibility of having contracted HIV that I could speak to them about the importance of skillful action and their relationship with mortality. As well as working in the health department's drop-in clinics, I also began doing some street outreach and getting involved in needle exchange, counseling addicts about risk and ways to reduce the amount of harm they caused through drug use. I saw a lot of the people I used to do drugs with, still strung out, still struggling. It was sad to see but also gave me a lot of gratitude that I had escaped that lifestyle. I no longer had the holier-than-thou Straight Edge attitude. It had been replaced with a feeling of caring and the understanding that we are all doing the best we can to find freedom from suffering.

Still very confused and hurt by what had happened with Matthew, I struggled with my own spiritual practice and faith but continued to meditate and I became more involved in the Buddhist community. I had often thought about Ajahn Amaro and had recently read more about the Thai forest Buddhist tradition. All of the stories that Jack Kornfield told of his teacher Ajahn Cha and the deep and simple practice of living in a hut in the jungle were inspiring. It was so completely foreign to my way of life, and the most extreme spiritual practice I had heard of yet. As a punk rocker, I had always had an anti-establishment ideal, and these Thai monks were putting that ideal into practice, owning nothing, relying on the generosity of the community for their daily meal, and committing all of their time to an inner revolution against attachment, fear, and confusion. To me it sounded like the perfect balance of outer simplicity and inner rebellion. So I started fantasizing about going to Thailand and becoming a monk.

Being sexually active was overrated. I was still so full of judgment and fear of my desires. It sounded great to just live the simple life of a Buddhist monk. The truth is, I had been thinking of myself as a punk monk for years. Why not take it one step further and submerge myself in the Buddha Dharma? I didn't really think I would be a monk forever but like Jack and many of the other teachers I had met or heard about, I wanted to ordain for a few years and then come back and share the insights I had found with others.

15

the Inner Revolution

Micah had come to Santa Cruz for a visit and fell in love with the West Coast. He had decided that the rock band—touring, recording, getting rich, and being surrounded by beautiful girls—was not the life for him. He truly wanted to live the simple life and commit more deeply to his spiritual practice. Vinny was still living back in New Haven so Micah moved to Santa Cruz and we got a house together with my friend David, who was an old punk rocker who had made the full transition to B-boy, hip-hop graffiti hooligan. We all lived in a ghetto neighborhood near the beach flats for a few months and then

Micah and I got a place of our own that was a lot nicer up the hill, in a quiet residential neighborhood overlooking the boardwalk.

I think this was really the beginning of the integration of our punk ethics and spiritual practice. We would go to meditation groups and then go to punk rock shows and do stage dives and slam dancing. I was reading a lot of Buddhist books and Micah introduced me to the Sufi teachings of Islamic mysticism. In one of the stories about the Buddha's enlightenment I came across a line where he said that his awakening was "against the stream," that the spiritual path that leads to liberation is against man's selfish, deluded ways. That was it, exactly what I was looking for: an inner rebellion that would bring me to liberation. I had been experiencing that through my spiritual practices but there it was in black and white, the Buddha had actually described it as the path. I knew that I was on the right track. My early life's external rebellion had only led to more suffering; the Buddhist spiritual path was the perfect way to realize my goal of the real revolution.

Micah and I often stayed up late discussing spiritual teachings. He taught me about the Indian Sufis' beliefs that all of the religions are talking about the same thing and that spiritual experiences are universal and just spoken about in different terms by different traditions. I liked that a lot. I didn't know enough about any of the religions to know whether it was true or not but it sounded good.

I was spending more and more time with Mary Orr and attending her meditation group regularly. My meditation practice and devotion to truth were strong but I was still quite confused about my sexuality, feeling that the highest form of practice was total renunciation but being caught in the web of satisfaction of desire. I had definitely learned from my period of celibacy that I had the ability to allow desire to pass, but I was also dealing with the residual self-judgment that I had laid on myself for seeking happiness in pleasure. I was also getting a bit more into Hindu devotional practice, chanting the names of the gods and studying the Bhagavad Gita. In the Gita, Krishna teaches that we must look at the material world as illusion and act according to our Karma. That was also a teaching that helped me understand and integrate my love of punk. I was just fighting the battle against society, just as the gods Krishna and Arjuna had fought against Duryodhana, the evil warlord in the Gita.

To a lot of the kids in the Santa Cruz punk scene Micah and I became the "spiritual ones," so we started organizing little meditation groups at our house. We would invite a bunch of people over, cook dinner, and practice meditation or do some chanting. It was hilarious because the group would inevitably fall into a pillow fight or wrestling or fart jokes or something. Hardcore punk kids can handle only so much spiritual shit before we need to act out some. We all hung out at the coffee shops downtown. Micah and I would talk to kids about Dharma stuff and when the next punk shows were. Joe and his little brother, Luke, were both sober and the more punks who got clean, the bigger our crew became.

I was doing a lot of soft-belly meditation, a body-centered meditation practice of relaxing the belly every time you notice fear, desire, or confusion arising, thereby making space and acceptance for whatever is present in the body rather than meeting it with aversion. My father had taught me the soft-belly meditation practice and it made a huge impact on my life. I would practice it all the time, no matter what I was doing, I could always soften. The more I began to accept my emotions and mind states, the more my relationship to them changed. I was no longer a slave to my mind. I was gaining the ability to respond rather than react. The soft belly taught me that.

I joked with my friends about trying to masturbate with a soft belly, or go into the slam-dancing pit with a soft belly. I even came up with a whole philosophy about slam dancing as spiritual practice. "The way I see it is that one of the first things we must understand is that we are not the body. That our true identity, our true self, is beyond the physical or mental formations. So by slam dancing and experiencing all of the pain and pleasure involved in such an activity we can use it as an opportunity for non-identification. As for all of the other poor little runts I am tromping on, they aren't their bodies either and perhaps one of my boots to their ignorant little heads will help them awaken to that fact."

All kidding aside, my relationship to violence and thrashing about had drastically changed by then. I didn't really want to hurt anyone anymore. I hadn't been in a fight in several years at that point and while in the pit I was usually smiling and happy as could be, not acting out of anger but just releasing some energy.

Although we kidded around a lot about our practices we were very sincere about them. Having had a glimpse of the freedom that was possible I knew that my life's work was to awaken from this confused dream I had been living and to help others to also awaken, to see clearly our life's potential and the true nature of existence.

Micah and I started talking about going on an extended pilgrimage to the East. We started looking at the maps of Asia and dreaming about what it would be like to visit the holy pilgrimage sites of India, Nepal, Thailand, Sri Lanka, and Burma. We dreamed of doing retreats and visiting ashrams. I continued fantasizing about ordaining as a Buddhist monk, as part of me really wanted to just live the life of renunciation.

Micah and I got more and more into the idea of selling all our stuff, putting the record collections into storage, and leaving. We told Vinny, who was still living on the East Coast, about our plans. He had just sold his hip-hop store and was doing construction again. He had lived the dream of being in the center of the hip-hop scene and saw that the happiness he was seeking was not going to be found there either. The game was catching up with him and he too had started looking inward. He, like Micah and me, was starting on the Eastern path of the wisdom traditions.

Vinny had been reading my dad's books and had really gotten inspired by what he was learning. He had recently met a man in New Haven who had done a lot of spiritual practice and had recently returned from some travel in Southeast Asia. When we told him that we were thinking of going to Asia, Vinny instantly said he wanted to come too.

He hopped a plane out to San Francisco and together we all started planning "The Pilgrimage."

Micah and I met a guy named Aaron who had recently returned from traveling in Asia. He was living down the street from us with a mutual friend, Punk-Rock-Mike. Aaron was also in recovery but not very interested in going to meetings anymore. Once when I spoke at a meeting he came up to me afterward and told me that it was the first meeting he had been to in months. Aaron was tattooed head to toe by a really famous artist up in San Francisco named Eddie Deutsche. When I saw his tattoos, mostly of Hindu deities, I knew I wanted to get some ink from Eddie. Every time I hung out with Aaron I would ask him to tell me about Asia but he would always just say, "Go check it out for yourself, it is too incredible to explain." Finally he consented to show us some beautiful photos and he shared a couple of stories from his adventures. What we saw and heard was more than enough to solidify our plans. Aaron was our messenger. We parted company, intending to keep in touch.

16

Wander Lust

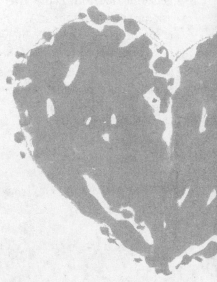

Going to the Far East clearly represented a pilgrimage for me. I wanted to experience the places that had birthed the spiritual traditions I had dedicated the last several years of my life to studying and practicing. I called my dad's friends Ram Dass and Jack Kornfield and they both gave me all sorts of advice and suggested places to visit. Ram Dass, who is one of the most influential spiritual teachers in America, having introduced tens of thousands of hippies to serious spiritual practice in the sixties with his foundation-laying book *Be Here Now,* even wrote me a letter of introduction so that I could stay at the ashrams of Neem Karoli (his teacher) around India. Jack told me all about the Buddhist monasteries in Thailand and Burma, and where I could ordain if I wanted to and told me about a book that I could get that was a guide to the monasteries and meditation centers in Southeast Asia. I was really excited about going. I was looking for enlightenment all the way.

Micah was a little less interested in the whole monastery and ashram circuit and seemed to be just into checking everything out. He certainly planned to do some retreat practice, and in particular to visit a Sufi mosque in Delhi. We had all been reading a lot of Hazrat Inayat Khan books, about the Universal Sufi tradition, and wanted to visit his tomb. Micah always seemed to lean toward the mystical teachings of Islam.

Vinny was just up for anything, the whole experience, but when it came down to it he was more aligned with Micah's agenda than mine. I think I was beginning to push them away a bit. I was so focused on going and getting enlightened or being a monk that I had some atti-tude with them because they didn't share my purpose. Maybe I was still playing out some of the drama from my relationship with Matthew, trying to be and look and act spiritual because I was still not convinced that I was okay just as I was.

Before we left we got a lot of attention from our friends, coworkers, and families. We were the first kids in the Santa Cruz punk scene and recovering community to go off to Asia. Some of our friends were re-ally impressed and others thought we were fucking insane. All of my meditation teachers and the group that I meditated with were very supportive of my desire to go deeper in my practice. I had to tell the guys I was helping with the steps to get new sponsors, because I had no idea when I would be back.

A few nights before we left there was a party at my ex-girlfriend Lola's house. We all went and it was very cool but sort of strange for me. I knew that I still loved this woman and yet I was heading off to Asia to renounce the material world. A part of me was already gone, but when I saw her I knew that I would really miss her. A part of me was still holding on to the possibility of our relationship. She was obviously sad to see me go but playing it cool, joking around about how I was going to get enlightened and all that stuff. The party was fun. I felt a little bad because it was her party but everyone seemed to be focusing on us and our trip.

Vinny was in a similar situation with this girl Jennifer he had been seeing. They really liked each other yet he was leaving, not sure when he would be back. Micah was the only one without much attachment. He had gotten his heart broken about a year earlier and hadn't been in a relationship since.

So the three of us each in our own way said good-bye to family and friends and embarked on a journey that would change all of us forever.

The week before we left I went to New Mexico to say good-bye to my parents, Stephen and Ondrea. Ondrea picked me up at the airport in Albuquerque. She looked beautiful wearing her favorite sweatshirt, jeans, and a pair of Converse. On the three-hour drive toward Taos we spoke of how everything was going in our lives. She said that she was excited for my big adventure overseas. We caught up on all the family gossip. I spoke about my other mom, Patty, and Aaron and Becky, my younger brother and sister. She told me about her visit with James and what was happening with my big sister Tara.

When we arrived at their home in the mountains of northern New Mexico the sun was setting on the plains below. We were greeted by my parents' three rottweilers and my dad. Stephen embraced me and gave me a big kiss; it felt so good to be home, although I had never lived at the house they now lived in. They had moved out of town and into the boondocks as soon as the kids had moved out, many years earlier. We made our way to the couches in the living room and that's where we stayed for most of my visit.

Over the previous several years of my life I had been attending their workshops, reading their books, and had adopted more of a student attitude toward them than the rebellious child I had previously incarnated as. To be with them for a few days was almost like being on retreat, except for the TV.

They were doing a practice that they called "A Year to Live," which called for very intentionally and consciously living as if you only have a year left of your life, and writing a new book about this experience of consciously turning toward death. We spoke at length about death, healing, and spiritual practice as well as all the other things that mattered to us. They were both empathetic about my breakup with Lola but said that they had the feeling that that one wasn't going to work out. I was really interested in their dying practice. I think a part of me was also preparing to die. I was about to embark on a journey into unfamiliar territory—the exotic temples and foreign lands of the Far East.

The night I flew back to California I was picked up at the airport by Vinny, Micah, and my friend Jimmy. We had a few hours before our flight left so we all went into San Francisco for dinner at Viva, our favorite Italian restaurant in North Beach. It felt like the last supper for a bunch of hooligans, sitting around a big table, laughing until we were crying. I was so excited and so nervous I almost made myself sick.

After a fifteen-hour flight our first stop was in Seoul, Korea, for an eight-hour layover before arriving in Thailand. We decided to leave the airport and go wander around Seoul for a few hours. We were all silly with anticipation and exotic delusions about Asian Buddhists. What we found were some really cool outdoor markets filled with everything imaginable. We were especially impressed with the pigs' heads and fake Adidas. We saw some cool kung-fu posters and ate some good noodles and Kim-chi. I was so tired it was hard to really believe I was there. It was sort of surreal and of course nothing like what I had expected. We all laughed a lot and Vinny was truly buggin' out about food and stuff. Vinny is the type of guy who has a hard time eating in a dirty restaurant in the States, so when we were trying to eat food from street vendors he was really struggling.

A few more hours back on a plane and we were in Thailand. At the airport we got picked up by a Thai family that Micah knew from New Haven. We arrived in Bangkok at midnight and this lady, named Tim, whom we had never met, was at the airport waiting for us. She picked us up and took us to her house, which was more like a compound; there were several small houses and they gave us one all to ourselves. It was a small place but we each had a bed. Before we went to sleep we went into town and had a meal at a restaurant with Tim and her mother and her brother. It was the middle of the night and we were eating dinner with the family, which was fine with me because I was starving. I had lost track of what time it would have been back home but my stomach told me that it was time for dinner.

It was a surreal scene: two o'clock in the morning and the streets were packed with people and street vendors busy cooking and selling wares. We were in some kind of open-air night market. I had read about them in the guidebook. We sat down at a little food shop with the whole family, only one of whom spoke much English. I had to try to explain that I was a vegetarian. I remembered the word in Thai was "jay" so that's all I was saying when they are ordering: "Jay, please."

We were completely exhausted after the seventeen hours of flying but the stimulation of the new environment kept us awake. The street was full of people on mopeds; some had whole families on them. The smell of deep-fried food and open fires filled the air. We were the only foreigners around and groups of people stared at us as they walked by, my bald head and tattoos probably adding to their curiosity. Some old folks stopped at the table and spoke with our hosts for a few minutes. When the food arrived I was shocked that it looked nothing like Thai food I had eaten at home. Needless to say Vinny was near his wit's end, since that place was far from clean. They pushed a dish my way and told me it was "jay." I guess it was okra or something. Not my favorite vegetable, but I ate it anyway to be polite. Micah was really enjoying the whole thing. He just seemed to feel at home with these folks. Vinny and I were a bit more culture shocked.

Back at the compound there were little albino lizards crawling on the pale blue walls and flesh-eating mosquitoes patrolling the airspace above our cots. We had been warned about the mosquitoes so we were prepared with our mosquito nets and repellent. But the lizards were a surprise and they made an eerie sound all night. Once I got used to them they were just like crickets and they didn't bother Micah or me much anymore but we laughed really hard at Vinny's irrational fear of these harmless little monsters.

In the morning the whole family greeted us with a delicious traditional Thai meal that seemed more like lunch than breakfast. We had rice and several kinds of curries. The only thing that resembled the kind of breakfast we were used to was an omelet-like dish that I wouldn't eat because I was still a practicing vegan at that point and not eating eggs. The whole first day was spent with the family, being carted from temple to temple seeing the Thai wats (monasteries). It was great to have tour guides and translators to explain all of the traditions and ceremonies to us. Most people we met were very friendly but a little shy. I could tell by the way they stared and pointed that my tattoos were shocking to most of the people we ran into.

There were a few kids in the family and none of them spoke much English. Actually, only the two older sisters could really communicate with us. But we had a blast making up names for the kids. We called the littlest girl Nikki Fresh. She mostly just rode her bike around in the courtyard and got picked on by her older cousin and big brother. Her brother's name was Willie so we called him Willie Bobo, after the famous jazz musician.

Micah was totally into the whole chillin' with the family thing. Vinny was down for it too, but I was feeling like I wanted to be out on our own, exploring. I was ready for the Dharma adventure to begin. Of course it already had but I wanted to be deep in it. So after a couple of days with the family we got dropped off in downtown Bangkok and checked into a guesthouse in the tourist area that Aaron had told us about.

We explored Bangkok for a few days, checking out all the temples, markets, and museums, eating tons of great food. Bangkok was a trip.

As soon as we got dropped off on Kao San Road we were in the mix of international travelers. There were lots of Westerners everywhere. I was kind of surprised to see a group of Thai kids skateboarding down the streets. I think I had expected a bunch of Asian folks pulling rickshaws or something. I had heard that as a pilgrim you are supposed to wear white, so I went out and bought a bunch of traditional white cotton Thai clothes. But I quickly noticed that I was the only one wearing that kind of clothing. None of the other travelers were dressed like that and certainly none of the Thai people were. The locals all wore button up dress shirts and slacks or T-shirts with American logos on them.

I really wanted to go north and stay in some monasteries but Vinny and Micah both wanted to go south and hang out on the beaches. The tensions between Vinny and me got pretty high; I was feeling like he was not there for the same reasons that I was. He felt like I was being a self-righteous dick. Both were true. So I decided to go by myself to the monastery that Ajahn Amaro and Jack Kornfield used to live in, planning to meet up with them in a couple weeks. They were going south to check out this resort where we had a hookup from a lady I used to work with at the hospital in Santa Cruz. They wanted to enjoy some time on the beach. I wanted to go north and stay at the monastery. When we parted ways in Bangkok I was not sure whether I would ever see them again, still thinking that I just might decide to ordain and stay at the monastery for a while.

We split up in the middle of downtown Bangkok. They were headed back to Kao San Road and I was going to the train station to find a train north into Ubon Rachatani. After our hugs and good-byes they jumped on a bus and I just stood there watching them go. All of a sudden it struck me that now I was alone. Truly fucking alone, in the middle of Thailand. "What was I thinking? How the hell am I supposed to do this?" I was starting to freak out so I threw my backpack on and started walking. I had no idea where I was going, I just walked. When I got tired I sat down at a little noodle shop, ordered some fried rice, and pulled out my guidebook to find out how to get to the train station.

After chowing down on my veggie fried rice and getting a little bit of a hand on the realization that I didn't know what the hell I was doing I flagged down a motorcycle taxi and did my best to explain to him that I wanted to go to the train station. The ride to the depot didn't help my anxiety at all. My backpack was doing its best to pull me back-ward off the bike and splatter my head on the concrete. Not to men-tion that the maniac in control of the bike was weaving in and out of traffic at a speed that would have been unsafe even if the roads were completely empty. Death seemed imminent and my prayers seemed trivial as we sped through the city streets. I was shocked when we ar-rived intact at the train station, perhaps even a little disappointed.

After haggling with the driver for a few minutes about the price of the kamakazi ride I agreed to pay him what I knew was more than I should have. Fifty bhat, seventy-five cents American. But at least I was rid of him. In the station I was attacked by touts wanting to carry my backpack but I trudged on, trying to ignore the insistent offers. My timing was lucky, there was a train leaving for the northeast, where I wanted to go, in thirty minutes. What I didn't realize was that it was going to take me a half-hour to find the platform it was leaving from.

When I finally tracked down the illusive platform the train was just beginning to jerk into motion. I ran and jumped on the slow moving vessel. I made my way to an empty seat by the window to catch my breath before trying to find the sleeper bunk that I had booked for the trip.

After a friendly conductor showed me to my bunk I secured my backpack and lay down in my bunk. I caught my breath and tried to soften my belly, which was hard with fear and anticipation. My mind was swimming with the day's events and fantasies of what it would be like and what I would feel like at the monastery. For some reason I had this idea that once I was at the monastery I would feel as peaceful as the Buddha. I made my way to the dining car to sit down and write in my journal for a while. As the train pulled out of Bangkok the sun was beginning to set over the seemingly endless suburbs. For miles and miles all I saw were the substandard shacks of lower- and working-class Thais. I wasn't really hungry but I ate some curry anyway. After dinner I retired to my bunk to get some rest. I looked through my

"Lonely Planet" guidebook for a little while before being rocked to sleep by the train's gentle side-to-side motion.

I didn't sleep very well. I think I woke up every time the train stopped, which seemed like every ten minutes. I was thinking about what it was going to be like at the monastery. I had sent them a letter asking for permission to come for a visit but it was just before we left the States so there was no time for a reply. I hoped it was going to be cool for me to just show up. When it started getting light in my bunk I gave up on trying to sleep any longer and went and sat on a bench next to a window. It was dawn and as far as I could see were rice fields in every direction. Occasionally we passed a small group of buildings that the farmers must have lived in but for the most part all that met the eye were never-ending fields. This was the Asia that I had come to see, not the bustling cities. I was groggy from lack of sleep but feeling much more relaxed and soft-bellied, still dreaming of enlightenment and the peace I would feel at the monastery.

When I got to Ubon I was back in a city—nothing like Bangkok but a city nevertheless. I had the address of the monastery written down but none of the taxi drivers seemed to know where it was. I hadn't thought this far ahead. I was just expecting to get off the train and walk into the monastery, but no such luck. Finally a Thai man who spoke some English came to my rescue. He knew of the monastery and said the best way to get there was on one of the pickup trucks with benches in the back that pass for public buses. He walked me over to a place where I could catch the right one and bid me good luck, bowing to me with hands together before he departed.

On the truck/bus the driver kept making motions of shaving his head, raising his hand over his head in a repeated motion. My head was already shaved so it took me a few minutes to realize he was asking if I was going to become a monk at the monastery. I told him that I didn't know yet, but since he didn't speak any English and I spoke no Thai, the shrugging of my shoulders seemed to be our only common language. The monastery was located about ten miles outside of town. The whole way there I was waiting for us to get to the forest— this was supposed to be a forest monastery after all. But the forest never arrived. When he stopped the truck in front of two big gates and a high wall with a large sign that said "Wat Pah Nana Chat," which I assumed meant "International Forest Monastery," I was still wondering where the forest was.

As I arranged my backpack, waved good-bye to the taxi, and walked through the monastery gates I was instantly transported into the midst of a Thai forest monastery. I later came to find out that all of the surrounding forests had been chopped down for firewood and cleared to make more rice paddies, that all of the miles and miles of fields I had just passed through were once heavily forested land. The monastery was protected land, the last patch of jungle in the area.

I was arriving just before the morning meal so everyone was quite busy preparing for the mealtime ceremony. The monks don't eat after midday so it is important that the meal be served promptly at 8:30 A.M. A friendly European monk welcomed me and showed me where I could put my bag down. He said he would notify the monk in charge of guests that I was there and that in the meantime I could just relax or get ready for the meal.

I had never seen so many white guys in robes before in my life. There were only a few Asians among them, and of those only a couple were Thai. I came to find out that most of the Thai monks stayed at another monastery nearby and this one was specifically founded for foreigners, by Ajahn. As I waited for the meal to be served I just took in the place with my eyes. I was exhausted from the struggle to get there but also intrigued. There were a few other people around who were not in robes and several Thai women busily preparing the dishes to be offered to the monks and nuns.

I wandered into the kitchen area, on the ground floor of where I would be staying for the next few days. In front of me was a huge temple with no doors or walls. Open to the elements, a large statue of Buddha sat at one end surrounded by smaller statues. These were clearly Thai Buddhas but ones that I had never seen before. The hardwood floors were beautifully clean and shiny. I could see right through to the forest that continued in every direction surrounding the temple. I felt a sense of reverence, a feeling of humility, in the presence of an ancient tradition. Walking trails cut through the forest in several directions and I could see a few little cottages perched high in the air on thick wooden stilts, each one with a ladder or stairs that led to the small single room above. I knew that these cottages, called kutis, were where the monks lived. I had heard about them from Jack, Ajahn Amaro, and my father. It was unbelievable to be there. I had been reading about all of this for so long and had come all the way around the world to experience it for myself.

The meal was served first to all the monks and nuns and then, while they were eating in the temple, the rest of us were offered our meals in the kitchen. Everyone seemed to be eating in silence so I did the same. The food looked good but questionable as to whether it was all-vegetarian. I knew that since the monks eat only what is offered to them, they accept everything, even meat. Since I was trying to practice simplicity and letting go of preferences, I ate what looked like it was veggie and left the rest.

After the meal the monk in charge of guests approached and welcomed me. I introduced myself and asked if they had received my letter. They had and were happy to host me for a few days. He showed me to the men's guest room upstairs from the kitchen area. It was just a big empty room with hardwood floors. There were a couple of mats laid out where other visitors were obviously staying. He handed me a mat and told me that I could stay up there for a couple nights and if I wanted to stay for a longer time he could probably arrange a kuti for me to stay in. I thanked him and fished around in my pack for the bag of good ink pens I had brought to offer the monks. He was delighted at the offering and remarked how good it was that I had the forethought to bring offerings. After a few questions about my travels and my parents he gave me a brief tour of the place and said I could meditate or do walking practice until tea at four o'clock.

Before he departed I bowed to him three times in the traditional way. I made my way to the meditation hall and after checking out the statues took a seat and meditated for a while. My mind was loud and abusive, insulting me for thinking I could just come to Thailand and become a monk. I tried to pay attention to my breath but with little success. My body was filled with a heavy weight of fear and anxiety.

After some time I got up and decided I would go and do some walking meditation instead. But rather than finding a walking path I began walking on the trail through the forest. I just kept going, with no idea where I was headed. I passed several monks who were sitting in peace in their kutis or gracefully walking back and forth on the walking paths. I tried to pay attention to the sensations of walking, to the present moment, but my mind was filled with thoughts of the past and fears of the future. I felt so alone and lonely. At some point I realized that I was completely lost, deep in the forest, all by myself. The trees swaying in the breeze and the hum of the insects gave me no clue about what to do next so I just kept moving. I was beginning to get scared when I finally came to the outer wall of the monastery. There I found a path that eventually led back to the main temple and my room.

I went upstairs to lie down for a bit and found another guy sleeping. I lay down on the hard floor, cushioned only by my flimsy quarter-inch-thick mat. I tried to soften my belly and investigate why I was so freaked out about being there, but to no avail. All I could think about was life back at home: cars, music, comfortable beds, my friends, and . . . Lola. "Where did that come from?" I thought. A sudden memory of Lola filled my mind. I was consumed by thoughts and feelings about her, about us, about love and children and a family. I was really taken off guard by that shit. I reminded myself that we had tried our best several times but it never seemed to work out. We just weren't capable of being in a relationship. The more I tried to reason with myself, the more depressed I became. There was a battle raging between my heart and my mind. I was consumed with fear that I would never know love again, that I was just here trying to run away from myself.

I heard the bells ringing for teatime so I got up and followed the monks to a large room off to the left of the main hall. I took a seat in the back and when the tea and coffee came around I helped myself like everyone else. One of the monks gave a talk about the joys of renunciation or something and many of the other monks chimed in with comments or questions. I felt a little better after the talk and tea. I tried to remind myself that I had just gotten there and that it would probably get better.

But things just got worse and worse. The next morning I woke up at 3:00 A.M. for chanting to the greatest sense of loneliness I had ever experienced in my life. It was as if I was being submerged beneath a vast and deep pool of water. I could see the surface but I knew that by the time I reached it I would have already run out of air.

I wanted to run away from all of those feelings but instead I made my way from my room through the pitch-black forest to the meditation hall. It was a different hall than the one they had the meal in. This one was set farther back in the jungle. But it too had the open walls on every side. It felt like we were sitting in the forest yet sheltered by the safety of the hall. At the front of the room there was a large standing image of the Buddha doing walking meditation. I had never seen one before and I instantly had the thought about what a cool tattoo it would be. I didn't know the chants they were doing but the sound of the monks chanting was very soothing. I felt a little bit better and even dozed off for a little while in the most restful slumber I had had in weeks. Of course I was supposed to be meditating not sleeping but I was beyond caring. I was just trying to survive at that point.

When I came to, the sun was rising, dawn over the jungle, so strikingly beautiful with the hum of the insects becoming a low roar. I was told that it was time for a short period of work before the meal. I was put to work carrying water from the well in five-gallon buckets and dumping it in the large containers that the monks used for their bathing and for washing robes. While I was busy the inner critic seemed to subside. I met a few other guys who were also just visiting. They were pretty cool, one Canadian, one German, and a couple of Americans. I didn't have much to say. I was still feeling pretty bogged down by my experience but at least I wasn't alone.

At the meal I noticed a young monk with a huge Anti-Nowhere League tattoo on his shoulder. I assumed he was English since the Anti-Nowhere League is an old English punk band. I wanted to talk to him, maybe he could help me sort out some of these feelings. But after the meal I didn't see him again and by that afternoon I really started freaking out. Too much time alone, nothing to do between noon and four but meditate, which for me meant the torture of thinking about Lola and listening to the constant abuse from my own mind. I didn't know what else to do so the next day after lunch I packed up my stuff and left, rationalizing my swift departure by saying that I had just wanted to check out the place where my teachers had been monks. Now that I had done that, it was time to see the next place; perhaps in the next place my meditation would be better. As I walked out of the gates and past the walls that surrounded the monastery I paused for a moment. I turned to look back at the monastery and I bowed to the sign on the wall. I tried to reflect on the gratitude I felt for all of my teachers who had spent time there, but it didn't feel genuine. I just wanted to get out of there.

I walked away and just kept walking. Buses were passing me by on the road but I didn't try to stop any. My pack was heavy and I was sweating but the farther I walked the more I was able to relax. There were periods of time when no one else was on the road and I was alone, walking through the endless fields of rice paddies. I walked all the way to town, which must have been a few miles. I was tired and hungry but the noise and business of the city was a welcome distraction.

It was beginning to get dark so I found the bus station and I jumped on a bus that was headed south. The moment I boarded the bus I was overwhelmed by the feeling of failure. I had come to Asia for enlightenment, not all this anguish and suffering! The bus was packed with people and the small narrow seats that were barely big enough for two people were seating three. I found a place next to the window in the rear of the bus and stared out the window, watching the sunset as we pulled out of Ubon, driving south toward Bangkok.

Not yet ready to surrender, I decided that what I really needed was to do a long retreat, to face all the fear that was coming up. I had read about a meditation center near Pataya where you could do self-retreats. They gave you your own little cabin and brought you some food every day. I decided that it would be the perfect place for me to relax into my meditation practice and let go of all those thoughts of Lola. At least there I would be able to sleep in and practice on my own schedule. So after a sixteen-hour bus ride I arrived at the center. I was really grubby from the overnight bus trip. An older lady greeted me at the office and after questioning me for a while about my knowledge of meditation she consented to allow me to stay for a few days.

The room that I was shown to was sparse but very clean. I had my own bathroom, a table, and a bed. There was a deck outside that was long enough to do walking meditation on. The retreat manager gave me a couple books on meditation and brought me some metal containers full of rice and fresh curry. I took a shower, had some food, and went to sleep.

I don't know how long I slept but I woke up experiencing a terror like nothing I had ever felt before. I felt imprisoned by my mind and submerged in a deep internal isolation even more intense than at the forest monastery. I attempted to do some sitting and walking meditation practice but the room felt like a cell and I needed to escape. Before I even really knew what I was doing I had packed my bag and was leaving, again.

Now I felt like a real fucking failure—two meditation centers in two days. "Am I totally freaking out?" I fretted. I didn't know what else to do so I decided that hanging out on the beach with Vinny and Micah sounded pretty good. I didn't even say good-bye or tell the center that I was leaving. I really felt like I was escaping. "What am I running from? Why am I so scared to be alone?" I caught a cab to the train depot and jumped on a train back to Bangkok and then down to the south to try to find them. I knew they were in a town named Hua Hin and the name of the resort, but that was all.

Just the thought of being back with some familiar faces was really comforting. On the train I was able to lose myself for a little while in a book I was reading.

A day and a half of traveling later, I arrived in the small town where I thought they might be. I rented a motorcycle near the train station and set off to find the resort.

When I finally found it I was amazed. This was a serious five-star resort. I was filthy from the train. I parked the motorcycle out front.

As I walked into the dining room brunch was being served, an American-style buffet. I was starving and hadn't had anything but rice and curry for about a week.

"Where the fuck are Micah and Vinny?" I wondered. Just then I saw them sitting at a table on the patio. They bugged out when they saw me wandering around, looking more like a homeless kid than a tourist. I was so relieved to see them that I wanted to cry. I tried to choke back the tears and tell them what had happened. But it was hard to explain; it didn't seem to make as much sense when I put it into words but the experience of it had been so overwhelming. They couldn't believe that I was there; they were really happy to see me again and very supportive and understanding about all my confusion and struggles.

We all had breakfast and I tried to tell them all of what I had been going through, the travels, the monastery, thinking about Lola, the second meditation center, and finally how good it was to see them again.

They had some stories of their own adventures; mostly they had just been hanging out at this plush-ass resort. But Vinny has a way of telling stories that makes anything seem like the most incredible experience ever. It turned out that the guy who ran the place was so cool he was letting them stay in his apartment and he had taken another room.

They had their own pool and all the amenities of home and more. We spent the days playing Ping-Pong, swimming, and just hanging out. It was so good to be back with my friends. I knew I needed their support and encouragement. But I was still hesitant to accept it and I felt a little guilty that I wasn't out tracking down enlightenment. I still thought I should be able to do it all on my own.

One day Vinny and I rented motorcycles and took this long ride into the jungle, where we found an incredible waterfall that we swam in. It was a very important time for us because we were still having some difficulty communicating. Mostly it was because I was putting some trip on him about not being spiritual enough or something. But there was also another dynamic. Vinny was used to being the one in charge, or at least the one who knows what's up. It was hard for him to let go of that role. That day on the bikes we spent a long time talking about our friendship, the trip, and life. It felt like a huge healing in our friendship took place.

After a few days at the resort we decided to go farther south, down to the islands. There was a meditation center on Ko Phan Gan that we had heard about and wanted to check out. I was back on the pilgrimage kick. I had a really hard time just hanging out on the beach, even though that was exactly what I needed to do. I felt like I was wasting my time. I knew that I had a lot of inner work to do and thought that it could only be done in an intensive meditation practice setting. The guys were both happy to check out some temples and meditation centers but weren't so hell-bent on practice as I was. I was really striving for something. I had been dreaming about doing intensive practice in Asia for years and now I was here and just hanging out on the beach. I felt like a tourist, not a pilgrim.

We found the meditation center on Ko Phan Gan but it was closed for the season. Vinny wanted to go scuba diving on Ko Tao, a smaller island off the coast. Micah and I wanted to go back to Bangkok to try to meet up with Kerri, who was our friend Aaron's girlfriend. We all planned to meet up at the guesthouse we had stayed at before in Bangkok.

It was good for Micah and me to have some time together, one-on-one, and talk about the dynamic that was happening with the three of us. The problem was difficult to pinpoint because although it was usually just between Vinny and me, Micah got caught in the middle. He was always so mellow about everything, it was hard to have conflict with the guy. But Vinny and I were anything but mellow, we were both more like the alpha males battling for position in the herd.

In Bangkok we met up with Kerri, covered in tattoos and looking more beautiful than I had remembered. She was one of the first girls I met who had more tattoos than I did. We had met once or twice at Aaron's place in Santa Cruz but didn't really know each other very well. She too had become inspired to travel to Asia by his stories and her own personal quest for meaning. I was very attracted to her but she was his girl and I still couldn't stop thinking about Lola.

A day later Vinny joined us. He was in pretty bad shape. He had gotten really seasick on the boat and tried to make them stop it in the middle of the sea. After barfing all over himself he had what he recounted as a near-death experience. When they finally reached solid land he got a mini-van transport instead of the train back to Bangkok and about halfway the driver hit someone and then got out of the van and took off running. So Vinny was stranded on the side of the road at the scene of an accident and the police were questioning everyone. When he met up with us in Bangkok he looked like I had felt a week earlier when I met up with them at the resort.

We all chilled in Bangkok for a couple days, visiting the main temples, spending hours walking through the markets, and sitting around at the guesthouse trading stories and discussing spiritual practice, movies, music, and relationships. It wasn't enlightenment but I was learning a key to it—sitting in the moment calmly.

The family we had stayed with when we arrived came and picked us up. We stayed with them for a day and then decided to all go and do a retreat together. There was a huge meditation center just outside of Bangkok that was really popular with the Thais and our hosts wanted to take us there. We all put on our white clothes and went to the center with the intention of staying for a few days. The day we arrived was an incredibly large celebration, there were thousands of people there. For lunch, the only meal of the day, we were served pork-fried rice. We were starving and since this was going to be my only food of the day, I ate the rice and picked out the meat but felt a little sick. This was the closest to eating meat that I had come in years. The practice there was challenging. The teachings were all in Thai so it was difficult for us with no real guidance.

We were given the opportunity to meet with an English-speaking monk once a day, but none of us were very inspired to practice there. The whole place had a weird vibe. On the second day we started planning our escape. This was becoming a pattern for me: I couldn't seem to stay at a monastery for more than a few days. We all packed our bags and hitched a ride to the train station in the back of a pickup truck.

Micah and Vinny wanted to go straight to Nepal and I wanted to go to Burma next. I had this whole plan for my pilgrimage of visiting all the Theravadan Buddhist countries first and then checking out the Mahayana, Hindu, and Sufi scenes. So we once again decided to part ways, making plans to meet up in India a few weeks later. The plan was that we would meet up in Bodhgaya for a Vipassana retreat and if for any reason we missed each other there then we would hook up in Delhi at the Hazrat Inayat Khan mosque a couple weeks after that. Our good-byes were uneventful. I was feeling a little disappointed that they didn't want to do what I wanted to do and they were probably feeling the same way about me.

I had gotten an extension on my Thai visa so I stayed and traveled with Kerri for a week or so before going to Burma. She and I took the train to the far northeast, where the Mekong River separates Thailand and Laos. We spent most of the time at a guesthouse in Nong Kai that sits at the end of an alley, on the shores of the Mekong. We met a very cool guy from America named Michael Wassambe, who lived across from the guesthouse and owned a funky little bookstore.

We spent hours with Michael talking about spirituality and then telling stories about our own lives. He had come to Thailand to be in the Peace Corps and loved it so much he never left. He'd grown up in Detroit and had been a roller disco skater or something. He asked us all about our tattoos and wanted to know about punk rock and Straight Edge. I think his biggest interest was getting into Kerri's pants, and I didn't blame him.

But Kerri wasn't interested at all, she was really heartbroken about leaving Aaron at home. She knew she needed the experience of this sacred travel but was torn between her heart and her head. I too was still being molested by incessant thoughts of Lola and how we probably could work everything out if we really tried. At a certain point I stopped fighting the thoughts and began writing her postcards, admitting my love and longing for her, expressing my desire to try to work things out. I felt a lot better when I stopped the inner battle of resistance and denial of my love for Lola. But once I wrote those letters I knew I couldn't take it back and was struck with feelings of doubt and confusion about what to do next.

Kerri and I were having a lot of fun exploring the local temples and ruins together. In Nong Kai there is this crazy theme park that consists of all of these statues and sculptures from the Buddhist and Hindu traditions that are several stories high and all tell a tale. We had a great time at that Buddha park. We met a Swiss heavy metal couple who were on their honeymoon and had dinner with them a couple times.

I had been in Thailand for about five weeks and I still hadn't done any intensive meditation practice other than a couple days here and there. I was feeling guilty about that but was hoping to get to do a longer retreat in Burma. I guess I still had the fantasy that things would magically get easier.

I bought a plane ticket that allowed me to stay in Burma for a few weeks and then continue on to India. Kerri stayed in Thailand with plans to go the other way and check out Cambodia and Vietnam. We said our good-byes, hoping to catch up in India or Nepal in a few months.

In Burma I had a connection with some friends of my mom's who lived there and were working for UNICEF. It was actually a really great hookup because they lived only three blocks away from the meditation center that I wanted to visit. So I stayed with them and went and meditated at Sayadaw Upandita's monastery every day. My meditation practice was still really challenging. My mind was full of fears and fantasies and my body was filled with pain from the long sessions of sitting. There was no meditation instruction given and the one American monk I was introduced to was kind of a jerk. He made some comment about how my father had said something about Theravadan Buddhism being a limited tradition; he had obviously been offended and took it upon himself to be self-righteous and uppity with me. That was all the excuse I needed to decide that I was in the wrong place. I began to accept that I was not going to ordain, that all I really wanted to do was grow old with Lola and have a simple life.

I had the good fortune of being in Rangoon during a small window of time when the elected political leader, Aung San Su Ji, who had been under house arrest for many years by the fascist military dictators who were controlling the country, was allowed to make public speeches from a platform behind the gate at her home. Thousands of people would come out to hear her speak every week. This lasted for only a short time before the military would no longer allow it. So I got the rare chance to see her in person and hear her talk. Since she was speaking Burmese I didn't understand what she was saying, but based on the energy in the crowd and the cheers when she finished it must have been important. I was on the front lines of a political revolution. The streets were being patrolled by armed forces. I felt like I was in the movie *The Killing Fields*.

I was enjoying Burma and my meditation practice was starting to get a little better. I found that a daily practice of a couple hours interspersed with exploring the city suited me a lot better than trying to practice intensively all day. I was still thinking about Lola a lot. She was so deeply imbedded in my mind, I missed her and longed to see her again. It was in Burma that I began to actually consider inviting her to come out to join me in India or Nepal. I was still fighting myself, judging my loneliness as weakness and a distraction from the path of awakening. Although that may have been exactly what was happening, I was not able to be very compassionate with myself about it.

After a week in Rangoon I traveled to the north to see some ancient ruins and possibly visit some monasteries. In Pagan, the ancient capital, where for miles and miles in every direction incredible ruins of temples and pagodas permeate the countryside, I spent the days wandering through the temples and taking photos. At one of the ruins I met a man who was selling art and I bought a couple of paintings to send home. He was incredibly friendly and invited me to come and meet his family and see how the Burmese people lived. I had dinner with his family and got a full tour of his art studio and the various crafts that they made in his village. I gave him all of the ink pens I had left and bought several handicrafts from his family. It was an amazing experience to be taken in like that by a family. Later I found out that he was actually risking serious consequences from the military government for having a foreigner in his home. But for him it was more important to be kind and generous than to live in fear of the fascist regime that ran his country.

Some of my best Dharma teachings came from outside of the monastery walls.

I spent my last few days in Burma in a small town built around a huge lake called Inle Lake. I explored the small villages and markets that surrounded the lake. On the far side was a Buddhist monastery called the Jumping Cat Monastery. Several monks at the monastery had trained cats to jump through hoops in exchange for delicious snacks. It was kind of entertaining but also a little questionable. Weren't those monks supposed to be meditating or something?

On New Year's Eve I left Burma and flew to India. On the plane I met a Swedish girl named Emily. She had been in Southeast Asia for several months traveling around, mostly alone. She told me of a horrific experience she had while traveling in the Philippines a couple months earlier. She was on a public bus in Manila and a man sat next to her and began asking her about her travels. She woke up several days later in a small motel room a hundred miles away from where she was going. She had been drugged and raped and all of her belongings were gone. After realizing what had happened she made her way to the embassy and got some help. I was shocked that she was still on the road after such a traumatic experience. She said that she had planned to travel for a year and that was what she was going to do.

I talked with her about Buddhism for a while and was trying to empathize with what she had been through. We decided to try to find a room or dorm together in Calcutta. Arriving late at night, we got a cab at the airport and directed the driver to a guesthouse from the guidebook. The streets were full of people celebrating the New Year. I was surprised that it was such a big deal in India. I guess I thought that it was only a Western phenomenon. After all it is all about Christianity and the Western colonial powers that have forced the whole globe to abide by the oppressors' calendar year. I was hoping to escape from the modern world and looked to Asia for a reprieve from the ignorance of America, but I found that ignorance is a universal phenomenon.

Eventually we found the guesthouse and paid for a couple beds in the large dormitory. I washed up and chilled in my bunk, looking at my guidebook. Emily went out for a drink and wanted me to come but I was too tired. I just lay there thinking about my life, all that had brought me to this strange land. What was a guy like me doing in India? And that thought was confirmed by a group of young wanna-be hippy kids who entered the dormitory. Fucking hippies were all I had met in Asia so far, not a single punk or anyone even sort of cool.

Calcutta was a hardcore introduction to India. I had read a book about Calcutta called *City of Joy* so I thought I had some idea of what I was in for. But nothing had prepared me for the masses of beggars, touts, and thieves who were constantly in my face. I was reminded of my days of panhandling in downtown Santa Cruz as a teenager, harassing the passersby, begging for my drugs and booze. Now I felt ashamed that I had so much when these people had almost nothing.

I found no comfort or resonance with the groups of travelers on the circuit. To me they were just a bunch of stoned-out tourists and I was on a serious pilgrimage. On New Year's Day we went to the Kali temple, where there were thousands of people celebrating, making offerings to the fierce goddess Kali. We watched as they sacrificed lambs to the goddess's images and found out that it was also what was being served for prasad, the sacred meal. I was disgusted with the whole thing. "What's so fucking spiritual about killing animals?" I fumed. Although I was struggling with my own meditation practice at least I wasn't killing. I tried not to be so judgmental, but my years of vegetarianism and understanding of the importance of nonviolence from my study of Buddhism left me feeling incredibly self-righteous.

My plan was to get to Sri Lanka and then come back to India in a few weeks so I got a train ticket to Madras in the south. Emily wanted to go to the south also, it was a forty-eight-hour trip, and we decided to go third class with everyone else. I became deathly sick on the train and spent most of the time going back and forth from the bathroom to my bunk. I was really lucky to get a top bunk so that I could lie down, because the bottom bunk gets folded up and everyone sits on the first bunk during the day. Seven people often sat on a bench that was really meant to hold four. I was getting delusional with fear and constant diarrhea. I couldn't get anything to eat on the train that wasn't deep-fried or full of chili and spices so I just drank tea and prepared for my imminent demise. Death sounded good at that point. I just wanted out of that hell realm of the constant onslaught of sounds, sensations, and feelings.

Two days later, when we finally arrived in Madras, I was starting to feel a bit better and decided to go directly to Sri Lanka the next day, wanting to complete my pilgrimage of the Theravadan Buddhist countries. It was clear at that point that I was nowhere near ready to ordain. While I was disappointed in myself, I was also relieved. I saw that it wasn't right for me at that point of my spiritual development and that what I really wanted to do was be in the world, in relationship, and of service. But I was still holding strong to the fact that I wasn't a tourist, I was on pilgrimage. I hadn't come to Asia for a vacation. I needed to lighten up.

I was reading *Zen and the Art of Motorcycle Maintenance* and started seriously considering getting a motorcycle to travel around India on. They have these great old Royal Enfield bikes in India so when I was in Sri Lanka I rented a bike to see what it would be like to do some touring.

Sri Lanka is a little bit better developed than India and therefore the roads are a lot safer and well maintained. Even so, it was just way too tiring to ride a motorcycle all day to get to a new place when I easily could have just sat on a train for a few hours and got there rested.

Sri Lanka was amazing with rice paddies carved out of the jungle and mountains of tea plantations, great beaches, and incredible Buddhist temples, ruins, and caves. When I arrived I stayed at a guesthouse for a few days that was owned by some Sri Lankan folks I knew from Santa Cruz. They had told me about a little meditation hut that they had built behind their place and offered it to me free of charge for as long as I liked. I had thought I would try to do a little retreat but as it turned out the building was being used as a classroom for some local children so I stayed in the guesthouse instead. Since I had rented a motorcycle in Colombo I mostly just traveled around visiting ancient Buddhist ruins and hanging out in the jungle or on the beach.

I had been on the road for a few months and was really beginning to get homesick. I pulled my motorcycle up in front of a guesthouse called the Surfer's Hostel. As I walked down the long corridor of the hostel to the back porch to check out the beach and ocean I began to relax a little. To my great surprise a bunch of Australian surfers were sitting around on the patio, listening to some good old American punk rock. One of the Aussies had a tape that had Good Riddance, my friend Russ's band, on one side and Shelter, my favorite Hindu punk band, on the other.

I got a room there for a couple of days and felt right at home. It was great to chill on the beach and do some surfing but I couldn't seem to allow myself to just enjoy it without feeling like I should have been doing some more intensive practice or at least visiting the major pilgrimage sites. Still unwilling to surrender and just enjoy my time in Asia, and unable to accept that I was not ready for the level of practice that I thought I should be doing, I trudged forward with the unrealistic expectation that everything would be different in India.

A couple days before I left Sri Lanka there was a huge suicide bombing in Colombo. Afterward, there were checkpoints everywhere and men with machine guns roaming the streets. Another wake-up call to the universality of hatred and war. When I thought of going to Asia I had all these visions of gentle Buddhist monks everywhere, of peaceful villages with happy people, and I had certainly seen a lot of those but I wasn't expecting all the violence and fear that I also encountered. It made me appreciate America a little bit more. Even with all the corruption of our government and the sexism, racist politics, oppression, and greed that make up so much of the Western society, at least I usually felt safe walking down the street. Even if the cops were going to harass me for being a punker they probably weren't going to kill me. Of course I knew that for many people in America, people of color or gays or even women, it isn't always safe to walk down the street. So basically I came to the conclusion that everywhere is fucked! Just as the Buddha taught, this whole world is a realm of Samsara, a place of suffering and death. That's why I was over there, trying to escape from this realm and awaken to the realm of Nirvana.

India was a constant assault on the senses. Unless I was way out in the country or hidden away in an ashram somewhere, I swam in a sea of people, animals, cars-trucks-bikes, smells (both pleasant and putrid), people dying on the streets, children working harder than most people ever have or ever will, and the loudest music blaring out of the worst speakers in the world. Hectic. Yet at the same time I couldn't turn a corner without seeing a beautiful shrine, an incredible temple, or at least a picture of one of the many Hindu gods and goddesses. It got under my skin. I began to realize that just being in India was the intense spiritual practice I had been looking for.

My first stop was a weeklong retreat at the Ramana Maharshi ashram. I had grown up with pictures of Ramana around the house and had been reading a lot of his teachings. Ramana had been enlightened as a teenager and then spent a few years living in caves on Arunachala; the rest of his life was spent teaching others to awaken as he had. It was a meditation practice of self-inquiry through repeating the question "Who am I?" So I spent my time at the ashram practicing self-inquiry and being mindful of the constantly unfolding process. As I went deeper and deeper with the question "Who am I?" I found myself in a process of negation. It went something like this: I'm not this body, I'm not this mind, I'm not this personality, I'm not these thoughts, I'm not these sensations, I'm not this, I'm not that. All I could say I was, was the continual unfolding process of being, the Self or Selfless.

The ashram was built at the base of Mount Arunachala, which is said to be a manifestation of the Hindu god Shiva; I was told that one of the pilgrimage practices is to walk around the base of the mountain remembering God with each step. I spent my days in meditation or hiking around the hill and looking at all of the things that I am not. I'm not sure why, but being at the ashram was much easier than being at the monasteries. Perhaps because I was begging to accept that I just wasn't ready to become a monk. I took comfort in seeing how impersonal everything was. It was a lot better for me at that point to do inquiry rather than mindfulness. Also, the ashram was much more active; people were socializing. Every day all of the local poor people and the wandering holy men and women would come to the ashram and the devotees would feed them and help them get any care that they needed.

Through all this I was still being chased by my mind and the painful heartache of desire to be back in relationship. By this time I had been writing Lola regularly and had even spoken to her on the telephone a couple of times. I was expressing my love but still not asking for us to get back together. It seemed to be easier for me when I wasn't alone and at the ashram I met an Englishman by the name of Steve. He and I had several conversations at the ashram and then decided to do some traveling together. Steve was practicing Tibetan Buddhism and was on his tenth journey to India. I was very inspired by his love of the Dharma and the Indian culture. It was great to have a friend again. I spoke to him at length about my struggles and feelings of still being in love with a woman who I had already broken up with three times. He was a good listener and once in a while offered some supportive comment but did his best not to give me any advice.

I had to decide if I was going to leave the south right away in order to get up to Bodhgaya where I was supposed to meet Vinny and Micah at the Vipassana retreat. If I hadn't met Steve I probably would have but since we were getting along pretty well and he was on his way farther south to check out some other ashrams, I chose to stay and travel with him for a few more weeks, hoping to catch up with those guys in Delhi at the Sufi mosque the following month.

From the Ramana ashram we traveled deeper into southern India, visiting various Hindu pilgrimage sites. I found a lot of the things we ran into difficult to understand, like that they wouldn't allow women and Westerners into some of the temples. This seemed inconsistent with the Hindu teachings on reincarnation and not being the body. "If I am not this body then why are you treating me differently because I was born into a Western family? If you are so fucking spiritual then why don't you start acting like it?" I got frustrated a lot in India. I wasn't meditating every day when I was traveling around a lot and it was easy to get annoyed with the people who were constantly invading my personal space.

Steve and I spent several days at one ashram where a female guru named Ama Ji was giving blessings to all the people who came to visit. There were hundreds of people there and many of them were Westerners—some Americans but mostly Europeans. During darshan (a blessing ceremony that means "seeing" or being seen by a saint) I waited in line for a very long time and when it was my turn to get my blessing the guru took my head in her hands and whispered something in my ear, gave me a hug, and then it was over. I had a feeling of new energy in my body and felt kinda high on the experience. I didn't really know what it was that she had said in my ear but it didn't matter. This was my first experience with a living Hindu guru and it was really interesting but by no means transformational. It was a lot like what I had experienced with Matthew. I was still feeling pretty burned by that whole experience. I knew that just because someone has some spiritual energy or powers doesn't necessarily mean all that much.

After visiting a bunch more temples, ashrams, caves, mountains, and holy sites I said farewell to Steve and left the south, taking a two-day train ride to the north that landed me in Varanasi, the holiest city in India. Varanasi is built on the banks of the Ganges River and is said to be the best place to die and/or be cremated so that your ashes may be spread in the river. I spent a few days in Varanasi watching the ceremonial "burning ghats" where all of the families come to have their loved ones cremated. The bodies are burnt out in the open on the banks of the river and the Hindu priest oversees all of the funerals, saying prayers and doing traditional chants and rites. It smelled like a huge human BBQ pit. There were wild dogs and cows everywhere and the grief of thousands washed through those alleys every day. I was told that in the old days, if a man died, his widow was supposed to throw herself onto the funeral pyre and join him in the next world. I didn't know what to make of all that. It seemed strange and inconsistent with what I thought I knew about Hinduism. I was beginning to see that what I "knew" and what there was to "know" were very different. In Varanasi I began to feel more like the tourist I really was. I was just looking at everything, not really connecting with anything or anyone. It was humbling.

From Varanasi I went to Bodhgaya, which is the place where the Buddha gained enlightenment. This was where I was supposed to meet my friends but I was about a month late. In Bodhgaya I spent a week at a Tibetan Buddhist meditation center practicing meditation and learning more about the Mahayana Buddhist tradition, which came about after the Buddha had died; it incorporated scriptures that were revealed by later teachers. During that retreat I was introduced to the theory and practices of Tibetan Buddhism, much of which I had already read about. I was inspired by the focus that was put on compassion. My understanding in the Vipassana practice was that compassion is a by-product of the spiritual life, but in the Tibetan tradition compassion is taught to be the path itself. I had been beating myself up so much, it was refreshing to be reminded about caring about my own suffering and the suffering of others. It was also very interesting to see the differences in the way the monks of the different traditions interpreted the precepts or rules for conduct. In the Theravadan tradition, for instance, the monks don't eat any food after noon, and at the Tibetan center the monks were eating dinner with the rest of us. This was a little bit of a shock to me at first. I thought that the monks were breaking the precepts but I found out that the different traditions just have different interpretations of the Buddhist scriptures. (I figured that maybe all these differences made room even for someone as weird as me. I mean, come on, who has ever heard of a Buddhist punk rocker anyway?)

I spent a few days just hanging out at the Bodhi tree, the main temple, which is built on the place where the Buddha gained enlightenment twenty-five hundred years earlier. The huge tree at the center of the temple grounds is a direct sapling from the original Bodhi tree that the Buddha was sitting beneath during his final awakening. Every day there were hundreds of pilgrims coming to the tree to pray for their own awakening and for the liberation from suffering of all beings. Surrounding the temple were Tibetans doing prostrations and chanting mantras. On the upper level dozens of people were doing walking meditation around the temple.

The smell of incense filled the air and butter lamps burned on several different altars around the temple. As I sat there contemplating all that I had seen and experienced in the three months I had been traveling so far, one thing was clear: I was on the right track. I had been humbled by my fears, desires, and the vanity of my "knowing." I had felt and seen suffering and it wasn't personal. I had learned that awakening has many paths and I felt encouraged that I too could follow the path of liberation even if it wasn't in the form that I had thought. No matter how difficult my time had been, all of the anguish and grief, all the fear and loneliness, on a cellular level I knew I was fighting the battle that would end in victory over suffering. I offered a prayer to that ancient tree and set my own intention to awaken in this lifetime.

I had finally surrendered, and with that surrender came an acceptance of myself, as I was, just a beginner, not ready to ordain, not even close to enlightenment, just a confused kid looking for happiness. I knew I had to give the relationship with Lola another shot.

After the retreat I invited Lola to come and meet me in Nepal. At that point I was willing to risk everything for the deep and sincere love that I felt for her. I had tried to ignore it, suppress it, and rationalize it away but it was still there stronger than ever. So I decided to just go for it. She said that she would come if I promised to never leave her again. I promised and said that maybe we should get married and she agreed. We both began to weep while on the phone. Her voice was so delicate and sensual; I could almost smell her perfume and taste her tears. I felt that everything was finally going to be okay. I would be reunited with my heart's desire and everything would be perfect. She accepted my proposal and we began planning to meet in Katmandu a couple weeks later.

I was finally going be with the only woman whom I had ever loved. I knew that this meant that my pilgrimage was over but felt that I must have come to Asia to find the love that I had left behind.

While I was in Bodhgaya I heard that His Holiness the Fourteenth Dalai Lama would be giving public teachings at his home monastery in

Dharmsala. I had gone to see him once in Berkeley a couple of years earlier and was looking forward to seeing his home and receiving teachings in a Tibetan community. Along with a couple of Canadian kids I had met at the retreat in Bodhgaya, I traveled up to the far northwest of India, where the Tibetan government in exile is located at the base of the Himalaya Mountains. My plan was to attend the teachings from the Dalai Lama while I was awaiting the arrival of Lola.

Dharmsala, where the Dalai Lama lives, was very different from anything I had experienced in India so far. It was almost completely Tibetan: the smell of butter lamps and incense permeated everything and in the center of the village stood a huge prayer wheel that was constantly being walked around by devout Tibetan Buddhists. Shops and restaurants lined the main street and for the first time since I had arrived in India I wasn't being hassled by beggars and touts. I was met with the warm smiles and friendly "tashi delek" ("hello" in Tibetan) of the locals. I saw a lot of other Westerners around and it seemed like some of them had been there for a long time, making a home among the Tibetan refugees.

I shared a room at a small guesthouse with the two Canadian kids. They were both ready for a nap but I wasn't tired so I went out to explore my new surroundings. Walking through town, I stopped a Western woman who looked like she had been there for a while and asked about where the good restaurants were. In her thick German accent she directed me to a path off the main street where I would find a nice place to hang out and get some food.

After some time wandering around, I found what I hoped was the path that she had told me about. There were several little buildings that had signs out front in English that I assumed were the restaurants she had spoken of. They were actually just people's homes that had been opened to travelers and set up as restaurants.

I decided upon the place that had a sign out front that said "tofu." I hadn't had any real tofu for months. In the restaurants there were several tables occupied by groups of travelers. In the corner a middle-aged white guy was playing Beatles songs on a guitar. A young Tibetan woman offered me a handwritten menu and some tea. I ordered some noodle soup with tofu dumplings and relaxed into the bench, leaned against the wall, and closed my eyes. I was feeling better than I had in a while, comfortable and happy. I was looking forward to seeing Lola, but since I knew she was coming it felt like I could just enjoy the few days there in Dharmsala before she arrived.

The soup was incredible, made with homemade noodles and fat dumplings stuffed with tofu and veggies. I was in heaven. I hadn't enjoyed a meal that much as long as I could remember. At the table next to me I overheard some people talking about going to meet the Dalai Lama the next day. I asked them about it and if I could come too. They told me about where I needed to go to sign up and get cleared with the Tibetan security.

The next morning I waited in line for an hour to get cleared for meeting the Dalai Lama. They just wanted our passports and we had to sign something. I was told where to go in the afternoon for the event. When I arrived there were a couple of hundred people lining up at the gates of the Dalai Lama's home monastery. It was mostly Tibetans, but dozens of Westerners, like myself, were also in line. I came to find out that we were all being welcomed to Dharmsala. Many of the Tibetans were refugees who had just escaped from China-occupied Tibet. The excitement in the crowd was thick and as the line slowly moved up the driveway people began coming back down the other way, crying and clutching some sort of gift they had received.

At the top of the driveway the line became a semicircle and I could see the Dalai Lama, standing in front of the building and taking a few moments to personally greet each person in the front of the line. Some of the newly arrived Tibetans were overwhelmed with reverence for their leader and spiritual guide, having walked for weeks over the Himalayas, risking death, for this very moment of seeing His Holiness the Dalai Lama in person. It was incredibly powerful and inspiring to witness the way he was completely present with each person he met. When it was my turn I felt a little dizzy and my body became filled with warmth. I was greeted with a bow and blessing that included some sort of handshake. I was given a Buddhist protection cord that he had blessed. He looked directly into my eyes and smiled. No words were exchanged and the whole transaction was very quick. I walked away feeling elated and filled with wonder.

"How did I get here?" I thought. My mind filled with awe at how far I had traveled in the years since I started walking the spiritual path.

The next day the public teachings by the Dalai Lama began. Hundreds of people gathered around in the outdoor Dharma hall to hear the Mahayana scriptures and commentary. As Westerners, we were given our own small section to sit in and on our radios we could hear the teachings translated into our native languages. Not being so familiar with the Mahayanan tradition, I found a lot of the teachings difficult to understand. But the heart of the teachings were clear: wisdom, compassion, and kindness are the path to awakening. It was so amazing to be sitting in the crowd with so many hundreds of Tibetans; just being surrounded by so many people who had dedicated their lives to uprooting ignorance was as inspirational as the teachings themselves. His Holiness the Dalai Lama was such an amazing being to be in the presence of; he had transformed so much suffering into so much peace in his life. I couldn't imagine all of what he must have gone through, having had to flee his own country from the invading Chinese, yet he continued to teach that the ignorance of violence must be met with the wisdom of nonviolence. A teaching that, as a young punk rocker, I had never grasped. While I was sitting there among the community of Tibetan Buddhists it was clear to me that I would do all I could with my life to bring this teaching to my generation.

One afternoon I called my mom's house and Lola, Vinny, and Micah were all there waiting for me to call. It felt strange to be speaking to all of them. I apologized to the guys for not having met them when I was supposed to and asked about how the rest of their travels had been. Micah had come home right after the Sufi celebration in New Delhi and Vinny had continued on, alone, for a couple weeks, hooking up with some crazy hippies and exploring northern India.

Vinny got on the phone and asked how I was doing; he sounded concerned. I felt defensive, like he knew I must have really been freaking out to invite Lola to come join me. He knew how much I had struggled with that relationship in the past. I just lied and told him that everything had been great, that I had just realized that Lola and I had to be together. He switched his tone and became supportive, wished me well, and told me how much he missed me. I was really moved to hear that from him. I was afraid that he and Micah were going to be pissed at me for not meeting up with them.

Micah also got on the phone and said hello. He told me that he had decided to go back to New Haven for a while to see his family, but that he looked forward to hearing more about my travels when I got back.

Lola had purchased her ticket and it was only a matter of days until we would see each other. None of it seemed real. I was still on the opposite side of the earth. I was so excited about being with her again, there were no words for how I felt and too many things to tell her. She sounded really happy and was joking around with Vinny and Micah about what it would be like out here. She had a bunch of questions about what to bring and what we were going to do. I told her that I loved her very much and that we would be together in a few days, not to worry.

After the teachings in Dharmsala I went to New Delhi and spent a few days at the tomb of the Indian Sufi master Hazrat Inayat Khan, where I was supposed to have met Vinny and Micah a month earlier. I spent a couple of days there before I went to go meet Lola in Nepal. There were some lectures on Sufism happening, a much smaller scene than the one I had just come from, but it was a wonderful experience to be in the place of a teacher who had deeply inspired me in my spiritual quest. Hazrat's teachings consist of seeing that all world religions hold the same universal truths. He talked about what Buddha, Jesus, Allah, and Krishna have in common: that they were all trying to point us back to our own true nature.

A lot of the time I was lost in my own fantasies of love. Making plans and recalling the good times we'd had. When doubts or fears would arise I did my best to ignore them, rationalizing everything as God's will and my own Karma unfolding. I felt very hopeful about my future with Lola. Envisioning marriage, children, and a life of spiritual practice and service.

I arrived in Katmandu a few days before Lola, but I had started feeling sick on the plane and didn't make it out of my room very much. At one point I was actually throwing up and spewing diarrhea at the same time. It was one of those times when I was grateful that the bathroom was so small that I could reach the sink while still sitting on the toilet. When I was feeling a bit better I began to explore Katmandu. I found a nicer room for us and rented a motorcycle to meet her on at the airport.

I had been anticipating Lola's arrival for so long, it was hard to believe it was actually happening. Even at the airport while I was waiting for her flight I noticed thoughts of doubting that she would really show up.

As she walked down the corridor I saw her from afar and a great joy arose that was mixed with the anxiety of my expectations. We embraced each other and tears filled both of our eyes. She was trembling in my arms and for a moment we were both speechless. I whispered promises of love in her ear and we had a long look at each other. I felt naked and exposed, the intimacy was almost more than I could handle after so many months of being alone. Before beginning the small talk about the trip, we just stood there hugging and kissing. She looked great; her hair was much shorter than it had been the last time I saw her and it was bleached blond. She was wearing a light-colored summer dress that slightly revealed her beautiful figure.

For the first couple of days we stayed in the motel room making love and cuddling for hours at a time, interrupted only by the occasional need for food.

We spent about a week in Katmandu talking of plans for our future together: our wedding, our children, and our love. We visited some of the main temples and Tibetan Buddhist centers but now I felt like I was just another tourist on vacation with my sweetheart.

Lola found it very difficult to adjust to the hideous poverty and different cultural traditions of Asia; although she had lived in Japan for some time years earlier, she had never been faced with the realities of being in an undeveloped country. She was unprepared for the strict dress code enforced upon women and ended up having to buy some long skirts to cover her legs.

We decided to go to Pokhara, where we were told that we would get a better view of the Himalayas. The ten-hour bus ride to get there was extremely difficult for Lola and I was already beginning to get impatient with her. I had been on the road for five months alone and was used to all the discomforts and concessions of traveling.

In Pokhara, Lola just wanted to rent some movies and stay in the room for a few days. I was realizing that she wasn't very interested in traveling around and seeing the sights. She really just wanted to be with me. I felt the same way to some extent; I was very happy that we were together again but just thought that, since we were in Nepal, we should explore and enjoy it.

The bus trip out to Pokhara was so traumatic that we decided to fly back to Katmandu. The view of the mountains from the plane was spectacular. We were in awe of the soaring peaks that surround the valleys of Nepal. The snowcapped ranges stretched as far as the eye could see, reaching into the heavens.

It was looking like it wasn't going to just be smooth and easy for us, that we still had some drastic differences that were going to be challenging to deal with. We obviously had our work cut out for us but were both willing to do whatever it was going to take to make the relationship work. I was committed to being her partner, lover, and friend. I had no choice, she was all I had thought of for the last several months. I had flown her halfway around the world and we were in love. So what if she wasn't all that interested in the sight-seeing, big deal, we were in love and that was all that mattered. Or at least that was what I kept telling myself.

We decided to go to India for a couple weeks and then back to Thailand before returning home. I really wanted to see the Taj Mahal and thought that she might enjoy seeing Varanasi.

In Varanasi she got really sick and decided that she wanted to go home ASAP. She had a really high temperature and was throwing up. I had been in the same place so many times. I understood that she just wanted to be back at home with clean food, clean clothes, and a comfortable bed to hide in. I guess I just had never given myself the option of going home. I was out here for the count, no illness or fever was going to send me home early. But looking at her frail little body wracked with pain and shaking with fever in the little shanty room we had rented, I did my best to take care of her and arranged to fly to New Delhi and from there to Thailand for a few days before going back to the States. I really wasn't ready to go home but I knew that if we were going to work everything out that it would be much easier once we were on familiar territory. Our time in India was mostly spent in hotels; we never made it to see the Taj. Lola started feeling better while we were in New Delhi but still felt very weak and wanted to get home as soon as possible.

There was a certain point when we were in Bangkok, when she wanted to go out shopping and this time I wasn't feeling well and wanted to stay in, that we got into a fight. For the first time I allowed the thought to enter my mind that I had made a mistake. That there was no way we were ever going to be able to work things out and that I really just wanted to stay and continue my travels and practice. I knew that I couldn't do that. I knew I had to get her home safely and give the relationship a shot. After all those months of longing for her, here she was and we were stuck with each other now, with our decision, with our Karma.

The day before we left Thailand we did do some shopping, buying presents for all our family and friends. I had started collecting miniature statues of Buddha so I bought a bunch of those. Lola mostly bought gifts for other people. On Kao San Road where we were staying you could get just about anything you might want, everything from traditional Thai handicrafts to bootlegged American cassettes and CDs.

I bought the only punk tape that I found, Rancid's *Out Come the Wolves*. My friend Jessica used to talk about Rancid a lot but I had never listened to them before. I was and still am to some extent stuck in the music that was produced from 1977 to 1988. I was actually quite surprised by how much I liked the tape. The Clash influence was pretty clear but that was fine because the Clash had always been one of my favorite bands and Rancid was doing the ska-influenced punk better than I had ever heard it done before, other than maybe Operation Ivy. So when I realized it was a couple of the guys from Operation Ivy who had started Rancid, I put it all together.

The flight home was long and uneventful. We slept a lot and spent the hours fantasizing about our future together and making plans. With a layover in Korea, I reflected on how six months earlier I had been there with Micah and Vinny, excited about our first pilgrimage to the East, full of fantasies and expectations. Now, on my way home, nothing had been as I had expected it, neither inwardly nor outwardly. Returning home with my girlfriend, so much for the monastery, so much for enlightenment. But I did have a new sense of meaning and purpose; my monk fantasy was replaced by an understanding of the importance of my work in the world, in relationship, in family, in engaged service. Maybe my path was more like my father's: practice and service, relationship as spiritual practice.

We made it home intact and moved into the extra room at my mom's in Santa Cruz. We were still talking about getting married but we were starting to fight more and more. Lola wanted all of me all of the time; she felt threatened by my friendships with both men and women. This caused a lot of problems between us; no matter how much I assured her of my love it wasn't enough, it seemed like she wanted me to give up all of my other relationships. I wasn't willing to do that and the more we fought the more I needed to hang out with my friends to get support.

We lasted like that for only a few weeks before I gave up for the last time. My love for her was as strong as ever but it was just too clear that the relationship was not working for either of us. We broke up, she moved back into her old apartment; I stayed at my mom's for a little while and then moved in with my old friend Joe.

The breakup was ugly; I completely shut down and just walked away. Within weeks I was dating someone else and trying to act as if the whole thing had never happened. I just rationalized the whole engagement thing as a temporary lapse of sanity.

Lola didn't take it very well and it wasn't long before she turned back to booze to drown the anger and pain.

I felt confused about all that had happened in the last year: the relationship at its final demise, all that I had seen and learned in Asia, still trying to make sense of what had happened with Matthew, and the continued deepening of my insight into the spiritual dimensions of life. I did all that I knew how to do, putting one foot in front of the other and continuing to walk the path of recovery and spiritual practice.

17

Meditate and Destroy

t he small beach community of Capitola where I had spent so many days of my youth surfing, getting high, and running amuck had slowly been transformed from a run-down little surf ghetto into an all-out tourist trap. The arcade I loved as a kid was gone, and the old shit house that we used to get high behind had long since been replaced by a heavily manicured, overly landscaped park for all the tourists to enjoy their high-priced picnic lunches from one of the many restaurants that now lined the esplanade. I had witnessed the transformation of Capitola over the years, hanging out in the parking lot and

watching the construction and face-lifts take place, but after returning
from India it was like I had never been there before. Almost nothing
of the place I knew as a kid remained except the ocean and beach itself. I had spent countless days on that beach, first as a junior life-
guard, running around, swimming the buoys, learning nothing about
lifesaving and everything about having fun in the sun, and later drinking beer on the north side of the pier with Toby and the crew of 'Tola
rats and more recently playing Frisbee with Vinny.

Although I had dropped out of junior lifeguards as a kid, my little
brother, Aaron, had continued all the way through his teens. Eventually he became an instructor in the program, teaching the kids what he
had been taught, sharing his reverence for the ocean and his love of
physical fitness with the hordes of local kids who made their way to the
beach every morning during the summer to join the long lineage of junior lifeguards. So it was with great enthusiasm that, when offered, I
accepted a job on the beach that first summer back from the East.

Working on the beach and living with my old friend Joe and his
new guitarist, Jeff, from Fury 66, a local punk rock band, was a nice
change of pace from the months of travel and confusion that had pre-
ceded that summer. The breakup with Lola was still weighing heavy
on my heart so the constant activity of the beach and our apartment
was a welcome distraction. Our apartment was completely insane. I
slept in the laundry room, Joe lived in the living room, and Jeff had
the bedroom, until their new drummer, Joe Fish, moved up from L.A.
to play with Fury, then Fish and Jeff shared the bedroom. For most of
the summer we had four guys in a one-bedroom apartment. I was
gone most of the time anyway, on the beach all day and at some meditation group, meeting, or training in the evenings.

On Thursday nights we had a small meditation group at the house.
I would give meditation instructions and then we would talk about
spiritual teachings or practice for a while. There was a growing interest in the punk and hardcore scene in understanding life from a spiritual perspective. And I wanted to follow up on the intention I had set
in India to share the Buddhist teachings with my peers. The class was
almost always followed by some sort of chaos, charlie horses, dead
legs, double fisters, cup checks, and pillow fights. Not exactly nonvio-

lent, but at least our aggression was consensual. Eventually the group got too big and too crazy to continue. I was moving anyway so I started looking for a new venue for the kids to meet and meditate.

That summer I was invited to attend a teacher training for mindfulness-based stress reduction (teaching meditation and calling it relaxation) with Dr. Bob Stahl. I had met Bob at a Jon Kabat-Zinn retreat a couple years earlier and had expressed an interest in further development and training in teaching mindfulness. At the time I was still working in the medical field and had intended to bring it into my work at the hospital. But now I was becoming much more interested in sharing the mindfulness techniques with my peers and thinking about doing some classes in jail.

I was learning a lot of helpful techniques in teaching and really gaining the vocabulary of the experiences of meditation. I was often so tired and burnt from running around all day on the beach with the kids that during our meditations I inevitably fell asleep, snoring and nodding out. Being the only young person in the room, I think I was given a little extra space to show up as best I could. Bob was incredibly supportive and that training gave me the foundation of how to offer meditation instructions.

I also got my old job back at the county health department so I was even busier but it felt great to be home. Everything began settling around the confusion I had experienced in Asia and a new sense of meaning and belonging began to infuse my life. It became clear to me that everything was happening perfectly. I had learned what I needed to learn during my time in Asia: I wasn't supposed to spend my life in a monastery, I wasn't supposed to be in relationship with Lola. All I knew was that I was supposed to use my life's energy to help others. I had a growing sense that my place was in the world, that I was to follow the example of my parents to live my life, to practice and serve.

After doing the teacher training I offered an eight-week meditation class to some friends and coworkers to test out my teaching skills. We gathered each week in the living room of Jeri, my boss at the AIDS program. Vinny and Jennifer were there as were some other friends and a couple of guys I had been sponsoring. This was my first real meditation class. I had done a lot of little groups for friends but this was the first time that I taught a several-week class on the practice of meditation. I was nervous but confident in my ability to share the simple and deep practice of mindfulness that had brought such an incredible transformation to my life.

Around the same time my friend Soren Gordhammer asked me if I would co-lead a weekly meditation group with him at the Santa Cruz Zen Center. Since I had moved out of Jeff and Joe's place and was living downtown, this was a perfect opportunity to continue offering a group but raising it from a goof-off session to a real opportunity to explore spiritual practice with a group of friends and the occasional college student or random civilian who dropped in.

Life was full of great opportunities to practice and serve. I was counseling at the AIDS program, teaching meditation with Soren, working with kids at the beach and then after the summer at a Montessori school, living in a nice little studio apartment in downtown Santa Cruz; it seemed like things couldn't get much better. The simplicity and focus on practice and service felt balanced and fulfilling.

Micah had decided to return to the East Coast after getting back from our trip and Vinny had moved in with his girlfriend, Jennifer. He and I had started getting tattooed by Eddie Deutsche, the tattooist our friend Aaron had introduced us to before we went on our travels. I got a tattoo of a Japanese-style standing Buddha on my forearm, inspired by the statue I had seen at the monastery in Thailand, and Vinny got a Tibetan-style sitting Buddha on his shoulder. We both already had lots of tattoos but these guys in the city were a whole level above the tattooists I had been to in the past.

Prior to that tattoo all of my other ink was concealable by a T-shirt and pants. I had decided when I started getting tattooed that it would be better to hold off on visible tattoos until I was either older or set in a good job. I had thought that I might be in the medical field and knew that it would be challenging to get jobs and perhaps intimidating to my patients if I were covered in tattoos. But while I was in India I had realized that I was no longer willing to live my life for anyone else or out of fear of how I would be judged or oppressed for being tattooed.

I loved the fact that being visibly tattooed set me apart from the mainstream. I had awakened from the delusion of wanting to fit in so that I could be of service. I realized that the community that I most wanted to serve, my generation, didn't have the same ignorant judgments as the generations before. Being heavily tattooed with images of Buddhas and religious icons has actually helped me to spread the Dharma rather than hindered me.

I started hanging out and getting tattooed at 222 in San Francisco, the shop that Eddie had recently opened. Scott Sylvia was working at 222 as well. I had met him way back in '88 when he was apprenticing at Miller Cottons in Monterey. But this was when we really began to establish a friendship and I came to find out about his story, recovery, and deep spiritual convictions.

Scott grew up in the Santa Cruz Mountains with two older brothers who tormented him sufficiently. He was sort of a hick in high school, played football and everything. He used to drink a lot of Jack Daniels and once had his stomach pumped at a Charlie Daniels–Alabama concert. His family moved to Monterey while he was in school and he was introduced to a whole new world of punks, skins, and drugs. His drinking got him into a lot of trouble and was out of control even before he graduated. He was sent to rehab at seventeen, caught up in the heavy trend of shipping your kids off to recovery centers in the mid-eighties.

When Scott was eighteen years old and about a year sober his friend Alicia started teaching him how to tattoo. They both worked for this crazy biker named Miller who gave me some of my first tattoos. Scott worked there for a couple years, then hooked up with Eric, an old Nazi skinhead I knew from hardcore shows at Gilman Street in the eighties. Eric had also gotten sober and begun tattooing. He worked for Miller in Berkeley for a while and then he and Scott decided to open up their own shop in Sacramento called American Graffiti. Eric had changed his fascist ways and he and Scott ran a very successful shop for several years. Both were staying sober and trying to open up to the spiritual dimensions of art and recovery, channeling their creative energy into tattooing, painting, and building hot rods.

(Years later, after Scott had moved away from Sacramento, Eric was murdered in his own front yard, shot down in the early morning hours as he returned home from a night of hanging out with the wrong people. Eric had stopped addressing his alcoholism and burned most of the bridges behind him. His death was a tragedy but not a shock. He will always be remembered and missed by the countless friends and family he left behind.)

By the time I reconnected with Scott he had been tattooing for about ten years and had become one of the best tattooists around. He had also become deeply involved in the punk rock scene and his art could be seen on the covers of many records and countless T-shirts and on the skin of hundreds of punks around the world.

Scott and I became very close friends. I would often stay at his house when I was in the city. It took me a while to really get to know him. As with me, recovery from addiction has played a central role in his life. Scott is almost completely covered in tattoos and he recently got the word "Kindness" tattooed on the palm side of his fingers and "Remember" in bold black letters covering some old work on his forearm. Both serve as a constant reminder of where he came from and his intention to transform his life's energy from self-centered fear to service and compassion. Remembering God and his place as a passenger and not the captain of the ship that carries him through life.

I was spending so much time in the city that I decided to move up there. Everything was great in Santa Cruz but I was just ready for a change. A room opened up in Gary Kosmala's house, who also worked at the tattoo shop, so I decided I was ready for the change of scenery and moved to the city. I started working at the tattoo shop full-time for a couple of months while I was looking for a real job in the city.

Living in San Francisco was exciting. I had been going up there from Santa Cruz for shows and shopping since I was a kid but it was a whole different thing to be living there. There were a couple of really great meditation teachers who I started sitting with on a regular basis, Howie Cohn and Eugene Cash. I was not doing any teaching at that point and that was fine with me. I had begun to feel like it was a bit too soon for me anyway. It was nice to be more anonymous, I could just be myself, no one knew my story. In Santa Cruz I had such a long history, people remembered me from being a street punk, a junkie, a biker, a graffiti vandal, sober, Straight Edge kid, counselor, meditator, teacher . . . in San Francisco I was just me, today.

Lola was also living in the city. We had tried to have some conversations and to be friends but it almost always turned out bad, with her getting angry or one of us being mean. She was drinking again and told me that she had made some suicide attempts, that when she got drunk she would cut herself with broken glass or razor blades.

It broke my heart to hear that she was in so much pain but there was also a feeling of relief that I wasn't in that relationship anymore. Finally closing the chapter of my first love and the ongoing delusion that one day we might be able to be together. I had finally accepted that we would never be a couple and was becoming more and more skeptical about our ability to even be friends.

One night she called me up and told me that she had just cut her wrist and that she was bleeding and that she needed to see me or she would kill herself. I was scared and hesitant but I agreed to see her if I could take her to the hospital.

We met near my house and she was going on and on about how we were supposed to get married and how she still loved me and wanted to know when we were going to get back together. She was very drunk and her wrists were still bleeding so I took her to the emergency room. I was feeling scared and didn't know what else to do. We walked the couple blocks from my house to the hospital but she was refusing to go in, until I explained to her why I left her and why we couldn't be together. I did my best to calm her down and get her to go into the ER with me but she kept refusing. I started to get pissed off and told her that I was going to leave if she wouldn't go in. She seemed to be somehow satisfied by my anger, the response that she could understand, probably reminiscent of her childhood.

In the hospital she admitted to having cut herself and they wanted to put her on a suicide watch. She was really freaking out, blaming me for everything. She continued to say that we were supposed to get married, that I was supposed to love her and take care of her. My anger and confusion was mixed with caring. I did love her but also knew that we could not be together. I began to shut down, feeling helpless and not knowing what to do or say. After some time I left the room they had put us in to ask a nurse about what they were going to do about her cuts. When I left the room she lit a cigarette and started burning herself with matches. When I walked back into her room she put the cigarette out in the open cut on her wrist. Immediately I called the nurse, not knowing what else to do, and they had to fully restrain her, tying her to the bed so that she couldn't continue to hurt herself. They tied her arms and legs down to the hospital bed. She was screaming and kicking, trying to fight them off; they asked me to help but I couldn't. It was so painful to see her like that and I certainly couldn't tie her down to a bed while she was crying out for help.

She was screaming at me and spitting at the nurses. It was completely surreal, I felt like I was in a bad movie. Unable to stay present in the face of so much suffering and feeling like I was somehow responsible for her pain, I began to disassociate, almost having an out-of-body experience. Like I was watching the whole thing happen from a distance.

At about 3:00 A.M. she was transferred to the psych ward at San Francisco General and I walked home through the empty streets. Climbing the stairs to my apartment, I began to cry. Crawling into my bed, I wept until I fell asleep, replaying all of the events of our relationship and questioning how something that felt as pure as our love could bring about so much despair.

The next day she called to let me know that she had been released and that she was okay. After that we didn't speak again for some time but I heard that she was doing better and had gotten back into recovery.

18

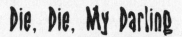

Die, Die, My Darling

When I got my dad's new book in the mail I was living in a spacious apartment in Japantown. Sitting in my room and reading *A Year to Live,* I was unprepared for the profound effect this book would have on my life. Things were going incredibly well and I was happy to be living in the city, meeting a lot of new people and enjoying my new surroundings.

After finishing the book I put it down, feeling inspired by it, but I didn't think I was going to actually do the practice. It was my dad's new book so I read it, but that was that.

I was still working down at the tattoo shop, a bit adrift. I had traded some work for tattoos and ended up getting a full sleeve of Krishna and Rhada in the Jungle surrounded by gopis and animals with a huge tree full of flowers and little birds that Rhada is swinging from. The tattoo was incredible but I didn't really feel fulfilled with the work. I knew that I needed to be doing work in the world that I felt made a difference.

I had interviewed at all sorts of community health centers and hospitals around the city and was just sort of waiting for someone to offer me a job. In the meantime I had a lot of free time and was practicing meditation regularly. I didn't plan it but I began to really contemplate my dad's new book. I started to ask myself, "What if I did have a year to live? Is this what I would be doing?" At first the answer was yes; I was enjoying San Francisco, being involved in the punk rock tattoo scene. Working at one of the most prestigious tattoo parlors in the country with some of the best tattoo artists in the world. Occasionally a rock star or someone from one of the punk bands that I liked would come into the shop. It was exciting to be around so many people who were around my age and into similar things.

My decision to do the year-to-live practice snuck up on me. I wasn't planning on it, but it just made sense. I felt like it could only be useful and I didn't seem to have anything more important to do than prepare for death. So I went for it, committing to really live my life each day as if I were truly dying. When I told my folks that I was going to do the practice they were very supportive—they thought it would be a great exploration for me at that stage of my spiritual practice.

I started my journal on July 1, 1997, twelve months to live. I immediately took inventory of all my relationships and quickly saw a few places where there was some unfinished business, where I owed amends or needed to extend forgiveness. I had been taking inventories and making amends for many years as part of my recovery so this wasn't a huge undertaking but I did see that if I were going to die there were several apologies to make and thanks to give.

My father was very clear in the book that it was fine to stay in one's present life situation during the practice so as to not accumulate more unfinished business. At the beginning of the first month that was my intention: to just stay in San Francisco, get a job, and live my last year in an ordinary way, discovering what was to be found through this shift in perspective. But by the end of the month I saw that if I had only one year to live, I would not stay put and work a nine-to-five. I wanted to do some traveling and attend some meditation retreats. After all, if I had only one year left to get enlightened, I better get busy.

July 27, 1997
"GOING FORTH INTO HOMELESSNESS"
With eleven months left to live, I have fully committed myself to this practice, to this moment. I have given notice on my apartment in San Francisco. I have given up my possible place at the East-West House. Decided not to take the job I was offered at St. Mary's Hospital, working with AIDS patients. I plan to sell my car and spend the rest of the year going to meditation retreats around the States and possibly Europe and to be in India by the winter. This is where my head and heart are telling me to spend my last year. Learning to be alone, letting go of all the doing. I've been thinking a lot about the traditional phrase that Buddhist monks say when ordaining, "Going forth into homelessness."

So that's what I did. My grandmother had died earlier that year and my mother had inherited a large sum of money. She was incredibly generous to all of us kids. With the money she gave me I had bought a new car. I decided that I would sell the car, get rid of the few belongings that I had, pack a backpack, and hit the road. I knew that I wanted to go back to India, feeling that I had come back earlier than I should have the last time. I felt that my trip had ended prematurely. I also wanted to visit a few meditation centers and communities around the world, including the Insight Meditation Society in Massachusetts, Plum Village in France, Hanuman Temple in Taos, New Mexico, and some Mayan ruins in Mexico.

I began the second month of practice with a ten-day Buddhist meditation/Vipassana retreat with Mary Orr in the Santa Cruz Mountains at a Tibetan center. We spent the days in sitting and walking meditation, the practice being to attempt to stay mindful of the present moment, letting go of the past and future and exploring with bare attention the experience of being, allowing wisdom and compassion to arise naturally. Sitting, walking, eating, and taking a few short hikes in the redwoods. I had come a long way from India.

At night I slept in a tent perched on the side of the mountain, affording me an incredible view of the valley below and the clear and bright phases of the moon above. My meditations were mostly filled with memories of the past and fantasies of the future. As each graphic memory of the years of drugs and violence filled my mind I attempted to bring my attention back to my breath, noting with as much compassion as possible my "thinking or remembering," thus returning to the present moment.

I thought a lot about Toby, who had been in prison for the last couple of years, and I sent him wishes for peace and healing. He had never been able to get sober. He had even stayed with me and Micah for a while when he was homeless and strung out on the streets of Santa Cruz—until the day we came home and he had robbed our house. I wasn't as mad at him as I was scared for him because I knew that for him to steal from me meant he had lost all hope. I was his last connection to the life he used to know, to sanity. In some way I felt kind of glad he was in prison—at least I knew he was probably still alive and hopefully safe. We had been writing to each other some and I planned to send him some books on meditation soon.

When my mind wasn't filled with grief for the life that I had lived it was busy making plans for how I was going to spend the last ten months of this incarnation. There were, of course, many moments of mindfulness and milliseconds of satisfaction, finding some peace and inspiration in this simple and profound meditation practice.

After the retreat I planned to spend a few days with my mom in Santa Cruz and then attend another meditation retreat, one led by the Vietnamese Zen master Thich Nhat Hanh in Santa Barbara.

I couldn't afford to take off traveling without selling my car, but the day before I was supposed to leave I still hadn't sold it. I was driving across the Golden Gate Bridge and this guy in a little old beat-up Toyota was waving at me, so I waved back, not recognizing him. When he finally caught up with me he pointed at the "For Sale" sign in the car window, which I had totally forgotten about. So I pulled over after the bridge and he took a test drive and asked me a bunch of questions about the car. He said it was exactly what he and his wife were looking for. I told him that unfortunately I would be out of town for a couple of weeks so he would have to wait until then, but he was insistent about buying the car. I was asking $6,500 but was planning on getting only about $5,500. He asked what the very bottom price was; if he was to buy the car today, how much? I said that since I was leaving and everything I would sell it to him for $5,000. He offered $4,500 and I said no way. He was trying to talk me into it so I said I'd take $4,500 if he gave me his Toyota in trade for the other $500. He thought about it for a minute and asked his wife, telling me all about how it was their first car and that they'd had it since college. After some deliberation he said yes and we went to his bank, where he got the money, and then to his house, where we exchanged pink slips, and I drove home in my new beat-up old '81 Toyota.

This was another one of those times in my life that felt like I was being taken care of, like I was surrounded by grace. With all of the Buddhist practice I had been doing I began to think of these events less as God's will and more as Karma.

So instead of hitch-hiking around the country I packed up the Toyota and headed down to Santa Barbara, stopping in Santa Cruz to say good-bye to friends and family. My mom said that she might even come and meet me in Nepal in a few months.

The Thich Nhat Hanh retreat was awesome but huge—1,300 people. My mind tended toward judging and resenting all of the rich, white Buddhists who were there with their brand new BMWs and designer clothes, yet in my better moments I realized that maybe there was some hope for our country if the ruling class was at least trying to wake up. I saw how clearly all my judgments were just creating more suffering for myself.

I knew a few people at the retreat; Soren and some of the people from the Santa Cruz group were there. I ended up enjoying very much the teachings on mindfulness in every aspect of life. I realized that it wasn't the right community for me but I was truly inspired by the simple yet profound teachings. Up to that point meditation had been something I did on the cushion as my spiritual practice. I realized that I could practice meditation in all aspects of my life, in every action and with every breath.

The day I left the retreat I went to meet a bunch of hardcore kids in L.A., a Straight Edge gang called the Monster Crew. Good kids most of them—at times a little too violent for my taste, but politically aggressive and I liked that. They were blowing up fur factories and smashing windows at the fast-food establishments that are slowly destroying the ozone by all of the clear-cutting in the rain forest to graze their cattle. I wasn't into any of that stuff anymore, but I was a vegan, I didn't eat any meat, dairy, or eggs or wear leather, and I did believe in fighting for animal rights and ecological sanity. I had chosen to go vegan years earlier out of a deep desire to cause as little harm to other beings and the earth as possible.

The Monster Crew was on their way to Disneyland, so here I was, first day out of retreat, going to Disneyland, an adventure that actually sounded kind of cool. I found out that it was one of their regular hangouts, a good place to meet girls, I guess. They had some scam for us all to sneak in: one of them had a pass, went and got a stamp, then stuck a sticker over the stamp and the sticker picked up the stamp and rubbed off on all the rest of us. To me Disneyland is just another example of the American empire of lies and corrupt capitalist propaganda, so I felt all right about sneaking in. I knew it was incongruent with my vow of honesty and not taking anything that isn't freely given but somehow I rationalized it. When we got there it was very surreal—I felt like I was on acid. The rides were more intense than I had remembered; with my heightened level of mindfulness, it was an incredible experience, but not recommended for the weakhearted or elderly. I had fun with the Monster Crew and my buddy Andre. I felt both connected to them and also that I had in some ways outgrown the cliquish Straight Edge mentality. But letting loose and fully enjoying the theme park transported me back into a childlike state of pure excitement. I guess I learned to drop back from judging. Who was I? After all . . .

From L.A. I drove across the desert to New Mexico to see my parents and say good-bye. On the way I stopped at the Grand Canyon. It was incredible. I camped for a couple of days and hiked all the way down to the bottom. I was beginning to appreciate nature more; previously I had always preferred the city life to nature but as my meditation practice deepened that seemed to be changing.

September 9, 1997
"THE GRAND CANYON"
An amazingly beautiful place. I think being in overwhelmingly beautiful places helps me see things more clearly. Hard travel to sacred places is a perfect explanation of all this. My belly is fairly soft and my heart feels somewhat open. My mind is still a constant source of commentary, old songs playing themselves out—fear, lust, etc. Being alone is good, I don't always like it but it seems so appropriate. I heard once that it is better to meet God alone than with someone who wouldn't understand.

In New Mexico I had a wonderful visit with my parents and I spent a couple of days at the Hanuman temple attending the Maha Bhandara celebration of Neem Karoli's death. Neem Karoli, also known as Maharaji, was one of my father's spiritual teachers. I had grown up with pictures of him and wonderful stories about his spiritual powers. This was the first time since I was a kid that I had been to a Bhandara, and definitely the first time that I went for my own spiritual connection with Maharaji and not just because it was what my parents were into.

I spent a couple days with my big sister Tara, playing with her kids and talking about the crazy lives we had both led. I asked for and extended forgiveness and expressed gratitude for all the ways that she had taken care of me as a kid. In a moment of generosity she offered me a free plane ticket she had. Together we checked out flights and I decided it would best be used to get me down to Mexico later that month after my retreat in North Carolina.

At the mountain hermitage that my parents call home I sat with them feeling nothing but love. My relationship with my parents had become more and more wonderful over the years. We had been through so much together and we were all amazed at how things were turning out. My father joked about how there was a time when they were thinking I was "not gonna make it," and Ondrea tried to stick up for me by saying, "Of course we always knew you would." When she walked away Dad shook his head and mouthed, "No way," and Ondrea, without turning around, said, "I heard that." Dad and I laughed and Ondrea kept walking. I felt so much love for them and so much gratitude for their support and encouragement over the years.

I thought back to that phone conversation with my dad when I was in Juvenile Hall almost ten years earlier and how that one simple meditation instruction ("just watch the breath come and go; every time your mind wanders off gently bring it back to the breath") so drastically changed the course of my life. Ondrea and I talked about the early days of our relationship, when I was stealing from them, and how she knew but Dad didn't want to believe it. We had been over all this before but it felt good to be accountable for my past actions. I felt so much gratitude for Ondrea; without her in my life I might not have made it. I might have ended up in prison with Toby or dead with so many of my other friends.

After New Mexico I headed for North Carolina to spend some time at the Human Kindness Foundation with Bo and Sita Lozoff. They have been inspirational teachers to me and are old friends of the family. They focus mostly on bringing spiritual practice into prisons and it is my intention to eventually start doing some of that same work myself.

On the way out there I drove long hours, stopping to cook food at rest stops and use the facilities. The first night I made it just past Oklahoma City and pulled off the road and slept in a field behind some office building.

Lying on the earth, staring up at the sky, I felt a sense of freedom and a peace that I had never known before. I had let go of all responsibility of work and home and was truly free to die, or live, or whatever. The stars above reminded me both how small I was and how interconnected to all things I had always been.

The next day I made it to Memphis. I found a convenient campground and went into town to have a look around. I saw some of the

Martin Luther King Jr. memorial stuff and that was cool, and of course all of the Elvis stuff, which I was much less impressed with. There was a time years before when I had a poster of Elvis on my wall and thought he was the coolest ever. I didn't stay in Memphis long, just walked around downtown for a little while. There was an outdoor music festival going on so I checked that out for a while and had a conversation about the nature of existence with some drunk people I was sitting next to. The next day I drove to New Orleans, stopping in Jackson, Mississippi, on the way, where I called my mom because that is where she was born. She wasn't home but I left her a message of thanks and love for all that she had been through in her life and mine.

Mom had really been through some difficult things in her life, but I knew she had done her best with all us kids, and we had all turned out all right. She had also turned her life around and was healthier and happier than ever. Taking the inheritance from her mother's death, she built her dream home in our old neighborhood on Pleasure Point in Santa Cruz.

In New Orleans I stayed at a youth hostel and hung out with some traveling English blokes. Also met some local punk kids when I was hanging out at the cemetery contemplating death. They showed me around and took me to some good vegetarian restaurants. I spent a lot of time thinking about my friend Aaron, who had really inspired me to go to Asia the first time. Having been many years clean and sober and world-traveled, he had moved to New Orleans to finish college at Tulane University. Aaron came home one day to find his best friend dead, having shot himself in the head with one of Aaron's guns. A week later Aaron overdosed on heroin. He was found dead in his apartment. I reflected on our short relationship and how grateful I was that I had met him and how sad it was that he had killed himself. It was a great teaching for me as I looked at my own mortality and how precious human life really is.

One night in New Orleans I went out to a strip club with the English guys. I had never been to one before so I thought I better check it out before I died. It was funny that right away the dancer who started flirting with me had scars all up and down her arms and legs from where she had cut herself. I was more interested in what it was that made her do the cutting than seeing her naked. She wanted to give me a lap dance but I just wanted to ask her about her scars and her life.

I was thinking about Lola and about how she had done the same thing while she was drinking. This woman told me a similar story about how she would get drunk and cut herself. Never when she was sober. She said that she had been sober for a few months now and that those scars were a constant reminder of what happened when she drank. Her scars were almost decorative, straight lines up and down her arms and legs. They reminded me of the intentional scarification designs that I had seen in books. It was so clear at that point how I just attract and am attracted to women who are deeply wounded. She invited me to meet her after work, at four o'clock in the morning, but I used my better judgment to go back to the hostel and get some sleep instead. The whole experience left me with more understanding of myself, and more compassion for Lola. We hadn't spoken since that night in the hospital. I prayed for her happiness and went to sleep.

After a short stopover in Atlanta I made it to North Carolina, to the Human Kindness Foundation ashram. My plan was to stay for a week and then fly from there down to Mexico. I had the plane ticket that my sister Tara had given me.

Bo is an old friend of my father's and Ram Dass's; they had set up the Prison-Ashram Project together back in the seventies. Stephen and Ram Dass moved on to other work but Bo has remained committed to serving the incarcerated communities. The ashram is set up around both personal spiritual practice in a community and being of service to prisoners around the world. We had a simple schedule of waking early and doing some group meditation and chanting; afterward we had breakfast, worked in the office or garden, had lunch, did a little more work, and then had free time to practice or read or whatever. In the evenings we would often get together and play badminton or volleyball, then dinner, and after dinner we had silence until the morning practice period.

One night in my room I was reading by candlelight and I caught my reflection in the window I was sitting in front of and was startled by my resemblance to my father. For a moment I thought I was looking at him instead of me. I realized how much I was becoming like him, physically and spiritually.

Toby was doing some time in the California Men's Colony in southern California so I spent my free time writing to him. I sent him Bo's book, *We're All Doing Time*, and included a long letter of forgiveness, love, and encouragement.

A couple of months later, after he received them, he wrote me and asked some questions about spiritual practice and said that he was enjoying the book and trying to meditate some. He was going to twelve-step meetings and church every week in the penitentiary. He also asked for forgiveness for having ripped me off and told me that he really wanted my help staying clean and out of trouble when he got out. Reading that letter, I felt a mixture of sadness and hope. My heart was heavy with the weight of his suffering but my mind was open to the potential of his awakening.

October 12, 1997
"HUMAN KINDNESS ASHRAM"

I am inspired by the people here. Today fifty recovering addicts came from a nearby rehab to have a picnic. We had a great time. I am beginning to see God in everyone and everything, what a wonderful practice. To live simply and peacefully is my goal. To serve and to awaken, to love and share the merit of my life's energy with others. With only nine months to live, I am more alive than ever, right here, right now.

Toward the end of my stay I spent a couple of days in a small cottage off in the woods alone and decided to fast during that time. The hours passed slowly and the hunger pains felt overwhelming at times. Practicing intervals of sitting and walking meditation during the day, at night I lay awake feeling like I was really dying. I was forced to let go and all of the attachment I had around eating and being around people was right in my face. I was all alone dying into each moment, nothing to comfort me but my faith.

With less than nine months to live, I decided to hit the road and go hang out in Mexico for a couple of weeks. I wanted to relax and reflect on all that I had learned so far. I flew into Cancun and then took buses around southern Mexico, checking out the Mayan ruins and hanging out on the beaches or in the jungles. I often spent whole days wandering alone through the jungles and ruins of the ancient Mayans. There was some way in which their dead civilization was mirroring my own death, the passing away of all that I had once believed to be real and definitive.

From Mexico I returned to North Carolina, retrieved my car, and drove up the East Coast to NYC to see Micah. Pulling into New York, I was flipping through the channels on the radio and I heard my dad's voice. It was crazy, there he was on the radio in NYC, talking about the year-to-live practice that I was doing and I just happened to hear it. I took it as a sign that I was on the right path.

Being in NYC with Micah was a blast. We had been through so much together; he really knew me in a way that few people did. Our mutual commitment to spiritual awakening was the foundation of our friendship. Sitting in his apartment on the Lower East Side of Manhattan, we just laughed about silly shit and talked about our spiritual practices and understanding. Over the years Micah had really committed to Sufi practice; he was practicing at the Sufi mosque in Tribeka and I went with him to meet the sheikha.

Walking into the Masjid, we saw people in funny white hats standing around talking; the smell of Middle Eastern food being cooked upstairs permeated the temple. I was introduced to several people and told that it was almost time for the feast. We all went upstairs and sat around a low table. A young-looking woman in all white with some sort of shawl around her head sat at the head of the table. Micah told me that she was Sheikha Fariha, their teacher. As the food was served she began to speak of the blessing we had all received to be fortunate enough to have so much food and a loving community to share it with. She said that it was due to the compassionate Allah, that Allah had personally blessed each one of us. This was news to me, but I did feel blessed and internally translated what she called Allah into the great mystery of the spiritual dimension that, for lack of a better word, or perhaps lack of my own understanding, I had taken to calling God. She went on to personally speak to different people around the table about their lives. After a while she turned to Micah and said, "Brother Mohamed, who have you brought with you this evening?" For a moment I felt like an intruder, like I had been discovered, put on the spot. Micah introduced me as his friend from California, Noah, and told her of our travels together. She welcomed me and told the congregation that the prophet Noah had joined them.

After dinner we all went downstairs to the mosque for a ceremony called Zikr, the chanting of Islamic prayers. Although I had studied Universal Sufism as taught by Hazrat Inayat Khan, I had never participated in anything like that before. We sat in a circle and moved our heads from side to side, chanting "La Illaha Ilallah" (There is no God but God). I got extremely high, partially from hyperventilating because we were chanting so fast, and also from the temporary release of my ego into the spiritual realm of the prayers.

After the Zikr a couple of people were being initiated into the community of Sufis through a ceremony called "taking hand." Micah asked if I wanted to join the ceremony to be initiated into the Sufi tradition. Having only months to live and having had a profound experience in the Zikr, I decided to go for it. But first I told the sheikha that I did mostly Buddhist practice, that I was concerned that being initiated into the Sufi tradition was contradictory to my commitment to that path. She said that there were many Buddhists in the community and that the "taking hand" ceremony was just a deepening of one's commitment to the spiritual life.

The ceremony consisted of some prayers and blessings from the sheikha, as well as a few movements back and forth and prostrations. At the end I was given one of the white hats I had seen on everyone else, some prayer beads, and my Sufi name, Tariq (the mystic). I felt a sense of calm and belonging, not so much to that community as to the world. It was like when I had done my steps years earlier—a release of self-centeredness and a relaxing into the care of God's grace and mercy, a complete acceptance of the truth of my Karma.

November 7, 1997
"NEW YORK CITY"

I would like to throw caution into the wind and experience life fully in each moment. No longer postponing life, allowing for all the possibilities. . . . Letting desire have its satisfaction. Seeing the true nature of wanting and inquiring deeply into the intention of each action. I am uncovering that which has been lying beneath the surface of awareness and beginning to see more clearly in the light of conscious living and the investigation of the deathless.

From NYC I flew back to California for a week to surprise friends and family before leaving for India. In San Francisco I caught a great punk rock show, Fury 66, AFI, and Good Riddance, two of my best friends' bands. I was doing these huge stage dives off the monitor speakers, smashing the delusion out of the kids in the crowd I landed on. I hung out with Joe, Scott, and Russ and had a great time talking shit and being crazy. I spent a couple more days with family and friends in Santa Cruz, saying good-bye and expressing my love and gratitude.

The flight to India was long and painful, a good preparation for the travels that lay ahead. I arrived in India the hard way: in the middle of the night in Bombay. Waiting for the train at five o'clock in the morning, I was surrounded by a group of Indian boys who just stood around me, staring and speaking in Hindi among themselves. The aroma of curry, fried food, and open fires mixed with the smell of human feces and filled the platform. It was a familiar scene, one I had experienced many times before. Either I could choose to try to ignore them or I could interact with them, asking them questions about their religion, age, etc., and answering the same old questions: "Your country?" "Oh yes, USA, Michael Jackson," or maybe the odd political comment about Clinton. I decided that I was too tired for all that right then and tried to ignore them. I couldn't wait for my train to arrive so I could just lie down for a while.

I had just gotten there but I was feeling the abuse my body had taken from the trip. I had already been traveling for two days straight, from NYC to London to Bombay, with a layover in Dubai. The group surrounding me kept growing and I occasionally smiled, feeling a little bit like an animal in the zoo. Finally one of the boys worked up the courage and started asking me questions. "How long in India?" I told him that I just got in but that I had been there for a few months two years earlier. Then it was on to "What country are you from?" and "How old are you?" and "Are you married?"—the same questions I would have to answer a thousand more times on that stint in India. Behind them I could see people starting to line up on the platforms and coolies stacking huge containers that were covered in burlap. I knew that meant that my train must be coming. Of course it didn't mean that I would actually be going anywhere. I once sat on a train in India for five hours, until finally the conductor came on and told us the train was broken. That morning I didn't even care about going anywhere, I just wanted to fight my way into the train and snag an upper bunk so I could lie down, turn on my Walkman, and rest my weary body.

When the train finally arrived, after some intense scrambling onto the train while people were still trying to get off, I secured an upper bunk. I felt a little bit like a rude American, but in India you have to be pushy to get what you need sometimes. When you are competing with the highly skilled and very aggressive Indian families you do what you need to do.

After locking one bag to the bench down below and stashing my small bag with my music, book, and the rest of my stuff up on my bunk, I folded up a sweatshirt for a pillow and tried to get a little rest. My body was exhausted on a cellular level. Of course, I wasn't actually going to be able to get to sleep because vendors were walking up and down the aisle screaming the name of their wares, chai, chai, chai, chai, or samosa or chapati or café.

It felt so good to get to rest for a few minutes and I began to re-member why I had come back to this beautiful and strange country. So far I had just been on survival status, trying to get to where I was going. I was on my way south to Goa, where I was going to meet up with, of all people, Vinny, who was traveling with his girlfriend, Jennifer. They had been traveling for a few months already, coming through Europe, North Africa, and the Middle East. They had bought one of those around-the-world tickets. I'd been on the road for about the same amount of time.

As the train pulled out of the station and bumped its way down the tracks, I began to reflect on the last few months and all that had brought me to that moment. My mind was a little cloudy and jumped from one thought to the next. It's actually quite interesting to watch the mind when the ego is too exhausted to defend its position.

I reflected on why I had started the year-to-live practice at a time in my life when things seemed like they couldn't get any better. I was surrounded by people who cared about me, I was almost ten years sober, my level of happiness was extremely high, and my dedication to spiritual practice and service was the main priority in my life. I guess that was why I was doing it. Waking up had become the only thing that I found fulfilling; the exploration of the many levels of self and my relationship to God or the Universal Truth were my passions.

For a moment I questioned if I was running away from anything at home but it was clear that things in my life were really settled. I wasn't running from anything, I was just exploring the path to freedom.

My plan was to spend a few months in India and then head home to do another long meditation retreat at the Insight Meditation Soci-ety, the center where so many of my teachers, including my father, had practiced and taught over the last twenty-five years. That would be near the end of my practice. I would have found what there was to be found in this incarnation and prepared myself for the next, projecting my consciousness up, up, and away, out the top of my head, through the Bardo, and headfirst into another womb, just to do it all over again. This being human is so strange.

I reflected back on Juvenile Hall, the group home, therapy, work-ing the steps, my early meditation practice, meeting Ajahn Amaro, my monastic teacher, the Santa Cruz Vipassana Meditation Sangha, Ramana Maharshi's teachings, Maharaji's grace, Lola and all of our failed attempts at relationship, the hospital and AIDS project, the streets and all the kids I had worked with over the years, the punks, skins, mods, rockers, skaters, B-boys, breakers, surfers, all the suffering and all the peace. I thought of Toby in prison and Shooter, Billy, Mark, Aaron, Vanessa, and Darren who were all dead. I didn't ask why anymore, I just asked how could I wake up in each situation, how could I use all of it as a teaching, the good and the bad, all of it.

As the train continued to rock on down the tracks I was not quite sleeping but drifting in and out of consciousness. As I headed somewhere, sounds, smells, tastes, all filled my senses. I wanted to watch the sunrise but my body wouldn't let me.

In Goa I hooked up with Vinny and Jennifer. It was comforting to be with two of my best friends in the world. I almost cried when I saw them, tears filling my eyes but not overflowing. They were incredibly happy to see me as well. They had been together 24/7 for four months and the tension between them was quite obvious. We were all relieved to be together again. We spent a few days on the beach, just relaxing and exchanging travel stories. Vinny, in his usual fashion, made each of his adventures sound like the most exciting or terrifying experience of his life. I was really aware of how much we had both changed over the years of our friendship. The competitive ego battles had subsided and we had both matured into dedicated spiritual practitioners.

In the evenings we played chess and made each other laugh until we were crying. After several days in Goa, a good sunburn, and all the fresh fruit and curry we could stand, we took the train south into Kerala.

December 1, 1997
"INDIA"

Having a wonderful time . . . just relaxing on the beach. Enjoying the deep conversations about God, Karma, and Fate. We have been practicing sitting meditation together, thirty minutes every day. I am so happy to be here with these two. Goa is an entirely different India than I experienced last time.

In Kerala things got kind of hectic for Vinny and Jennifer and she took off and spent a whole day alone. She wandered through temples and markets, looking for answers to the dilemma of her love for Vinny that wasn't being returned. They had begun to grow apart. Vinny was no longer in love but staying in the relationship out of his own sense of duty and guilt. Jennifer on the other hand was still very much in love with him but, feeling the growing distance, was already beginning to grieve the loss of his affection. I was sort of acting as relationship counselor for them and it put me in an awkward position. I did my best to make peace between them.

I decided to give them some time alone to figure things out, plus I needed some space to process all that had happened in the last couple of weeks. I jumped on a train headed south to another town at the southernmost tip of India called Trivandrum. On the train I met three girls from Sweden. We hung out and ended up sharing a room in Trivandrum. When the lights went out the cutest of the three, who had taken the bed next to mine, rolled over into my bunk and cuddled up with me. We began kissing and groping around in the dark. Unthinkingly, I went down on her, but she began to moan so loud that it was waking up her friends. We cooled it and just cuddled for a while until we fell asleep. It was nice to have a woman in my bed again; it had been a while. Even though we didn't have sex and it was a little frustrating to get so turned on without satisfying the desire to come, it was still a lot of fun. They split the next morning but I had to wait for Vinny and Jennifer to arrive. We said our good-byes, hoping to catch up with each other at the beach.

That day I became violently ill, with vomiting and the worst diarrhea of my life. It was then that I realized what I had done: oral sex in India! Of course I had gotten sick, I had probably picked up dysentery. By the time Vinny and Jennifer showed up I felt like I was half dead, completely dehydrated, but too sick to get out of bed, other than the regular trips to the bathroom. Since I was in the middle of my dying practice I tried to use the experience as an opportunity to let go and explore the helplessness of illness and dying. I saw the tremendous resistance I have to being sick and letting go. It was also a huge lesson in my relationship to sexual desire. I had completely lost mindfulness in the face of my lust. It was so much easier to practice dying when I was feeling well.

On the beach at Kovalum I met an Australian guy named Stu who had dreds down to his ass and a beard to his belly. He probably weighed only about ninety pounds. He had been traveling in India for a couple of years and had been sick with giardia for about half that time. We had a lot in common: he was a punk growing up and had also turned toward spiritual practice for the freedom he was seeking, practicing both Hindu yoga and Buddhist meditation.

We had a blast on the beach, eating fresh fruit and body-surfing all day. At night we sat in the restaurants by the beach, eating delicious curries and drinking frozen banana smoothies, and the conversations drifted from esoteric spiritual teachings to the roots of English punk in 1977. Stu and I decided to share a room. Vinny and Jennifer were still not getting along all that well and I needed my space from them as much as they needed their privacy to work things out.

Stu grew up in Adelaide, Australia. He had a couple of siblings and his parents were somewhat conservative folks, pharmacists, I believe. He had decided early on that he wasn't interested in their lifestyle and had become a punk in his early teens. He went along with the punk rock thing for a few years and then through his experiences with psychedelics found himself getting more into just being a freak and partying naked a lot.

Stu told me that he used to DJ at parties wearing nothing but a cooking apron. He said that he partied so much in college that when it came time to graduate with his degree in engineering, even though he had passed all his classes (some of them he took two or three times), his professors agreed to grant him his degree as long as he promised never to actually work in the field of engineering, which by that time he had no intention of doing anyway.

After college Stu had moved to this town in the middle of Australia called Alice Springs, where it is 100 degrees plus all year round. He told us stories of just traveling around naked in the bush, camping at little lakes with his crew of feral-type freaks.

He started doing yoga at some point and when I met him in India he had come to study with Iyengar. After completing a several-month training, he signed up for another one the following year and was just traveling around waiting for his next course to start. He had been in Nepal for several months but they had finally kicked him out for over-staying his visa.

Stu had been living in Pokhara with some other Aussies in a small place with a dirt floor. They hadn't changed their clothes in a couple of months and even the locals were afraid of them by the time they left. Stu was a perfect example of a punk who went off the spiritual deep end. For all of his crazy stories and the fact that he had had giardia for almost a year, he was really easy to get along with and we ended up traveling together for a couple of months.

Along with Vinny and Jennifer, Stu and I chilled on the beach for a few days, body-surfing, eating fruit and curries. In the evenings we listened to music, meditated, and talked about all of the crazy things we had all experienced in this incarnation. I think my practice was really affecting all of us; it was no longer just me looking deeply into the nature of life and death, we were all spending hours discussing our beliefs.

Stu was pretty sick, his frail body barely supporting life, but he really wanted to go to the Ramana Maharshi ashram with us. I was looking forward to returning to the ashram. It had been almost two years since I was last there and with my death looming closer I felt drawn to the nondual realms of that which was never born and will never die. Stu and I set off a few days before Vinny and Jennifer. I had written to the ashram before I left the States, so we were able to stay there. They gave us a small cottage near the main temple. Peacocks and monkeys roamed freely around the ashram's grounds. The Brahman caste priests who tended the ashram were scattered about performing rituals and practicing meditation. Stu and I settled into our room. I set up my small altar of pictures of my family and sat on my bed to meditate. My mind was filled with thoughts, desires, and fears. I began to do the self-inquiry meditation that was taught there, asking: "Who is scared? Who is wanting? Who is thinking? Who dies?" My mind became calm, the ego diffused of its control. I rested in awareness for some time before I opened my eyes feeling refreshed, peaceful, and in awe of the power of such a simple practice to transform my state of mind. Stu had fallen asleep on his bed so I didn't disturb him.

I spent most of the days meditating and practicing self-inquiry in the temple and hiking on Mount Arunachala to the various caves and temples. Some locals told us about a lake nearby that was nice to swim in. Eventually Stu and I found it and made that part of our daily ritual. His energy was really low from being sick for so long and having lost so much weight, so he was sleeping half the time we were there, and I would just hang out at the ashram and practice letting go of my identification with my body and mind. At times I felt restless about having only a few more months to live, about all of the things I would never do, never be, never see. It was clear that if I held on to any ideas, anything at all, I would suffer. All I could do was let go, let go, let go.

Easier said than done. At times I was feeling very free but at other times I was completely caught in the mind's web of desire for more of the pleasant and for freedom from anything that I didn't like.

After a couple of weeks at the ashram we had to move out because they needed the space for other guests. Vinny and Jennifer had spent about a week with us in the ashram. They were ready to hit the road and had decided that they wanted to go to Sri Lanka for a couple of weeks. Stu wanted to stay in the south for a while longer to try to heal himself. I was of the mind to go to Varanasi and spend some time on my own contemplating death at the burning ghats.

I made plans to meet up with Vinny and Jennifer in Varanasi a couple of weeks later and to catch up with Stu in Bodhgaya for a Vipassana retreat two weeks after that. We all said our farewells and I was off on the two-day train ride north to Varanasi.

In Varanasi I got a room at a guesthouse overlooking the Ganges that was full of young Japanese travelers. Every morning I woke up early and drank my chai watching the sunrise over the Ganges. Hundreds of devoted Indians were there every morning doing their prayers and rituals, bathing in the icy cold January water. I sat on the steps

near the water wrapped up in a blanket I had purchased in one of the
stalls that line the small alleys winding through Varanasi. After my
chai and morning meditation and reflection on the imminence of my
looming death, I would have some breakfast and walk down to the funeral grounds, find a place to sit, and observe the funerals and my own
mind. The site of the burning ghats where they perform the funeral
pyres for all of the Hindus who are fortunate enough to be burned by
the Ganges River is an awesome and disgusting place. It was a very
powerful practice for me to watch the bodies burning and to contemplate that my own body is just the same as those, impermanent and decaying. It was so different from my experience years earlier when I had
timidly checked out the burning ghats; this time I had a purpose and
pushed myself to sit through all of the revulsion and disgust. I went
through waves of understanding and non-identification and periods of
intense fear and regret for all of the awful shit I had done. One minute
I would be thinking about the awful hell realms I would surely be re-
born into for all of the negative Karma I had created and a few minutes
later I would be feeling very peaceful and filled with the sense that I
had purified all that shit through the many years of spiritual practice
and service. Being alone, I began to forget that my year to live was only
a practice, that I could die anytime, tomorrow or in fifty years.

When Vinny and Jennifer finally joined me I was so happy to see
them, all the contemplation of death and mortality had started to really freak me out. I had become overwhelmed with all of it and
started to feel sort of withdrawn and despondent. They were exactly
what I needed: a couple of really good friends to make me laugh and
to help me cry.

We all shared a room for a week or so. While we were in Varanasi
we found out that His Holiness the Dalai Lama was going to be giving
teachings in Bodhgaya at the same time as the meditation retreat we
had planned to attend. We all agreed that it would be wise to see His
Holiness teach instead of doing the Vipassana retreat. I decided to go
ahead and get some accommodations and meet up with Stu; Vinny
and Jennifer wanted to stay in Varanasi for a few more days anyway,
so I split.

From the train station in Gaya I took a local bus the several-mile stretch to Bodhgaya. The bus was completely full so along with several others I scrambled onto the roof. As the bus navigated the busy streets, avoiding cows, people, potholes, and traffic, I held on for my life to the luggage rack. When the bus finally pulled onto the long section of road between Gaya and Bodhgaya, I could relax.

Coming back to the place of the Buddha's enlightenment felt like coming home. Back to the familiar territory of the four noble truths and the eightfold path. I loved the Hindu rituals and practices, but Buddhism resonated at a higher frequency within me. It is kind of like my relationship to punk rock: I enjoy other forms of music but only punk can move me in that certain way that I feel in my bones.

It took me a while to find a place to stay. The town was packed with Tibetans and Westerners who had come to see the Dalai Lama. When I arrived the streets were filled with people carrying their bags around looking for somewhere to stay. For some reason I stumbled into a shack that was selling hardware. I think I needed a new lock for my bags or something. The man who ran the place asked me if I needed a place to stay. I told him that I actually needed two double rooms, for my friends and me. He called to one of his sons to show me to the guesthouse that they had recently built.

The place was still under construction, like so much of India usually was, but it had two beds and a bathroom down the hall and that was all I needed. I took a shower and settled in for a nap. It felt good to be back. I fell asleep reflecting on the story of how the Buddha had come to enlightenment in this very place some twenty-five hundred years ago. I awoke feeling disoriented and confused. The familiar yet vague feeling of fear clouded my mind. I threw on some clothes and decided to try to walk it off, thinking that I would feel better if I got outside of the boxlike room I was sleeping in.

I walked through town, past the various monasteries, temples, and shrines. When I came to the main temple, where the Bodhi tree is, I paused for a moment. Hundreds of pilgrims were walking around the temple, chanting mantras, spinning prayer wheels, doing prostrations and offerings. A group of Tibetans seemed to be performing a ritual near the tree; the smell of incense filled the air and the sound of bells and gongs greeted me out on the street where I stood watching the scene. But I wasn't feeling peaceful. I was getting angry, the fear was turning to rage, and then it became sadness. I started walking again, this time a little faster, ignoring all of the beggars and merchants. I just walked and walked until I was exhausted and far from town. Far from people, alone, walking through the fields on the outskirts of the village.

I might have just kept walking, but I was tired and hungry so I turned around and went back into town and found my way to the rows of tents the Tibetans had set up as a makeshift area of restaurants and shops. I entered a tent and sat at a table full of people but kept to myself. I ordered a bowl of noodles and soup with veggies and ate my food and left.

Back at my room I pulled my Walkman out of my bag and put on a tape of the Bad Brains, one of my favorite bands, and sat on my bed with the volume all the way up. The sadness again turned to anger. I felt all alone and alienated from all the nice Buddhists. Who was I fooling? I was a punk, not a monk. I felt like I didn't belong. I wasn't a fucking hippy like all the rest of the travelers I had seen. The music was my only refuge. As I rocked out to the hardcore rhythms and the mellow reggae beats I began to calm down, to relax and accept that I was just in a funky mood.

My bad mood and loud mind continued for a couple of days. I was full of judgmental thoughts and self-centered fears. I avoided the other Westerners and spent many hours alone, walking along the riverbed and listening to my music. I tried to meditate and pray but it didn't seem to help much. I was caught in a dazed space of confusion and doubt.

When Stu arrived I told him of my struggles. He listened and understood, reassuring me that it would pass. He also shared my contempt for the hippy crowd, even though with his dreds and beard he fit in much better than I ever would. Just being with him seemed to lift the funk. By the time Vinny and Jennifer arrived a couple of days later I was feeling much better and had returned to being excited about seeing the Dalai Lama. I began to be able to see that I was just freaking out about the focus on dying; the grief had become overwhelming and turned into depression and anger. I started doing the loving kindness and compassion meditations I had learned every morning. I began to see how I had created so much suffering for myself, pushing too hard, not accepting myself as I was. As I let go of my expectations and desires I settled into a place of more mercy and care.

January 22, 1998
"BODHGAYA"
Been down for a couple days. Confusion, feeling dazed, spaced out . . . Loud Mind . . . just not with it, no clear cause. Fear of some sort, I'm sure.

[A few days later] . . . the fog lifted just before the teachings started and a new clarity has taken its place. I've been highly inspired by the teaching on compassion.

The day before the teachings began I finally made it into the main temple to visit the place of the Buddha's enlightenment. There were hundreds of people sitting around listening to a Tibetan lama speak about the practice of Phowa, the Tibetan death meditation. It was the last day of a week of teachings. I could have attended the whole thing if I hadn't been so busy trying to avoid my grief. But it was nice to hear some of the final talk and witness the empowerment that the lama was performing.

Vinny was filming some rituals that were being performed at one of the smaller shrines and Stu and Jennifer had taken a walk around the temple grounds. I went and sat near the Bodhi tree and reaffirmed my commitment to the path of awakening. One thing was clear: spiritual practice was the only thing that had brought any amount of peace into my life. I still got angry, was still judgmental and full of lust and desire, but my relationship to the world had changed. My relationship to my mind had changed. I reflected on how far I had come in the ten years since I had begun on the spiritual path. I felt silly for judging myself for what I wasn't doing rather than rejoicing for what I was doing.

The next morning we all got up early and made our way to the large tents that had been constructed to house the couple of thousand people who had come to see the Dalai Lama. As Westerners we were given our own section to sit in. We set up our cushions and blankets on the ground and waited for the teachings to begin. As I glanced around the crowd that surrounded us, I saw many of the people who days earlier I had been so averse to; the aversion was mostly gone. Those I had previously seen as pretentious hippies I began to see as sincere seekers. I realized that I was no different from them; we were all there for the same reason. My feelings of separation began to melt into a feeling of interconnectedness. The costumes we chose were meaningless; the desire for freedom was our common bond.

As His Holiness the Dalai Lama entered and took his place on the elaborate throne that had been created in the front of the tent we all stood up, bowing low with hands together in reverence. After performing his own ritual he waved for us all to be seated and laughed a little in his childlike way. I was mesmerized by his presence; he emanated a sense of so much wisdom and compassion. I couldn't help but smile and feel like I was somehow blessed to be in his presence.

The teachings, which lasted for five days, focused on the cultivation of bodhicitta, the arousal of the compassionate heart, and ended in a bodhisattva vow of empowerment: setting the intention to use one's life and all subsequent lives to help alleviate the suffering of others until all beings are eventually liberated. I understood the teachings much better this time, being more familiar with the Tibetan tradition and also having had more direct experience of the wisdom of the compassionate heart that naturally arises out spiritual practice. It was a pivotal experience for my spiritual practice. Before those teachings I had been aware that my spiritual practice benefited others in unknowable ways but it was during the third day of the teachings that I realized that my motivation for spiritual practice could actually be for the benefit of all beings rather than just for myself. From that point on I began offering the merit of my life's energy to the liberation of all beings.

On the final day of the teachings I took the bodhisattva vow. With sincerity and faith I vowed to cultivate compassion for all living beings and to postpone my own final liberation until all beings had been freed from the cycle of rebirth in Samsara. I tied the red protection cord that had been blessed by His Holiness around my wrist as a constant reminder of my intention.

After the teachings we all traveled to New Delhi. Arriving in the middle of the night, we took a cab to a guesthouse in the tourist section of town. It was about four o'clock in the morning, so we just sat around waiting for the owners to give us a room. I decided to go to sleep in one of the dorm beds. After falling asleep for a few minutes I was awakened by the sounds of arguing at the front desk. The owners finally got up to give us a room but they were trying to tell us that Stu couldn't stay with us because he had dreadlocks; they were saying he was "a bad Sadhu." I got so fucking angry that they wouldn't let him stay there, that we had to deal with those prejudiced bastards in the middle of the night, that I grabbed a big stick and started threatening the owner.

We were all totally freaking out and yelling at that poor ignorant Indian fellow. They were yelling back, "You get out, no stay here, get out now!" We finally left, but not before Vinny defaced their sign with something like "Fascist Bastards."

Standing outside with all of our bags, with the sun rising over the city, I had to laugh at myself. The day before I had taken a vow to be compassionate and there I was threatening some crazy Indian man with a stick. The absurdity of it made me laugh. I was very far from being a bodhisattva but at least I was trying.

We sat in a café across the street, drinking chai and arguing about what to do next. Stu and I went in search of lodging and Jennifer and Vinny stayed with the bags at the café. We found a cool place to stay but that night it got hectic again. Vinny and Jennifer were on the brink of breaking up. He was ready to throw in the towel; with not enough sleep and too much drama, he wanted out of the relationship. She said she was going to go to Nepal alone to meet her mom. I was stuck in the middle; not wanting Jennifer to go alone to Nepal, I thought I might have to go with her.

For a minute there it looked like their relationship was over. I don't even remember what the fight was about. But right at the last moment

Vinny came around and decided that he needed to stay with her no matter what until they got back to the States. So they both went to Nepal and I stayed in New Delhi with Stu.

I'd had just about enough of India; my trip felt like it was coming to an end. I had been in India for a little over three months and I had only four more months to live. When I was on the phone with my mom, she asked me if I wanted to come home from India and go to Costa Rica with her. It sounded like a good idea. I mostly just wanted to try to spend some time with Mom, but hell, going to Costa Rica sounded pretty fun too.

The day I was leaving New Delhi, Stu said to me, "Well, mate, if nothing else, this whole trip has been worth it because I made a great friend." I knew exactly what he was talking about. It's so rare to meet a true friend. Although we hadn't known each other for all that long we had been through a lot together. Stu was the craziest punk rock Sadhu I had ever met. He taught me a lot about being willing to die for the practice that had saved our lives.

I stopped over in New York to visit Micah on the way home to California. The night after I got back to the States I went to a hardcore show in the East Village. It was one of those times when I really saw the extremes of my life: one day I'm in India chillin' with the Dalai Lama, and a few days later I'm in NYC seeing some hardcore bands called Bloodlet and Hatebreed.

Walking into Coney Island High on St. Mark's, I noticed the calm and openness of my months in India congealing into my old self-image of a tough punker. I took my place against the wall and tried to soften my belly; I wanted to practice being open to the moment even in the midst of the New York hardcore scene. The bands blasted out powerful anthems of grinding hate and rage at the injustices of our world. I wasn't fully connecting; at the time I was feeling sort of mellow. But it was a bit of a shock to my system and I liked that. These were my peers, my generation, the beings for whom I had vowed, while sitting beneath the Bodhi tree, to dedicate the merit of my life's energy.

The violent thrashing about of bodies, the release of so much pent-up aggression, began to spill over from the pit in the front of the stage and waves of people were being shoved in all directions. As I got smashed against the wall a couple of times some of my energy came to the surface and I shoved the crowd back toward the front of the room.

By the time Hatebreed was halfway through their set I was up front, swinging my arms and slamming about in the pit. It felt great to be able to completely let go of any ideas or concepts about being spiritual and just allow the raw power of my own aggression to be released. I had walked in feeling mellow but the music elicited the easily accessible energies lying just beneath the surface. It was great fun and a needed catharsis. I left feeling more alive, embodied, and awake than before.

Back in California I visited friends, sharing stories and pictures of my travels and practice. I saw some good punk rock shows, ate at all my favorite restaurants, and even picked up a couple of shifts at the health department. I felt a lot different than when I had left several months earlier. I felt more grounded in my spiritual practice, yet like I had a lot less understanding of how it all works. My faith was becoming verified through experience but a lot of what I thought I had known about spiritual practice began to seem much less certain. With only a couple of months left of my practice, I was opening to the mysteriousness of it all.

My mom and I planned to spend a couple of weeks together in Costa Rica. She had invited my sister Becky to come along. And one of my good friends, Darden, had also wanted to come. So the four of us set off on the Central American expedition. I saw it as my opportunity to try to deepen the forgiveness and gratitude practice I had started with my mother so many lifetimes earlier.

After arriving at the airport in San Jose, the largest city in Costa Rica, we spent the first night at a cheap hotel. The place was small and not very clean, which was fine for Darden and me, who had both done a lot of backpacking, but challenging for my sister's fine taste and my mother's expectation of cleanliness. The place was a lot nicer than the dingy little rooms in India I had been living in, but certainly substandard for the American tourist.

In the morning, after coffee and breakfast, we took a bus to the Caribbean coast, where we were staying with the son of my mom's neighbor, who owned a hotel down there. He put us up in his house, which was really nice but it was one of those open-air places with no windows so it was incredibly hot.

I shared a room with my mom and we spent lazy days under the fan and wandering the beaches and jungles. In the evenings we kids would go out to the dance club or hang out in the restaurants that were open late. Mom would retire early and curl up with her book. The heat was beginning to really get to her. With her natural, menopausal hot flashes, which already burned through her body, the ninety-degree-plus humidity was becoming unbearable.

After about a week Mom decided that she wanted air-conditioning and a pool. I tried to accommodate her as best I could. We found a place on the other side of the country, on the Pacific coast, that was exactly what she wanted: swim-up bar, fine dining, and air-conditioning. I was trying to see my practice as acceptance and appreciation. I wasn't doing anything special to heal any of the past difficulties, I was just trying to be a living amends for all of the pain I had caused her in my youth.

April 4, 1998
"COSTA RICA"
Soften the belly and let go. Mom's been up and down, between scream-ing and laughing. Me? I'm dying soon and still full of attachment fear, judgments, and ego . . . my life has passed with so much learned and loved and experienced. I am prepared to do it all over again and learn the truth over and over.

We spent the second week swimming and eating at the resort. A friend of mine from Santa Cruz, Nick, was working in the hotel next door, so he and I went out surfing a few times and checked out the discos with Becky and Darden. There were times when I had to ques-tion how all of that had anything to do with my investigation of my dying practice. Perhaps it didn't but I was having a good time and so was my mom and that was all that mattered.

I had registered for a meditation retreat at the Insight Meditation Society in Massachusetts, so I flew back to the East Coast. I still had my trusty little Toyota in Connecticut, at my friend Becky's, so I picked it up and drove up to Barre, Massachusetts, for my retreat. The retreat was on the practice of Metta (loving kindness). We spent ten days in silence cultivating love toward ourselves, our teachers, and our enemies, eventually extending it out in all directions to touch all beings. As in the retreats I had attended in the past, the practice was sitting and walking meditation, but rather than focusing on mindfulness this was a concentration practice of the heart. Most of the retreat was surprisingly pleasant. I was entirely pleased to see how much ease I had with opening to love and compassion, how very few obstructions, resentments, or fears remained. I had done my best to come to terms with my life and I was ready to let go into the unknown regions of death.

My year was coming to an end. With less than a month to live, after the retreat I packed up my car and headed back to California to die among family and friends. My buddies from Santa Cruz, Fury 66, were on a U.S. tour. Richmond, Virginia, was as far east as they were going, so I decided to drive down there and hook up with them for a week of punk rock on the way west. The tour was incredibly fun: slam dancing every night, bad food, silly kids. The shows were small so it was my job to get the kids dancing. I would just start running around in a circle and soon enough there was always a slam pit. I decided to follow them as far as New Mexico, where I stopped to see my parents in the final days of my practice.

I thought of what it would be like to see my parents for the last time if I were to really die in a matter of days. Driving into New Mexico from Colorado, where I had departed from the boys in Fury, I reflected on our relationship. My earliest memories of my father, his glowing warmth and wisdom, the struggles of my youth with Ondrea, all of the jealousy I had felt toward her. Our relationship had come full circle. I couldn't imagine what my life would have been like without her loving presence. I remembered sitting in the lawyer's office at sixteen, signing the emancipation document that was setting me free from parental rules. Little had I known about all of the rules and regulations I was trading them for as I headed into a couple of years of being in and out of the juvenile justice system.

My relationship with them seemed like it had already been through several incarnations. It felt like we had traversed the hardest of terrains and come out on the peak of a summit. Below us lay the past, all of the paths we had taken to arrive at the splendid view of the valleys and villages; above were the endless spiritual realms—so much more to experience, so much further to go.

Pulling off the highway and onto the long dirt road that wound through the pine trees and over the sage-covered mesas that surrounded their home, I knew I wasn't ready to say good-bye. I tried to comfort myself by thinking that we were not these bodies and that our relationship would continue regardless of our physical form.

I was greeted in the driveway by the rottweilers. My parents were at their bedroom window waving for me to come into the house. Leaving my bags in the downstairs office that would serve as my room for the next couple of days, I joined them in the living room. I savored their hugs, holding on a little longer than usual, my heart beating heavily in my chest. My father's eyes said that he understood. We probably could have just sat there and cried but I was still pretending to be okay. He had once told me that if someone says that they have their shit together, they are probably standing in it. I was standing in it, too, proud to be vulnerable, too scared to admit it.

In her usual, motherly way, Ondrea offered to make me some food, but I wasn't hungry yet. The burrito I'd eaten for lunch had been more than enough. We sat on the couches and spoke of my travels, all of the practice and adventures I'd had in the months since we'd seen each other. They were both glowing with pride in how my life was turning out.

Before sunset I took the dogs for a walk, hiking the hill behind their home. I sat on a large boulder that overlooked the house and wilderness in all directions. A strange calm came over me; the fear and trepidation vanished and as the sun began to set over the mesa I realized how blessed I was to have taken birth into my family. I had experienced the perfect amount of suffering to bring me to spiritual practice and the perfect amount of love and encouragement to continue on the path. I realized that the external support of my parents had been internalized, that I had all that I needed to deepen my exploration. The legal emancipation at sixteen was finally becoming a spiritual emancipation at twenty-seven.

After a two-day drive through the desert I made it back to Santa Cruz and to my surprise Micah was there too. He had decided to move back to the West Coast. New York had been fun but he was ready to get back to the lazy days in the California sunshine. Joe was back from tour. So for those final days of my practice we had most of the crew back together. We all hung out, going to the beach, sitting around sharing stories of our adventures, and joking around. I took some time and wrote out a mock will, leaving my records to Joe, my books to Vinny and Micah, and the rest of my belongings to my siblings. I asked in my will that my tattooed skin be removed and made into wallets for all my friends and that a fruit-bearing tree be planted on my grave.

My mom and I took some long walks on the beach at low tide, throwing the stick for her dog and talking about how wonderful life had become for both of us. I expressed my deepest gratitude for all of the love and support she had shown me over the years and told her how happy I was that she had overcome her own struggles and come out the other side an incredible woman and mother.

The last night of my year-to-live practice, June 30, 1998, the night that I was to die, I made a huge feast for my mother, brother, and sister and Vinny, Jennifer, Joe, his girlfriend Mikala, and Micah. At dinner I read to them my own eulogy and thanked each one individually for all that they had brought to my life. We all stayed up late looking at old pictures and telling stories of our lives together. A little after midnight everyone went home and I went to bed.

After contemplating all that I had learned and experienced in my year of investigating death, I died peacefully and awoke the next morning reincarnated, ready for the next teaching.

July 1, 1998
"Dead"

Nothing left unsaid, all has been done to the best of my ability. So much attachment remains . . . but it all floats in an openness that feels incarnations old. Through all of the searching I have finally taken birth . . . and I see that love is the only rational act of a lifetime.

19

Reincarnation

I stayed in Santa Cruz for a while, enjoying my friendships and the feeling of being at home with the people I love. On the fourth of July, Vinny and Jennifer finally split up and he and Micah decided to move up to San Francisco. I got hooked up with a great apartment in downtown Santa Cruz that needed some work done to it so I took it and ended up completely remodeling the place with some help from Vinny. When we were finished I had a great place to live, for cheap rent. I decided to stay in Santa Cruz, even though I was tempted to move back to San Francisco with those guys. I was working for the

AIDS program again, doing HIV testing, and I also started some drug and alcohol counseling groups at a couple of local high schools.

Through the county health department I got involved in some mentoring programs, working directly with young men who were struggling with school and drugs. I gathered together a few guys I was working with and we all went to a conference in Los Angeles to meet with all of the different mentoring groups around the state. The whole thing was funded by a program called the Male Involvement Project. They flew us down to L.A. and we attended the conference, meeting with mentors and teens from all the counties, attending workshops and performing rituals.

At the conference I led a small workshop on forgiveness, teaching the basic Buddhist principles of loving kindness and compassion. Eric, one of the other mentors attending my workshop, had a very powerful and emotional experience of forgiveness for his father during the guided meditation. He said that for the first time in his life he was able to really connect with the suffering he felt around his relationship with his father and began to touch it with some forgiveness. It was a healing that was just ready to happen and the meditation had allowed his heart to break through the long-held pain and separation.

After the class Eric and I spoke for some time about his experience. It turned out that we had a lot in common. He too had been a punk junkie in his youth and was also now in recovery. He was also tattooed and still into the punk scene. In college he had studied religion and through the steps was beginning to practice meditation. He was now working with young men, trying to be of service, just as I was.

Over the years Eric and I remained in contact, eventually even attending teachings from the Dalai Lama together in Mountain View a couple of years later. He became one of my closest friends, another brother on the spiritual path—another punk for the inner revolution.

In India, Vinny and I had spoken about how we could best use our life's energy to help others. I felt that for me it was through counseling and teaching spiritual practice so I decided to go back to college to get my degree. It just seemed that although I don't like school much it would allow me the opportunity to do the work that best fit my personal intentions. Vinny also spoke about the possibility of going to college but he seemed to feel less optimistic about the possibilities of really succeeding. He had been working construction for so long and making such good money that although he hated what he was doing and really wanted to do something that felt like it was more in line with his spiritual practice, he couldn't see how he could ever really get out of it. I encouraged him to just start taking some classes with me and he said he would try, but never did.

(A year or so later I told Vinny about an organization that I had been doing some training with called Challenge Associates that went into high schools and facilitated daylong workshops on understanding how oppression works, directly addressing racism, sexism, and all the other isms. Through a series of well-planned activities and group process they taught the kids how to live from a place of appreciating differences and often brought about a huge cathartic experience and healing. The organization was looking for new teachers and I thought it was a powerful and much-needed process and was convinced that Vinny, with his natural leadership qualities and maturing spiritual practice, would be a great teacher. He was interested in checking it out and quickly became a workshop leader for the organization.

Vinny realized his intention to be of service and use his spiritual understanding to help others. He now travels around the country leading workshops helping thousands of kids survive high school every year. His success is inspiring, in a lot of ways he has been one of my most important teachers.)

I remembered hearing about a school in San Francisco that was integrating Eastern and Western approaches to psychology and spirituality, called the California Institute of Integral Studies (CIIS), so I began checking into what they had to offer and found out about a program they offered that allowed you to finish your degree in one year of attending school on weekends. That sounded a lot better than another two years of university.

I applied to California Institute of Integral Studies to attend their bachelor of arts completion program. After being accepted, I started classes and was commuting to the city from Santa Cruz on the weekends.

My life felt like it had taken on a new dimension. With the year-to-live practice came an incredible amount of inner freedom. I was connecting with friends and family in what felt like an entirely new way; the subtle fears and posturing were gone. At work I couldn't have been happier, counseling people about safe sex and ways to be aware of risk and encouraging them to be wise and careful with the use of drugs and alcohol.

I sold the Toyota and picked up a 1965 Chevrolet Impala from a friend and began fixing it up. I was going to the city a lot on the weekends for school and to see friends up there. Joe and I were spending a lot of time together and eventually he ended up moving in with me for a while. My Dharma practice and the punk ethic were becoming seamless; it began to feel like one world instead of two. We would go to meditation classes and punk shows, hang out at the coffee shop or on the streets, and talk about Buddhism. The spiritual practice that once had made me feel disconnected from the punk scene was coming full circle and allowing me to feel more connected to punk rock than ever before. I understood more clearly, from the inside out, the discontent that fuels punk. My perspective had changed but my connection to the revolutionary music and lifestyle was growing even stronger. It became clear that it was the same energy, the same search for freedom, which I had once channeled into the rage of my drug-induced punk rock rebellion, that was being redirected into my spiritual practice. All of the anger at injustice and rage against the system

was still in me, only I was relating to it differently. I had found the solution to my once-hopeless situation and lack of faith had been replaced by a verified understanding of the path to freedom from
suffering. I knew that the path led upstream, against the current, and
was the most rebellious thing I had ever done.

When I moved to the city I called up Spirit Rock Meditation Center in Marin to see if there were any opportunities for me to work
with the kids or teens there. Jack Kornfield and some other Dharma
teachers had built Spirit Rock as a Buddhist retreat center and a
place for the Buddhist community of the Bay Area to gather, study,
and practice. They were offering classes and retreats for adults,
teens, children, and families. I had seen Jack a year or so earlier at a
benefit event for Ram Dass (after his stroke) that my parents were
teaching at. Jack had somewhat casually mentioned to me that I
should come help out with the teens and family program, so when I
was back in the city that's what I did. I started volunteering on teen
and family days and helping a woman named Lisa with the Monday
night kids' class.

On the weekends I often had school or retreats. I tried to get some
time to hang out down at 222 or go to punk shows or movies with
Scott and Vinny.

Shortly after moving back to the city I got a call from Lola. She had
been sober for a couple of years and wanted to make amends to me.
We got together at a coffee shop near my house and had lunch together. She looked as beautiful as ever, even after all of the shit we
had been through I still had a place in my heart for her, probably always would. In her amends she asked me to forgive her for all of the
ways she had been selfish, dishonest, or acted out of fear. She spoke
at length about some of the ways she had been confused, dependent,
and harmful and she went on to tell me about the insights, clarity,
and healing that had taken place in her life since she had gotten
sober, worked the steps, and been in therapy.

I accepted her amends and offered my own, also asking for forgiveness for all of the ways I had been unskillful. It was great to see her
doing so well. It was inspiring to see that she had come to a place of

peace with what had happened in our relationship and all of the difficulties she had experienced.

We departed with a friendly kiss, going our own ways, closing that
chapter of our lives.

Micah had moved to Thailand to be with a woman he'd fallen in love
with on his last trip out there. We were keeping in touch by e-mail
and Scott and I went to Thailand and visited them that year.

Scott had never been to Asia before. Neither of us had much time;
with his busy schedule tattooing, painting, and writing and my school
and work schedule, we had only a couple of weeks for the trip. We had
spoken about trying to go to Angkor Wat in Cambodia but with the
limited time we had to travel we chose to just stay in Thailand the
whole trip. Micah didn't know I was coming; I wanted to surprise
him. Scott and Micah had never met so I wrote to Micah and told him
that I had a friend who was going to be in Bangkok who he should
show around. Scott and I got a room at a guesthouse on Kao San Road
the night we arrived and the next day he called up Micah and his girlfriend, Boom, to let them know he was there and that he would like to
hook up.

The guesthouse we stayed at was clean but sparse; it had that familiar smell of Asian filth. The smell from years of tourists sweating
themselves to sleep in a drunken stupor on the sagging mattresses
and from the smoke-stained walls was barely hidden beneath the
freshly whitewashed walls and neatly folded terry cloth blankets. I had
stayed in much worse rooms over the years and it was certainly a step
up from the cells of my youth, but Scott was a little bit shocked by the
realities of the exotic land that he had expected, just as I had been
years earlier on my first trip to Thailand. But Scott took it all in stride
and was a great traveling partner.

When Micah showed up and Scott and I were both sitting at a table
in one of the open-air restaurants that line Kao San Road, he just

looked at me, in his usual cool manner, with a huge smile on his face, and said, "I knew you were coming." He met Scott and I met Boom. We all just sat around and laughed for a couple hours, catching up on our life's adventures and drinking banana milkshakes.

We spent a few days taking in the sights of Bangkok, checking out the temples, strip bars, and endless markets. Boom and Micah were both working but we talked Micah into taking a few days off and traveling up to Chang Mai with us. Our friend Keri, who we had traveled with years earlier, was also in Thailand on a buying trip for an import business she was trying to set up. Scott knew her from the tattoo scene in San Francisco; she had dated a couple of his close friends and they were old friends. So we made arrangements to meet up with her in Chang Mai.

Seeing Keri again was great. She had been living in L.A. with some famous actor. We all shared a big room in a guesthouse and stayed up most of the night laughing hysterically about stupid little inside jokes that we had all cultivated over years of well-practiced silliness. It was one of the funnest times I had ever had, just sitting around laughing, enjoying the absurdity of life with some friends.

We spent the days trekking through the multitudes of Buddhist monasteries, trying to find one where Scott and I could get tattooed in the traditional Thai Buddhist hand poke style. Although we were un-successful in getting tattooed, we had a great time seeing the sights and scaring the monks— these two big Americans, already tattooed from head to toe, asking if we could get tattooed at their monastery.

In the night market we ran into a bunch of Thai street punks, com-plete with studded leather jackets, tattoos, mohawks, and Rancid patches. At the time Scott was living with Lars, so it was even more striking to be on the other side of the world and see your roommate's band covering the back of kids' jackets. We even saw some kids wear-ing T-shirts that Scott had done the art for.

After a few days in Chang Mai we all returned to Bangkok, re-trieved Boom, and went to the ancient capital city of Ayutthaya to see the ruins of the once flourishing and simple Buddhist kingdom, which had been slowly replaced by the urban sprawl of Bangkok.

Walking through the ruins and recently excavated sites, sitting beneath the decaying statues of Buddha, sharing with Scott the limited information I had on the history of the ancient Thai kingdom, I felt a palatable sense of faith and devotion to the spiritual path that had become the focus of my life.

Our last few days were spent in the weekend market, shopping for gifts to bring home to friends and family. The market goes on for miles in every direction and you can find everything from Asian antiques to Air Jordan basketball sneakers. It was a lot of fun to spend a couple weeks with Scott, great to see Micah again, and especially nice to meet Boom. I was surprised by her quick wit and great sense of humor. She was strikingly beautiful and extremely friendly. Other than Micah, Scott, Keri, and I were the first Americans she had met. It must have been sort of shocking that all of us were so heavily tattooed. Micah doesn't have any ink but all three of the people she had met were covered. But she was unfazed, totally accepting, and even curious. Micah was her first boyfriend and they were completely in love and planning to marry.

The flight home was a day sooner than Scott and I had thought, a mistake on my part in the planning. We had a ten-hour layover in Hong Kong. I was excited to go and check out the city, never having been there before, but Scott was really pissed at me for fucking up the itinerary. He had really enjoyed Thailand and would have liked to stay but I had to get back to school and work. It took him a few hours to forgive me and start speaking to me again. In Hong Kong we got the train into town and walked around for a few hours, eating some good food and wandering through the endless malls and street markets.

20

Inside Out

toby got out of prison and we spent some time together. He was really starting to get into spiritual practice and had had some powerful experiences with meditation and prayer while he was locked up. He had been reading Bo Lozoff's books and also studying the Bible and going to twelve-step meetings but like so many others he found that it was much more difficult to maintain all of that when he was out of prison than when he was in.

A few days after he got out he hooked up with a woman named Alicia who we had both known from growing up. Toby called me up and told me that he had run into her at a coffee shop in downtown Santa Cruz and that he wanted to ask her out. My question for him was, "Is she sober?" because I knew that Alicia had been strung out at one point and the last thing Toby needed was a girlfriend who was using drugs. He said she was sober and they were even going to meetings together.

They started dating and the first time they had sex she got pregnant. When Toby found out he freaked out and relapsed, overdosing on heroin and getting sent to the hospital and then back to prison for a few months. I visited him in the hospital. It was hard for him to look at me, feeling like he had disappointed me or something. I was disappointed, but more than that I was scared for him. I just told him that I loved him no matter what and that I would always be there for him. He did a few months in the pen and got out about a week before Alicia gave birth.

The day their son, Gage, was born Toby called me and asked if I would be the godfather to his new son. I of course agreed and was honored to continue to be a positive influence in Toby's life. He had stayed sober for a few months while he was in prison and was really trying to walk the spiritual path of recovery.

Alicia and Toby got an apartment together and things looked good but he ended up relapsing again and the first time I saw my godson was to visit his dad, my best friend, in the Santa Cruz county jail. Instead of sending him back to prison they put him in a rehabilitation program for addicts. After a couple months in rehab he was released and reunited with his son and girlfriend.

Things were going very well for him for a while and he even came and stayed with me in the city a couple of times, helping me with some teen meditation and sweat lodge ceremonies I was leading at Spirit Rock. It seemed that he had hit his final bottom and was really ready to do what it took to stay clean. We were talking fairly regularly but I was very busy with school and work, and there were still some boundaries that I was keeping between us because I loved him so much and it had been really painful to see him going in and out of prison.

I had started getting invitations to do more teaching. I started a weekly meditation group and got more involved with the family program at Spirit Rock.

The year-to-live practice had helped me let go of all expectations of ever getting to teach. I decided that now I would just show up for whatever manifested in my life. I wasn't out looking for anything or really trying to do anything or be anyone. I was just showing up for the opportunities that presented themselves, just saying yes to life.

After only ten years of being in and out of college I finally graduated with a bachelor's degree from CIIS. And that was cause to celebrate.

After my graduation ceremony I had a big dinner party and about fifty of my close friends showed up. It was one of those incredible times when all of my worlds came together: all the guys from the tattoo shop, a bunch of folks from the Buddhist community, old punk rockers from Santa Cruz, sober friends, and of course my family. It was both wonderful and overwhelming to have so many people coming to support and celebrate my accomplishment. It wasn't just a celebration of graduating, it was a celebration of having survived my fucked-up youth and actually coming to a place of great happiness and a deep feeling of usefulness in the world. But considering I basically dropped out of school when I was fifteen, it was kind of impressive that I had actually gotten a college degree.

Shortly after I started working at Spirit Rock I got a call from the San Francisco Zen Center and was invited to help them start a rites-of-passage program for teenagers in their community. I felt incredibly honored and excited about working with the Zen Center. Although my main Buddhist practice was Vipassana, I had been deeply inspired by Shunryu Suzuki-Roshi's book *Zen Mind, Beginner's Mind.* The idea of creating a rites-of-passage and mentoring program felt like a coming together of all the work that I had been doing in the high schools, juvenile halls, AIDS programs, and Buddhist community. I was directly mentored by Norman Fischer, who had done a similar two-year group with some boys from the Zen Center that had inspired our program.

I interviewed for and was accepted into the master's program in integral counseling psychology at CIIS. I was really pleased to get in and grad school started the week after I finished undergrad. I felt like I should just keep up the momentum that I had started, so I went straight into it. My life was unrecognizable to me sometimes. How the hell had I ended up in grad school? It seemed so established and respectable, at times I felt like an impostor. "What is a punker like me doing studying psychotherapy with a bunch of hippies and yuppie do-gooders?" I often wondered.

When I moved back to San Francisco I ran into my old friend Mike from Santa Cruz, the guy who, in my youth, had mentored me in the ways of motorcycles and madness. I saw him at a twelve-step meeting and he asked me if I would be his sponsor, if I would help him work the steps. I agreed and it was really incredible to see what a full circle our relationship had come, from bikes and violence to sobriety and spiritual practice.

Mike eventually became very involved in meditation practice and has taken a prominent role in spreading the message of the spiritual revolution, often sending people from the bar he worked in to my meditation classes. After a couple of years of his own recovery and Buddhist meditation practice he quit his job at the bar and got involved in hospice work and community service. The full circle of our relationship has been one of the most fulfilling experiences of my life. He had mentored me all those years ago, and then it was my turn to mentor him.

At Spirit Rock I used my position as family program director to start a series of daylong meditation retreats exclusively for people in their twenties and thirties as a way of building community and sharing the

Dharma with my peers. It was incredible training for me to get to teach those days alongside some of my teachers. Probably the most important for me personally was when I began doing some teaching with Ajahn Amaro, who by then had moved to California, was in the process of establishing a monastery in Mendocino County, and was very involved in teaching at Spirit Rock. For me to get to study with him again, so many years after that retreat of his I had attended in 1993, was enough of a gift, but actually sharing the podium with him was truly incredible. He was very supportive of my teaching and to this day continues to be one of the teachers I connect with regularly.

21

Being Here Now

I woke up in a small, unfamiliar room, alone. For a moment I was confused and disoriented. Looking around, I saw that the walls were blank, giving me no clue as to my whereabouts. The small sink in the corner of the room reminded me of many cells that I had awoken in before, but in that room there was a door and it was not locked. I could get up and just walk away if I wanted to. I knew no one was forcing me to be there.

As I wiped the sleep out of my eyes I recalled that I actually had to get special permission to volunteer as Ram Dass's attendant to be there. It was the conference of "Buddhist Teachers in the West" at Spirit Rock Meditation Center. Just about every teacher from every Buddhist tradition had come and the Dalai Lama was going to show up today. I needed to get up and go help Ram Dass get dressed and ready for the day but I just lay in bed for a few minutes reflecting on how similar that room was to the cell I had begun meditating in ten years earlier and how strange it was that I was still alive. More than still alive: I was extremely happy, fulfilled, and walking through life with a sense of meaning and purpose that had just become natural and easy.

It hadn't always been that way. There were so many years of struggle and refusal of the work that I knew had to be done, and then the many, many hours of sitting on the cushion, with the therapist, at my meetings, and eventually with others. I was doing my best to work for the benefit of other people—teaching, using my life's energy to the best of my ability, being of service.

That's why it was such an incredible experience to be serving as Ram Dass's attendant. He was one of the people who had really inspired my father to teach and serve. So it felt like such a gift to be able to serve him after his stroke, to care for the man who helped open up the West to spiritual practice in the sixties. It was my hope that I would be able to do a tenth of the good for my generation that he had done for his. I'd known Ram Dass since I was a kid, but to me he had always just been like an uncle, Dad's best friend. To be able to help him, as an adult and a student, was a blessing.

In the meditation hall the excitement in the air was palpable; as I rolled Ram Dass in we were stopped many times by other teachers who wanted to tell him how much his work had influenced their lives. Maneuvering his wheelchair to our place in the back of the hall, I felt so incredibly blessed to have the opportunity to be there. I was hoping, like everyone else, to get a blessing from His Holiness the Dalai

Lama. The friendly looks I got from everyone there made me feel welcome and a part of everything, even though I was the youngest one in the room and the only one there who had not been teaching meditation for at least ten years.

As His Holiness entered the room everyone stood and with hands together in reverence bowed deeply for that simple Buddhist monk from Tibet, the fourteenth incarnation of the Dalai Lama. I was moved, both by my own feelings of respect and reverence for the Dalai Lama and also by the humility and love that was exuding from all of the teachers in the room, from so many countries and traditions, both monks and nuns as well as lay teachers. There were Zen masters, lamas and rinpoches, ajahns and venerable teachers, as well as most of the senior American teachers. It was one of the most inspiring moments of my life.

With my hands together in Anjali and my back bent to try to keep my head lower than His Holiness', my eyes followed his every movement. As he rose from the podium and prepared himself to exit the hall, he rearranged his robes and exchanged a few words with Jack Kornfield. We had been gathered to hear him address the Spirit Rock community. I'd somewhat unintentionally positioned myself on the aisle and I realized that as he exited the room he would probably touch my hands and bow to me, offering a blessing, as he would do with all the others in his path.

As the Dalai Lama approached, everything seemed to get very still and I could feel each minute sensation of my breath coming and going. My jaw was getting sore from smiling so much and my back was beginning to get slightly fatigued from bowing for so long. As he finished blessing the lady standing next to me we made eye contact and I had the experience of slightly leaving my body, like I was observing the whole scene from about five inches above the top of my head. His Holiness stopped directly in front of me and took my arms into his hands, staring at the tattoos of Buddha and Krishna, then looked back into my eyes and then again down at my arms, and exclaimed, "Very colorful!" My whole body was vibrating and I felt a warm energy that started at my toes and exited through my mouth in the form of laughter, joined by the laughter and praise of everyone else in the room.

I continued to bow, turning to watch him exit the room and turn the corner, followed by his Tibetan guards and the Secret Service personnel. As I straightened up I caught some of the approving glances and acknowledgments from many of my teachers and friends in the audience.

The next week I was the attendant and driver for a group of monastics, including Ajahn Amaro, who went to Los Angeles to see His Holiness the Dalai Lama give public teachings. For me the opportunity to spend so many days with my teachers was an incredible opportunity. It was on this trip that I began to find out a little more about the lives that some of the monks led before ordaining and what had inspired them to commit their life to monasticism. As I spoke about the Dharma Punx and the way I was trying to integrate the punk ethic and Buddhist practice several of the monks shared that they too had been into the early punk scene before ordaining. Ajahn Amaro told me of being in London in the mid-seventies at the inception of the punk movement and seeing some of the earliest punk rock bands live, including bands such as the Damned, Debby Harry, and Television. He spoke of listening to the Clash record daily the last few months before he went off to Thailand in 1977 and became a monk. Since he hadn't really listened to any music since then, he could still recite most of the lyrics from the record. I was more than impressed; he had been my teacher for many years but I never knew that we had so much in common.

Another monk I had just met who was with us, Ajahn Santikaro, had been the abbot of a popular monastery in southern Thailand for the past several years. He told me of his youth, growing up in Chicago and being involved in the punk scene for years before getting interested in Buddhism and going to Thailand to ordain. He said he had collected all the early vinyl of both American and English punk bands.

Needless to say I was very impressed and inspired by this discovery that I wasn't the only punk who had turned to the Dharma for answers to the questions that my life had brought up. We had long discussions about the ways in which punk and Dharma practice support each other. We agreed that at least to some extent the whole punk movement is based on the Buddha's first noble truth, the truth of suffering and the dissatisfactory nature of the material world. The punks see through the lies of society and the oppressive dictates of modern consumer culture. Very few punks though seem to take it further and attempt to understand the causes and conditions of the suffering and falsehoods; unfortunately punks rarely come around to seeing that there is actually a solution and a path to personal freedom.

My own life's experience with both Dharma practice and punk rock inspired me to try to bridge the gap between the two. I've tried to help point out the similarities, while also acknowledging the differences, and to show those of my generation who are interested that they can practice meditation and find there the freedom we have been seeking in our rebellion against the system. The monks were all very supportive and encouraging of this intention, while reminding me that only those who are ready will be able to understand the teachings of liberation.

It felt really good to me to be with monks, these guys who had committed their whole lives to following the path of the Buddha. They inspired me in a way that is hard to put into words.

Walking across the street in Los Angeles in the middle of the summer heat carrying the bags of Ajahn Amaro and Ajahn Passano, I reflected on how my life had brought me to that simple action of carrying the shoulder bags of Buddhist monks on our way to see the Dalai Lama.

Many stories and reflections arose and passed but I was just left with a sense of total satisfaction. For a moment I realized that there was nothing else in the world that I would rather have been doing. As I allowed myself to enjoy this glimpse of peace and freedom my mind began to analyze it, to try to figure it out, and as the attachment entered my mind the experience faded and was replaced by thinking about it rather than directly experiencing it.

In the winter, during my birthday month, I sat a monthlong silent meditation retreat at Spirit Rock, wanting to explore more deeply my inner world and see more clearly the nature of the mind. My retreat was surprisingly pleasant and I experienced an incredible amount of spaciousness and satisfaction. Of course on retreat there are always the moments of doubt, restlessness, and sloth that visit us but it was all held in a larger container of acceptance and effort.

On the day of my birth I took a walk through the rainy fields and came upon the namesake of our community, the huge boulder that sits alone in the middle of a field with a large oak tree growing up through the center of its solid mass. That rock, which is said to have been the center of sacred ceremonies all the way back to the time when the Native Americans inhabited the coastal regions of northern California, had long been a place I visited in times of seeking wisdom.

In the drizzle of the early morning I carefully climbed up the side of the old rock and took a seat beneath the shelter of the branches of the oak. Sitting there in the rain, I reflected upon my life, my parents, siblings, friends, and lovers over the years. Having already been in silence for almost two weeks, my mind was not cluttered with the usual business of life and I clearly and methodically reflected on the years of my existence, from my earliest memories of childhood: the five-year-old under the stairs with a knife, the eight-year-old smoking pot in the streets, the day I met Toby at Little League, the first time I heard punk rock, my first sexual experiences, the drugs that gave me the relief in the beginning and became nothing but pain in the end, Juvenile Hall, the group home, starting to meditate and finally finding some comfort, graffiti, working the twelve steps, school, service, all of my failed attempts at intimate relationship, the many meditation retreats, travel in Asia, my year-to-live practice, teaching, and the more recent experiences and opportunities.

Through all of this reflection the word "humility" came to the surface. "How do I remain humble?" I thought. I uttered a prayer: "In all that unfolds in my life, good and bad, pleasant and unpleasant, may I remain humble." As if in answer from what felt like the core of my being, a voice said, "Stay connected with your recovery. All of this is coming out of having worked the twelve steps. Stay involved in the program." It was true. I realized that I had begun to feel disconnected from the program of recovery. I couldn't remember the last time I had talked to my sponsor, and although I was still attending meetings here and there, I didn't really feel a part of the program anymore. There was a growing sense of separation; I had become so identified with my Buddhist practice that a wall had been created. Yet I knew I would not have been able to get to this place if it had not been for the years of twelve-step work that was the foundation of my spiritual practice.

At that moment I committed to attending more meetings and decided it was time to get a new sponsor, one whose perspective included both Buddhist practice and long-term twelve-step recovery. It took some time but eventually I met a man, named Kevin, through the meditation center who was teaching a weekly group in Berkeley. Together we began working the steps again, this time from a Buddhist perspective.

Working with Kevin was incredibly valuable to me in the integration of my recovery and Buddhist practice. He's writing a book about Buddhism and recovery from addiction and alcoholism that should serve a growing desire in the recovering community to delve deeper into contemplative meditation practice.

After having co-taught with Ajahn Amaro a weeklong retreat for families, I was helping gather his things when he turned to me and said, "Noah, you have a real gift for sharing the Dharma. You are doing all the right things with your life." He may or may not have known it, but that was the highest compliment he could have given me. It was the approval and encouragement that I needed at the time. Coming from him, my teacher for so many years, it was like the Buddha himself giving me the thumbs up and saying, go forth and teach.

I realized how lucky I was to be earning my full livelihood through teaching meditation and leading counseling groups. I had actualized the intention I set a couple years earlier on that beach in India when Vinny and I both committed to doing the work we knew we were best at. I was in graduate school studying psychology with the understanding that most of my peers would be more likely to see a therapist than come to a meditation retreat. I knew that I wanted to serve the population that could best relate to my experience of growing up in the insanity of the eighties punk culture. It was with that motivation that I continued school even though I was already doing a lot of the work that I wanted to do. The thing was, I hadn't yet begun to work with the people I really wanted to work with. And with the busy schedule of work at the meditation center, I wasn't able to do as many classes in the institutions as I would have liked to.

One night while having dinner at Spirit Rock I was introduced to a man named Jacques who runs the Insight Prison Project. We had met once with Bo Lozoff at a talk at San Quentin. Jacques invited me to join his project and lead some meditation groups at the prison. I had been wanting to start working more with adults, feeling that the Juvenile Hall work was great but that with adults there was more of a chance they would take on a serious meditation practice.

Entering the gates of San Quentin, I felt a familiar chill run up my spine. Jacques waved to the guards with automatic rifles in the tower and the electronic gate slowly began to open. Signing in at the checkpoint, I noticed that my hand was a little shaky. I was more nervous about this than I thought. I knew I had something to offer, and it wasn't that I was scared to teach. I realized that I was afraid I would see someone I knew. A lot of guys I hung out with over the years had done time here, including Toby, and there were a few friends who were still doing time and I was just waiting to see someone I knew from growing up walking the yard.

Looking around at the yard, I saw groups of men standing around; some were exercising, others just hanging out talking. Not knowing what to do or where to go, I followed Jacques along the path beside the building we had entered through. I noticed I wanted to keep my head down, to avoid eye contact with the inmates. It was so easy for me to slip back into the old institutionalized way of being.

22

Death Is Not the End My Friend

Driving fast with the music up loud, as usual, I didn't even hear my cell phone ring. Seeing that I had missed a call, I picked up the phone and checked my messages. I could tell by the sound of Alicia's voice that something terrible had happened; all she said was, "Noah, call me as soon as you get this, it's an emergency." Dialing her number, I could feel my belly get really tight, like I was bracing myself for a hard blow. When she answered the phone I heard the desperation in her voice. I said, "It's Noah, what happened?" and all she replied was, "Toby's dead." Everything became fuzzy and dark for a moment and I felt like my chest was being smashed, like a heavy weight was crushing my sternum. I didn't even reply. I couldn't speak; only a deep guttural sigh came out followed by a flood of tears. I started saying, "Fuck. What the fuck? Why? What happened? Fucking Toby." I had to pull my car to the side of the road and just cry and scream for a while. Alicia told me that she and Jerilyn, Toby's mom, had found him that morning, sitting up in bed, his skin cold and blue. They called the paramedics but it was too late—he had stopped breathing several hours earlier. She thought he probably overdosed but didn't really know; they hadn't found any dope or needles.

Alicia asked me to come down to Santa Cruz and be with her and Gage, Toby's son. I was crying so hard that I couldn't think. I was on my way to work at Spirit Rock, where I was supposed to meet with someone, but I couldn't remember whom. I was also supposed to be leading a weekend for a rites-of-passage boys' group at Tassajara Zen Center, but it didn't look like I was going to be able to make it to either commitment. I couldn't even think about trying to teach or work, my mind was foggy and confused, every cell in my body was in anguish.

I told Alicia that I would be there as soon as possible. After I got off the phone with her I immediately made several calls: to my dad and Ondrea in New Mexico, to my mom in Santa Cruz, to Vinny, Joe, and Micah. Mostly I just left messages telling them what had happened and asking for some support. I talked to Vinny for a little while and he was very supportive—it was so nice to just hear a friendly voice. I felt so alone, so overwhelmed and distraught.

My heart felt like it had just been torn from my chest. I couldn't believe it. I wasn't ready for this, not now. Toby had been doing so well. He had been out of prison and going to recovery meetings and counseling, and as far as I knew he had been sober for almost a year. He was so in love with his son, and every time I talked to him he spoke about wanting to start helping kids like I was doing. He was trying to volunteer at some teen counseling programs in Santa Cruz and going to church every week with his family.

Not now! There was a time a few years ago when he was on the streets and I was just waiting for the call to come, but not now. He had just spent the weekend with me a few weeks ago in the city and had come to a teen retreat that I was leading at Spirit Rock. I had led a day of meditation and a sweat lodge in the afternoon. Toby had been great, sharing his life's experience with the teens and expressing his hope that they would never have to experience what he had. The kids had really loved him and it was so great to be sharing my role of Buddhist teacher with my oldest friend in the world.

Just the day before I had gotten an e-mail from him, something about being a spiritual porn star, another one of his punk rock fantasies. I wrote back telling him of my love for him and encouraging his continued commitment to the steps and spiritual practice. I said that I had been thinking about him a lot lately because of the meditation groups that I was doing in San Quentin. Thinking of the time he spent there, I was so glad he was back in my life and I never wanted him to have to go back to prison. I said that above everything else I hoped he was putting his recovery first, because without staying clean it seemed inevitable that he, that I, that we all would end up back in a cell, if not physically then at least spiritually.

He probably never even got it. Or maybe he did and since he was already relapsing it made him feel so bad that he had killed himself. I would never know.

My whole body was flushed with guilt and the tears flowed out of my empty eyes, soaking my face and sweatshirt. I made a quick stop at work to let them know that I would probably be out the rest of the week and drove directly to Santa Cruz to be with Alicia and Jerilyn and all the rest of our friends and family. I tried turning my stereo up so that it would be louder than my mind, but every song, every chord, and each beat reminded me of Toby.

It felt like nothing had prepared me for this; no amount of meditation, no amount of therapy, none of the spiritual practices or experiences I'd had, prepared me to lose my best friend. I felt like without him nobody in the world really knew me. It seemed like when I was ten years old I had left home and found my real family. The day I met Toby I finally felt understood. We had been through everything together. When we were kids on the streets getting high, chasing girls, when we couldn't relate to our parents and they couldn't understand us, we always had each other. The first time I had sex Toby was there—the first punk rock show, first acid trip, first fucking everything. We fought together and stole together, we shared bottles, crack pipes, and needles. We did it all. Even when I got sober and turned into a fucking self-righteous Straight Edge asshole, Toby was still there. When he was strung out on the streets and needed somewhere to stay, my door was always open. Even when he ripped me and everyone else off and ended up in prison, our connection was still too strong and nothing could break our friendship; we were brothers. I sent him books in prison, he sent me letters. When he got out and met back up with Alicia and she got pregnant he asked me if I would be godfather.

We spent twenty years together, longer than with anyone else. My oldest friend in the world was dead. And with him died the only witness to see me both shoot dope and teach meditation. Now I was all alone, surrounded by people who I could tell about my past but who would never really know what it was like.

No amount of spiritual understanding or faith could make that feeling go away. I knew he was okay wherever he was, be it outside of his body or on to the next realm. But I wasn't okay. I was left behind to deal with his skeleton. I wished I believed that he was resting in peace, but I didn't. I knew that whatever his work was, it would be done, either this time or the next, in this realm or another.

When I finally spoke to my father he said that he felt that Toby might be feeling lost and confused and that what he really needed was my forgiveness. He suggested that I do as much forgiveness practice as possible to help set Toby free and guide him on his journey. I didn't even realize that I hadn't forgiven him, or that maybe I had but he just needed to hear it to help him navigate his strange journey, feeling confused and afraid. I hope my prayers and meditations touched him and helped him to let go and go back into the essence and into the next distressing disguise. I offered any merit that I might have accumulated to him, that he might take rebirth in a realm where he will come into contact with the Dharma.

In Santa Cruz I had to do everything for the funeral. Toby's mom was too overwhelmed with grief, his dad wasn't around, and Alicia had her hands full with taking care of Gage and getting them both out of the apartment where Toby had died. Lola was with Alicia when I arrived. Lola had been sober since just after that night in the hospital three years earlier. She was Alicia's sponsor. We had been in touch off and on and had been able to establish somewhat of a friendship. It was great to see her. I was in so much pain, her hug felt incredibly comforting. She just wanted to know what she could do to help.

We set up the funeral and got the word out as best we could, in the newspaper and by word of mouth. About two hundred people showed up, overflowing St. John's Church, the little chapel on the hill in Capitola where we grew up. People, some of whom I hadn't seen in fifteen years, lined the aisles and spilled out into the streets.

I stood at the pulpit in the front of the church. Pictures of Toby hung on the walls, and a large pile of flowers was being laid on the altar we had created. It was the most important talk I would ever give, remembering Toby and honoring his life and his search for freedom. Looking out over the gathering of his family and friends, feeling inadequate and afraid, I spoke of his love for his family and friends, his son and his girlfriend, his humor, his style, and his struggle with addiction. I told the story of how our friendship had been one of the most important things in my life, how I might not have made it through some of the more difficult times without him. How he'd saved my life so many times by just being understanding and supportive, by just listening when we couldn't relate to our parents or anyone else.

I spoke of how we met at Little League, of our first punk shows and our first sexual experiences. I shared with the gathering of punks and parents, skaters and surfers, what I knew of Toby's life journey, of his search for love and happiness that led instead to addiction and confusion. Of his many loves and his son, of the honor I felt to be godfather to his child. Through my own tears and the tears of a church filled to the brim with love and grief, I did my best to memorialize Toby's life, his incredible sense of humor, and his uncanny ability to make any-one feel comfortable in any situation.

Before we ended the service I led the whole gathering in a short meditation of forgiveness and gratitude and we all offered our love and forgiveness, ending the period of reflection with a funny sound that Toby was famous for making. Everyone was laughing and crying at the same time.

I took some more time off from work and spent a lot of it just cry-ing and reflecting on how lucky I had been to have such a good friend for so long, how rare and wonderful it was to ever connect with some-one in such a deep way.

I kept coming back to the feeling of being lost, like a part of me had died, and it began to hit me that all of our other friends were dead also: Shooter, Mark, Darren, and even Toby's old girlfriend Jamie. My mind started swimming upstream, asking the useless question of "Why?" Why them and not me? Why was I surrounded by such won-derful spiritual teachers, all only a phone call away, all available to me? All of them helping me on the spiritual path.

After some time I realized that I was experiencing survivor's guilt. It was as if I had lived through a war and was one of the only ones left. And on some level it was true.

Talking to my parents and my teachers about my grief process, al-though helpful, also seemed to compound my feeling of guilt. There I was, being supported by some of the most wonderful teachers in the world, and all my friends were dying alone in ghetto apartments, shooting some more dope so that they wouldn't have to deal with the suffering for one more minute. That was me and where I came from, and I felt like I was somehow betraying them by surviving.

The guilt and doubt began to fade fairly quickly and were replaced by the realization that it was for Toby and all my other friends, all of the punks and kids who didn't make it, that I was continuing my spir-itual quest, and for them that I had committed my life to sharing what I was finding with others—to teaching the simple meditation tech-niques that had so profoundly altered the course of my life.

Toby's death became the next teaching, opening my heart to the floods of grief and despair that we all hold at bay. No longer able to keep myself together, I fell apart and stumbled into a deeper understanding of what it means to be human. I began to see Toby's death and all of my life's experiences as teachings and tools to offer to others who will surely walk a similar path. I saw all of it as an opportunity for awakening, as grist for the mill.

Still processing all that had happened, I put one foot in front of the other and showed up for my life's work, using the grief and even the feelings of guilt and confusion over having escaped from a life of addiction and crime as the basis of my teachings. My heart was ripped open, raw and tender—I offered it to others so that they might benefit from my suffering.

A short time later Jack Kornfield invited me to join a small Buddhist teachers' training group that he was offering. I humbly accepted, knowing that it was the appropriate next step in actualizing my intention to share the Dharma with others. I decided that my time would be better spent working in juvenile halls and prisons, gave notice at Spirit Rock, and with a couple of friends started our own nonprofit organization to teach meditation to inmates, called the Mind Body Awareness project.

23

Stay Free

Going back into the same juvenile hall where I had begun my meditation practice so many years earlier was an incredible experience of my life having come full circle. As we walked into the gates of Santa Cruz County Juvenile Hall, I was feeling kind of nervous yet very confident. Memories of being handcuffed in the back of cop cars and all the court dates, probation officers, and piss tests of my youth flashed through my mind.

Tim, the same guy who had worked there when I was a kid, greeted me; he had helped set up the classes and was very pleased to see me. I was happy to see him also and it felt so good to be back there with something to offer other than insults. Tim walked me back to the unit and about forty young faces looked up to check me out as I entered the rec room.

Telling the kids that I was the real thing, Tim gave me a lengthy introduction, telling them about all the times I had been locked up as a teen and about my graffiti fame of later days. I recognized a couple of the kids from the drop-in center where I did outreach, needle exchange, and HIV testing or from one of the alternative high schools where I used to do drug counseling.

When it was my turn I stood in front of the room, feeling oddly old, and told them of my own struggles and search for liberation that had led me to exactly where they were right then. I shared that almost ten years earlier, while in that same juvenile hall, I had, through a conversation with my father, learned how to meditate. I went on to mention my recovery from addiction and said I had honestly found everything that I was looking for. Everything that I had been searching for that kept getting me locked up I'd found through this simple practice of mindfulness meditation.

I invited those who were interested to join me for an introduction to meditation. Looking around to see who else was going to come, several people stood up at once. Several girls and a couple of guys joined me in the classroom, where I was setting up some chairs. We sat in a circle and began by introducing ourselves, saying our names and stating how we were feeling at the time. Most of the kids said that they felt "bad" because they were locked up, and how bad that sucked, or that they were "happy" because they were going home soon. I spoke a little about how so many of our difficulties and sufferings are created by thinking about the past or the future, about court, our convictions, or pain and regrets from the past. I taught them that what we were going to do was begin to train our minds to be fully present in the here and now, that in the present moment it is possible to find some freedom, even when we are locked up.

After a fifteen-minute guided mindfulness meditation on the breath and sensations, we went around the circle again. I asked them to share how they were feeling now and if it was any different from when we had started. The reports varied from "I feel really relaxed and calm" to "I feel high, like I just smoked a big fat joint." No one claimed to still feel bad about being there and one young lady said, "For the first time since I have been here I felt safe and peaceful. I almost forgot I was even locked up."

I knew I had planted the seeds of mindfulness, the greatest gift I could ever give. I had no idea what would come from those seeds, whether they would be watered and grow into deeply rooted Bodhi trees or just be a few minutes of relaxation in a difficult time in their lives. Either way, it was clear that I was doing the best that I could to share the path to liberation that I had found.

Returning home from a three-month meditation retreat on the East Coast, I gathered my friends for a sweat lodge ceremony in celebration of my birthday.

The retreat had been incredible. I had sunk very deep into the silence and solitude of the unfolding experience of being. The New England fall had been a perfect mirror for the experience of retreat. When I arrived the forest was thick with foliage and the heavy fog of autumn. My mind was filled with thoughts, plans, memories, and trepidation. As the days, weeks, and months passed the leaves upon the trees began to illuminate with the most incredible hues of yellow, red, and orange. As I began to relax into the silence and fifteen-hour-a-day meditation schedule, a brightness and interest replaced the trepidation. By the last weeks of the retreat the leaves had all fallen and the wide-open fields, meadows, and woods were revealed, no longer obscured by the foliage. During my walking meditation and the occasional stroll through the woods to sit near the lake, I could see in the distance all that had been hidden when I had arrived. On my meditation cushion with eyes closed, watching each breath, thought, feeling, every thing that arose, pass back into the emptiness from which it had come, I too became more open, less-obscured and able to see that which had previously been hidden beneath the foliage of my being.

On my birthday, surrounded by some of the people I love most, we sat in a circle and I led the gathering in a Buddhist blessing-cord ceremony. Looking around the circle at Vinny, Joe, Micah, Mike, my brother Aaron, Eric, Scott, and many other close friends, I was filled with awe at how my life had turned out.

Inside the dark and safe confines of the sweat lodge I began to cry. It had been over a year since Toby had died but my heart was still tender with loss. The heat from the stones burned through us, as we went around the circle offering our prayers and intentions to the great mystery of spirit. The freshly tattooed open eye of the Buddha upon my palm burned with pain, the heat and the tattoo were painful, but not as painful as the journey required to open that eye.

As the sweat, prayers, and tears continued to flow, in the darkness all I could see were my hands. These hands that I once used to steal, fight, and do drugs with, now used only to serve and to love. On my wrist where I had once tried to kill myself, Toby's name is tattooed beneath the feet of the Buddha. My hands covered in sacred images, Dharma Punx tattooed on the edge.

Epilogue

Buddhism and punk rock obviously have some huge differences. But for me they are both part of a single thread that has been stitched through every aspect of my life. My search for happiness, which first led me to drugs and punk rock, is the same search that eventually brought me to spiritual practice. The truth is, going against the internal stream of ignorance is way more rebellious than trying to start some sort of cultural revolution. It's easy to hate and point out everything that is wrong with the world; it is the hardest and most important work in one's life to free oneself from the bonds of fear and attachment. Compassion is our only hope, wisdom our weapon. The inner revolution will not be televised or sold on the Internet. It must take place within one's own mind and heart.

All of this is to say: wake up! Look at your own life and see what is true about yourself. Freedom is available, the trick is to stop looking out there for it and to sit down, shut up, and see for yourself that your truest nature, however deeply buried or obscured, is closer to love than anything else.

It is my hope that these words will bring inspiration and faith to you, not in me but in yourself. May each one of us find the happiness, peace, and freedom that we have been seeking since birth. I dedicate any merit that has arisen from my story, from my life's energy, to the benefit of all beings everywhere, from the lowest hells of addiction and suffering to the highest heavens of love and satisfaction.

Mindfulness Meditation Instructions

These are the simple instructions from my father that so drastically changed the course of my life. May you too benefit from this practice.

Find a comfortable place to sit, with the back straight, but not rigid.

Allowing the body to just breathe naturally, bring the attention to the most noticeable point of touch where the breath makes contact as it enters the nostrils.

Bring the awareness to the sense of touch of the air as it passes in and passes out. Keep your attention at one precise point and note the sensation that accompanies each breath as it flows in and flows out of the body in the natural breathing process.

If the attention strays, bring it back to the point where you notice the breath as it comes and at the nostrils. Noting "breathing in; breathing out." Not thinking about the breath. Not even visualizing it. Just being with the sensation as it arises with the touch of the air passing in and out of the nostrils.

Sounds arise. Thoughts arise. Other sensations arise. Let them all be in the background, arising and passing away.

In the foreground is the moment-to-moment awareness of the sensation of the breath coming and going. Not pushing anything away. Not grasping at anything. Just clear, precise, gentle observation of the breath. Mindfulness of breathing.

Sensations arise in the body. Thoughts arise in the mind.
They come and go like bubbles.

Each mind moment is allowed to arise and allowed to pass
away of its own momentum. No pushing away of the mind, no
grasping at the breath. Just gently returning awareness to the sensations always present with the coming and the going of the
breath. Gently returning.

The awareness of breath is foreground. In the background,
everything else is as it is.

Each breath is unique: sometimes deep, sometimes shallow, always slightly changing. The whole breath felt going in, stopping,
and coming out; the whole breath experienced at the level of sensation, of touch.

Breathing just happening by itself. Awareness simply watching. The whole body relaxed. Eyes soft. Face relaxed. Shoulders
loose. The belly full and easy. No holding anywhere. Just awareness and breathing.

Just consciousness and the object consciousness, arising and
passing away moment to moment in the vast space of mind.

Don't get lost. If the mind pulls away, gently, with a soft, non-
judging, non-clinging awareness, return to the breath. Note the
whole breath, from its beginning to its end, precisely, clearly, from
sensation to sensation.

The body breathes by itself. The mind thinks by itself. Awareness simply observes the process without getting lost in the content.

Each breath is unique. Each moment is completely new.

If sensation should arise in the body, let the awareness recognize it as sensation. Notice it coming and notice it going. Not
thinking of it as a body or as leg, as pain or as vibration. Simply
noting it as sensation and returning to the breath.

The whole process occurring by itself. Awareness observing,
moment to moment, the arising and passing away of experiences
in the mind and body. Moment-to-moment change.

Surrender to the present. Experience the breath. Don't try to get anything from the breath. Don't even think of concentration. Just allow awareness to penetrate to the level of sensations that arise of themselves and by themselves.

The point of touch becoming more and more distinct, more intense with the coming and going of each breath.

The mind becoming one-pointed on sensations that accompany breathing.

If thoughts arise, clearly note their motion in mind, rising and passing away like bubbles. Notice them, and return to the mindfulness of the breathing.

If thought or feeling becomes predominant, with an open awareness, softly note what is predominant as "feeling" or "thinking," as "hearing," as "tasting," as "smelling." Then, gently return to the breath.

Don't tarry with thought. Don't identify contents. Just note the experience of thought entering and passing away, of feeling, of any sense, arising in the moment and passing away in the next moment.

Return to the even flow of the breath. Not grasping anything. Not pushing anything away. Just a clear awareness of what predominates in the mind or body as it arises.

Returning deeply to the intense point of sensation that marks the passage of the air of each full breath.

The eyes soft. Shoulders soft. Belly soft. The awareness crystal clear.

Subtler and subtler sensations become predominant. Thoughts become predominant. Each one noted clearly within the concentrated awareness of breathing.

Watch its motion, continual change from object to object, breath to breath, sensation to sensation. Like a kaleidoscope, continual change.

Moment-to-moment objects arise and pass away in the vast space of mind, of body. An easy, open awareness simply observing the process of arising and passing away. Awareness of whatever is predominant, returning to the sensations of the breath.

Feelings arise. Thoughts arise. The "planning mind," the "judging mind." Awareness experiences the process of their movement. It doesn't get lost in content. Observe thought passing through the vast space of mind.

These words arising from nothing, disappearing into nothing, Just open space in which the whole mind, the whole body, are experienced as moment-to-moment change.

Sound arises and passes away.

Feeling arises and passes away.

All of who we are, of what we think we are, moment to moment, coming and going, bubbles in mind, arising, passing away in the vast, open space of mind. Choiceless awareness. Moment-to-moment awareness of whatever arises, of whatever exists.

All things that have the nature arise have the nature to pass away. Everything we think of as "me" disappearing moment to moment.

Moment to moment, Knowing the truth of each experience.

Resources

For information about our non-profit organization that teaches meditation in institutions, go to:
www.mbaproject.org

For information about meditation retreats or classes, contact
On the west coast: *www.spiritrock.com* or call 415–488–0164
On the east coast: *www.dharma.org/ims.htm* or call 978–355–4378

Or contact Inquiring Mind for a free subscription to the journal of the Vipassana community at *www.inquiringmind.com*

For Noah's teaching schedule and Dharma Punx stuff, go to www.dharmapunx.com